The Ultimate Player's Guide to

SKYLANDERS®

SUPERCHARGERS

[Unofficial Guide]

Hayley Camille

que

800 East 96th Street,
Indianapolis, Indiana 46240 USA

The Ultimate Player's Guide to Skylanders® SuperChargers [Unofficial Guide]

Copyright © 2016 by Pearson Education

ISBN-13: 978-0-7897-5715-9

ISBN-10: 0-7897-5715-X

Library of Congress Control Number: 2016931454

Printed in the United States of America

1 16

Trademarks

All terms mentioned in this book that are known to be trademarks or service marks have been appropriately capitalized. Que Publishing cannot attest to the accuracy of this information. Use of a term in this book should not be regarded as affecting the validity of any trademark or service mark.

SKYLANDERS and SKYLANDERS SUPERCHARGERS are trademarks of Activision Publishing, Inc. This book is not affiliated with or endorsed by Activision.

Warning and Disclaimer

Every effort has been made to make this book as complete and as accurate as possible, but no warranty or fitness is implied. The information provided is on an "as is" basis. The author and the publisher shall have neither liability nor responsibility to any person or entity with respect to any loss or damages arising from the information contained in this book or from the use of the CD or programs accompanying it.

Special Sales

For information about buying this title in bulk quantities, or for special sales opportunities (which may include electronic versions; custom cover designs; and content particular to your business, training goals, marketing focus, or branding interests), please contact our corporate sales department at corpsales@pearsoned.com or (800) 382-3419.

For government sales inquiries, please contact governmentsales@pearsoned.com.

For questions about sales outside the U.S., please contact intlcs@pearson.com.

Editor-in-Chief
Greg Wiegand

Executive Editors
Rick Kughen
Laura Norman

Development Editor
Todd Brakke / Jackowski-
James Floyd Kelly

Managing Editor
Sandra Schroeder

Project Editors
Elaine Wiley
Lori Lyons

Copy Editor
Bart Reed

Indexer
Ken Johnson

Proofreader
Debbie Williams

Publishing Coordinator
Cindy Teeters

Interior Designer
Mark Shirar

Cover Designer
Chuti Prasertsith

Compositor
TNT Design, Inc.

Contents at a Glance

BONUS: Register your book at quepublishing.com/register to gain access to four online appendixes.

APPENDIX A Portal Master Rankings

APPENDIX B Trophies and Achievements

APPENDIX C Magic Items

APPENDIX D Skystones Overdrive

Table of Contents

BONUS: Register your book at quepublishing.com/register to gain access to four online appendixes.

APPENDIX A Portal Master Rankings

APPENDIX B Trophies and Achievements

APPENDIX C Magic Items

APPENDIX D Skystones Overdrive

About the Author

Hayley Camille is a dedicated writer, working from Australia. Her previous nonfiction work includes *The Ultimate Player's Guide to Skylanders: Trap Team* as well as various Minecraft projects.

Hayley has a strong interest in computers and gaming. She has collaborated on numerous software projects, including touch-screen and interactive games. With two young sons that are highly tech-savvy and mad about the *Skylanders* and *Minecraft* games, she is in a unique position to not only know the games well, but also to write from the different perspectives of what's important to a child gamer as the target audience, a parent-facilitator, as well as a strategy-focused teen forum player.

Hayley has several published works and is currently completing a screenplay adaptation of her award-nominated superhero novella *Avon Calling!*

She holds a post-grad university degree in molecular archaeology—the study of ancient residues (blood/DNA/plant) on prehistoric artifacts—which forms the underlying scientific theory behind her recently published adult fiction novel *Human*.

Hayley can be found haunting her blog at hayleycamille.com.

Dedication

This book is dedicated to Orrin, Eric, Finn, and all the children who love Skylanders so much that it makes grown-ups like me want to play it, too.

Acknowledgments

Many people have been involved in the creation of this book, without which, it would not be here. Thank you first, to Rick Kughen, for his kindness, encouragement, and professional expertise in bringing this SuperChargers guide to its readers. Hearing how much Eric enjoys the books makes them a joy to write.

The lovely editorial and publishing team at Que of Rick, Jim, Todd, Elaine, Bart, Brandon, Cindy, Lori, Laura, Greg, Sandra, Mark, Ken, Debbie, and Trina have put in so many hours on creating a wonderful, fun book for young gamers, and I am so very thankful. Your time and assistance are always much appreciated. Thanks, Jim, for your editorial notes that always made me smile, from one Skylander kid's parent to another. I hope your boys find this book useful, too.

A big thanks to Alex, for assisting me with all the tech needed to manage my game playing and recording, and for making me coffee each morning so I could keep writing.

Thank you again to my boys, Orrin and Finn, who spent so many hours exploring the SuperChargers game with me. We played the same sections over and over again to discover every collectible and mod, and then we raced each track until we knew them by heart. I think I must have the most fun job in the world to be able to share it with my boys.

Most importantly, thank you to all of the Skylander fans out there who love these games as much as we do, and who support this book. You've created such a vibrant and fun online community; I love being a part of it.

We Want to Hear from You!

As the reader of this book, *you* are our most important critic and commentator. We value your opinion and want to know what we're doing right, what we could do better, what areas you'd like to see us publish in, and any other words of wisdom you're willing to pass our way.

We welcome your comments. You can email or write to let us know what you did or didn't like about this book—as well as what we can do to make our books better.

Please note that we cannot help you with technical problems related to the topic of this book.

When you write, please be sure to include this book's title and author as well as your name and email address. We will carefully review your comments and share them with the author and editors who worked on the book.

Email: feedback@quepublishing.com

Mail: Que Publishing
          ATTN: Reader Feedback
          800 East 96th Street
          Indianapolis, IN 46240 USA

Reader Services

Register your copy of *The Ultimate Player's Guide to Skylanders SuperChargers* at quepublishing.com for convenient access to downloads, updates, and corrections as they become available. To start the registration process, go to quepublishing.com/register and log in or create an account.* Enter the product ISBN, 9780789757159, and click Submit. Once the process is complete, you will find any available bonus content under Registered Products.

Be sure to check the box that you would like to hear from us in order to receive exclusive discounts on future editions of this product.

Introduction

Our favorite heroes are back—only this time, they're SuperCharged!

Portal Masters, Ready!

Far away on the magical, floating islands of Skylands, a terrible villain has been brought back to life. Prepare for an adventure of huge (and sometimes tiny!) proportions as you lead a new team of heroes across the skies, seas, and land to conquer The Darkness and save the crazy inhabitants of Skylands!

This guide will explain to you all the ins and outs of mastering the *SuperChargers* game. You'll get to know every new Skylander and his or her specially customized vehicle. Use your new knowledge and combat skills to defeat the bad guys and chase down the Skylanders' hilariously evil nemesis, Kaos, to put an end to his ego-fueled quest for domination of the universe!

Skylanders is one of the biggest "toys to life" games ever created and has all the family-friendly features we love. The newest edition of the game, *Skylanders SuperChargers*, published by Activision, is no exception. Whether you're an expert Portal Master with years of villain-trapping behind you or a new explorer keen to throw yourself into the fray, this book will guide you on your journey.

Included in this guide are cheats for earning sparks in Live Wire Locks, a complete gameplay walkthrough, and tips on the best route to take throughout story chapters to make sure you don't miss any hidden collectibles or Red Toolboxes. Maps and tips will speed you through Pandergast's race tracks toward a victorious finish. There are hints on what to expect in Elemental Quests and Buzz's SuperCharged Challenges as well as advice on ways to combat even the trickiest villain battles.

What Secrets Will You Uncover?

The first couple chapters will give you some background on *Skylanders SuperChargers*—what to expect of your new game, how to play, where to find important features of your game (non-console specific), and how to use them. Different types of Skylanders, vehicles, and accessories are discussed with tips on how to best improve them in-game to boost your playing power. The multiplayer and co-op racing challenges and elemental symbols are explained, and you'll be introduced to the team of helpers (and a couple of troublemakers!) waiting for you at Skylanders Academy.

You'll meet all the new SuperCharged characters in Chapter 3, "The Good Guys," including bios, attack moves, speed and strength stats, Soul Gem abilities, and upgrade paths. Each SuperCharger has his or her own unique matching vehicle as well, and we'll look at their strengths and weaknesses, weapons, stats, and mods.

Chapter 4, "The Bad Guys," brings the heat on the villains burning up the racing tracks. Each track has one evil dragster to beat to the finish line. After you win, that villain is yours to race. In this chapter, we get the low-down on villain vehicles, weapons, and stats, along with tips on how to beat them and how best to use their attack moves for a quick win on the track.

Chapter 5, "Cool Collectibles," is all about uncovering secrets—use this chapter to aid a treasure hunt of collectibles hidden within each story chapter and racing track. Epic Treasure Chests, Wish Stones, Kaos Diaries, Red Toolboxes, Legendary Treasure, Winged Sapphires, and magic hats are all explained.

Spend some time at Skylanders Academy in Chapter 6, "Explore Skylanders Academy," where we'll search out some fantastic new areas built by the ingenious inventor Mags, including the Games Room, Eon's Academy, Sharpfin and Persephone's upgrade stations, vehicle and Skylander training zones, and much more. Gather gold in the Storage Room or bounce your way to riches in a mini-game. But whatever you do, don't let cranky Kaos defeat you at Skystones Overdrive (he'll gloat for days)!

If you're on the path for gold and glory, you'll find quests galore in Chapter 7, "Questing with Tessa, Hugo, and Buzz." Use the tables to track down milestones and challenges to earn extra rewards at Skylanders Academy. When you're ready to really test your skill, use the tips for Buzz's SuperCharger challenges to get the inside edge on how to make it through unscathed.

Haven't had enough of high-speed mischief? The Great Grizzo is waiting at Skylanders Academy with special vehicle challenges. In Chapter 8, "Great Grizzo's Elemental Challenges," we'll break down each of these, in turn, and look at ways of turning the odds in your favor to beat them.

The most exciting expansion of the *SuperChargers* game is the new world of racing. In Chapter 9, "SuperCharged Racing," we'll pay Pandergast a visit to learn all about the land, sea, and sky racing tracks—their hidden secrets, shortcuts, and where to find boost pads, magic boxes, and ammo pods.

When you're ready to get your game on, Chapter 10, "Gear Up for Adventure," has got you covered! A complete walkthrough of each story chapter includes how to manage Live Wire Locks, block puzzles and secret areas, battle tactics and hidden collectibles, as well as the best path through to make sure you never miss a step. Celebrate all your game achievements with Chapter 11, "Fully Charged!" and learn about more fun ways to expand your *SuperChargers* adventure.

Want to take your game further? Get the inside scoop on how to earn and use Portal Master-level rewards, additional challenges to score trophies, and achievements specific to your console, as well as how to play (and win!) Skystones Overdrive and how to use your old magic items from previous *Skylanders* games at the academy. Simply visit your very own online portal using the login details provided with this book to take advantage of all of this bonus information.

Bonus Material: To access bonus online resources, you first must register your book online by going to quepublishing.com/register and creating an account. Enter the product ISBN, 9780789757159, and click Submit.

Share Your Sky-deas!

As an avid *Skylanders* fan, I would love your feedback and ideas on ways to expand, improve, and get more out of your *Skylanders* games, as well as what you'd like included in future *Skylanders* guides. Feel free to contact me any time for a chat or to share your favorite *Skylanders* experiences.

For more *Skylanders* fun, you can find me haunting YouTube on my Skylanders Gameplay channel **SkyPandaAus** (www.youtube.com/SkyPandaAus). Drop by to watch some gameplay walkthroughs, enter giveaways, meet new *Skylanders* characters, and find out what's happening in Skylands!

To contact me personally, send an email to SkyPanda@hayleycamille.com. I can't promise that I'll be able to reply to every message, but I'll definitely *read* each email and try to get back to you!

Happy Skylanding!

Hayley Camille
(aka SkyPanda)

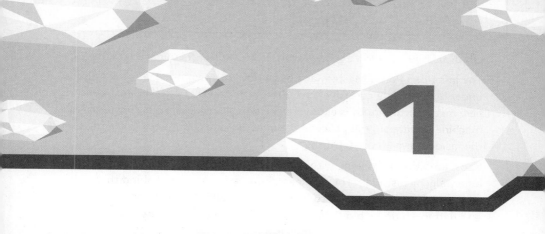

Skylands Is DOOMED!

Welcome back, Portal Master! You've arrived just in time—the future of Skylands is in grave peril.

That most despicable of pointy-toothed villains, Kaos, has finally succeeded in overthrowing Master Eon at Skylanders Academy. Far away in the Land of the Undead, the greatest Portal Master of all time is powerless, imprisoned in crystal inside a desolate castle overseen by Count Moneybone (see Figure 1.1). Meanwhile, his faithful crew of Mabu heroes are locked away in a jail cell on a transport ship, guarded by trolls!

FIGURE 1.1 Poor Master Eon is locked away in Moneybone's gravity-defying prison! You're going to have to turn topsy-turvy to break him out and save the day.

Oh dear. It just couldn't get any worse. Oh, wait... of course it could!

The infamous Portal Master Kaos has a new evil weapon to force Skylands under his complete control—The Doomstation of Ultimate Doomstruction! A fiery mechanical mouth is eating up the sky. Never before has such a terrible machine threatened the peaceful realm of Skylands—but what is lurking on the inside is even more terrifying.

Kaos' ambition is growing with each mission (see Figure 1.2) and he has a new ally by his side: "The Darkness." It is the evil power behind the Doomstation, which sparks to life and sweet-talks Kaos with smooth jazz and flattery to do its bidding. Time is running out as these two combine their strength. The race to save Skylands is on!

A slather of new villains will try to stop you succeeding in your quest—from the hard-hitting hammerheads to an axe-wielding pirate called Blubberbeard. CockadoodleDoom has a feathery fist of fights to crow about, and pompous Lord Stratosfear is lightning fast!

Are you up to the challenge, Portal Master?

Never fear! To help you in this dangerous mission, Master Eon created a super-charged team of Skylanders to fight alongside you. The SuperChargers and their customized vehicles are hot on the heels of the bad guys. Together, you'll shrink giant chickens, dive into storybooks, ride tidal waves in the clouds, pop colossal corn kernels, harpoon a Hydra, and battle Skybandits... and that's all before breakfast!

As you race through the game like a champion, make sure you take time out to explore Skylanders Academy. You can also collect magical hats, Winged Sapphires, Soul Gems, Epic Treasure Chests, Wish Stones, Red Toolboxes, and Kaos Diaries hidden throughout your journey.

If you need some racing practice, Pandergast has his checkered flags ready! Dive, fly, float, barrel-roll, sail, and rev across Skylands to discover a frozen fossil wonderland, speed down a dragon's spine, and zoom through Calamity Canyon.

You're in for a fast ride, Portal Master! But with the help of your friends at Skylanders Academy and some super-secret tips from this book, you'll be shrinking Kaos down to size in no time.

Let's get going!

Start Your Engines!

Playing *Skylanders SuperChargers* can be as simple as buying a starter pack for your console or device and playing through to the end with it, or as expansive as you like by collecting all the adventure packs, Skylander character toys, vehicles, and accessories (see Figure 2.1). There's a treasure-trove of fun within the game itself, including racing challenges, mini-games, villains to defeat and prisoners to rescue, hats and trophies to collect, and new locations to explore. You can also play online in multi-player races and adventures or join your friends on the same portal in co-op mode. Let's begin by looking at how to get started and what to expect from your new *Skylanders SuperChargers* game.

FIGURE 2.1   Expand your SuperChargers collection or focus on your favorites—from a basic starter pack to an epic collection of character toys, vehicles, and racing packs, there's an adrenaline-filled adventure waiting in Skylands!

Where You Can Play

Skylanders SuperChargers is compatible with PlayStation 3, PlayStation 4, Xbox 360, Xbox One, iOS tablets, and WiiU (developed by Vicarious Visions, with developmental support by Beenox) and published by Activision. The Standard Starter Pack for tablet devices is compatible with iPad Air, iPad Air 2, iPad mini 2, iPad mini 3, iPhone 5s, iPhone 6, iPhone 6 Plus, and iPod Touch 6. *Skylanders SuperChargers* will also work on iPhone 5, 5C, and iPad 3 and 4; however, only the offline functions (split-screen racing, single-player adventure mode, and co-op adventure mode) will work on these devices. A cloud-save feature allows you to use your game across connected devices.

A separate version of the game, *Skylanders: SuperChargers Racing* (developed by Beenox), was released for the Wii and Nintendo 3DS consoles. The 3DS and Wii versions have a unique racing storyline compared to the other platforms, and gameplay for *SuperChargers Racing* is therefore not covered in this book. However, we will look at their inclusions in this chapter.

Two versions of the Starter Pack are compatible with their respective consoles: the Standard Starter Pack and the Dark Edition Starter Pack (see Figure 2.2). The following sections detail what you receive with each pack.

FIGURE 2.2　Collector's dilemma? Begin by choosing either the Light or Dark Starter Pack. Keep in mind that the Dark character toys may be a little harder to find (or more expensive pre-loved) after the initial game release is over.

Console Starter Pack (PS3/PS4, Xbox 360/Xbox One)

You'll find the following character toys and inclusions in this starter pack, as shown in Figure 2.3:

- *Skylanders SuperChargers* game, specific to your console
- Traptanium Portal of Power
- Two Skylander figures—Super Shot Stealth Elf and Spitfire
- One SuperChargers vehicle—Hot Streak
- Two character BattleCast cards, stickers, and toy codes
- SuperChargers character poster

FIGURE 2.3 Super Shot Stealth Elf, Hot Streak, and Spitfire all come as standard inclusions with the PlayStation, Xbox, and Tablet versions of the Starter Pack.

Console Dark Edition Starter Pack (PS3/PS4, Xbox 360/Xbox One)

You'll find the following character toys and inclusions in this starter pack, as shown in Figure 2.4:

- *Skylanders SuperChargers* game, specific to your console
- Traptanium Portal of Power

⊗ Kaos Trophy

⊗ Two Skylander figures—Dark Super Shot Stealth Elf and Dark Spitfire

⊗ Two SuperChargers vehicles—Dark Hot Streak and Dark Sea Shadow

⊗ Two character BattleCast cards, stickers, and toy codes

⊗ Dark Edition SuperChargers character poster

FIGURE 2.4 The Dark Edition Starter Pack for PlayStation and Xbox comes with a bonus Dark vehicle (which is not sold separately) and a Kaos Trophy.

Console Starter Pack (WiiU)

You'll find the following character toys and inclusions in this starter pack, as shown in Figure 2.5:

⊗ *Skylanders SuperChargers* game, specific to your console

⊗ Traptanium Portal of Power

⊗ Two Skylander figures—Super Shot Stealth Elf and Turbo Charge Donkey Kong

⊗ One SuperChargers vehicle—Barrel Blaster

⊗ Two character BattleCast cards, stickers, and toy codes

⊗ SuperChargers character poster

FIGURE 2.5 Amiibo gamers rejoice! The WiiU SuperChargers include perennial favorite Turbo Charge Donkey Kong and his vehicle Barrel Blaster, which can also be played in other Amiibo-based Nintendo games.

Console Dark Edition Starter Pack (WiiU)

You'll find the following character toys and inclusions in this starter pack, as shown in Figure 2.6:

- ⊗ *Skylanders SuperChargers* game, specific to your console
- ⊗ Traptanium Portal of Power
- ⊗ Kaos Trophy
- ⊗ Two Skylander figures—Dark Super Shot Stealth Elf and Dark Turbo Charge Donkey Kong
- ⊗ Two SuperChargers vehicles—Dark Hot Streak and Dark Barrel Blaster
- ⊗ Two character BattleCast cards, stickers, and toy codes
- ⊗ Dark Edition SuperChargers character poster

FIGURE 2.6 The WiiU Dark Edition Starter Pack is the only place you'll find new Dark Donkey Kong and Dark Barrel Blaster, which are not sold separately. However, there is a fairly strong (but expensive) online resale market for these toys if you miss out.

Tablet Starter Pack (Apple iOS Devices)

You'll find the following character toys and inclusions in the tablet starter pack:

- *Skylanders SuperChargers* game, specific to Apple devices
- Traptanium Portal of Power with handheld controller
- Two Skylander figures—Super Shot Stealth Elf and Spitfire
- One SuperChargers vehicle—Hot Streak
- Two character BattleCast cards, stickers, and toy codes
- SuperChargers character poster

The iOS Tablet Starter Pack essentially has the same inclusions as the Standard Xbox/PlayStation Pack, with the exception of including a wireless Portal with removable game controller built in. There is no Dark Edition Starter Pack for iOS tablets.

Console Starter Pack (Wii, Nintendo 3DS)

You'll find the following character toys and inclusions in the Racing starter packs, as shown in Figure 2.7:

- *Skylanders SuperChargers Racing* game, specific to your console
- Traptanium Portal of Power
- Two Skylander figures—Super Shot Stealth Elf and Hammer Slam Bowser
- One SuperChargers vehicle—Clown Cruiser
- Two character BattleCast cards, stickers, and toy codes
- SuperChargers character poster

FIGURE 2.7 The Wii and Nintendo 3DS Starter Packs include another Nintendo favorite Amiibo—Hammer Slam Bowser and his vehicle the Clown Cruiser. Keep in mind, this version of the *SuperChargers* game is a special "Racing" game edition, not the full adventure story.

Console Dark Edition Starter Pack (Wii, Nintendo 3DS)

You'll find the following character toys and inclusions in this starter pack, as shown in Figure 2.8:

- *Skylanders SuperChargers Racing* game, specific to your console
- Traptanium Portal of Power
- Two Skylander figures—Dark Spitfire and Dark Hammer Slam Bowser
- Two SuperChargers vehicles—Dark Clown Cruiser and Dark Hot Streak

- Two character BattleCast cards, stickers, and toy codes
- Dark Edition SuperChargers character poster

FIGURE 2.8 Dark Hammer Slam Bowser and Dark Clown Cruiser are only available in the Wii and 3DS Dark Edition Starter Packs. By flicking a switch on the toy base, you can play Bowser as an Amiibo in your other Nintendo games.

Digital Starter Pack: "Portal Owner's Pack"

You'll find the following inclusions in the digital starter pack:

- *Skylanders SuperChargers* game, specific to your console
- One in-game digital character—Instant Spitfire
- One in-game digital vehicle—Instant Hot Streak

A digital version of *Skylanders SuperChargers* can be downloaded through the online store via your console. You can complete the main adventure in story mode with the digital character and land vehicle provided. However, if you would like to expand your game to include other in-game areas, you will need to buy additional character toys and use your existing Portal from an earlier Starter Pack (*Giants*, *Swap Force*, or *Trap Team*). This is the least expensive option to play the game, priced at approximately $50–$70, depending on your console type (see Figure 2.9).

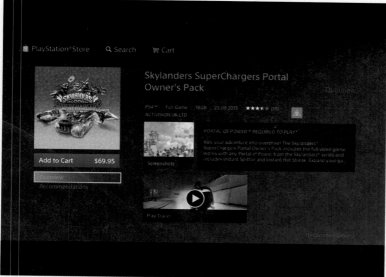

FIGURE 2.9   The Portal Owners Pack available as a digital download through your console gives you access to the game using your existing Portal of Power.

Nintendo-Specific Character Toys

There are some new kids on the block this year, with the inclusion of special Amiibo character toys Bowser and Donkey Kong. These toys are included in the Wii, WiiU, and 3DS Starter Packs (both Standard and Dark versions) and will only work on the Nintendo consoles. Not only do these Amiibo characters come with their own special vehicles (again, which only work on Nintendo consoles), the toys can also be used in other Amiibo games by flicking a switch underneath the base of the toy (see Figure 2.10). Each Amiibo character and its signature vehicle can also be purchased separately at major retailers in a double pack.

FIGURE 2.10   A small switch under the base of the character toy will allow you to choose to play within Skylanders or use as a general Amiibo character in other applicable Nintendo games.

The Best Starter Pack for You

Deciding which Starter Pack bests suits you will depend on a few important points. First, of course, you'll define your choice of collectibles based on which console you own. Because the Xbox and PlayStation starter packs do not include the Amiibo-based toys, you have a slightly more limited range of characters in your complete collection (you'll miss out on the Standard and Dark Bowser and Donkey Kongs, as well as their vehicles). Outside of this limitation, however, you can begin by choosing between the Standard and Dark Edition Packs for your specific console.

The Dark Edition Starter Packs (RRP $100) contain unique characters specific to each console that will be unavailable for individual purchase. Although the Standard Edition Super Shot Stealth Elf and Spitfire are also unavailable for individual purchase (a limited-edition Hot Streak is sold separately), they are far more likely to be accessible as resale purchases online due to the much higher quantity of Standard Starter Packs (RRP $75) produced. The Dark Edition Starter Packs (also known as the Collector's Edition Starter Packs) are typically more limited in production, so the Dark Edition variants (Dark Super Shot Stealth Elf, Dark Spitfire, and Dark Hot Streak, as well as Amiibo-based Dark Hammer Slam Bowser, Dark Turbo Charge Donkey Kong, and their vehicles, Dark Barrel Blaster and Dark Clown Cruiser) will be harder to source independently. There is a strong market online for resale of rare character toys, which are often sold at a premium price.

Similarly, the Kaos Trophy (see Figure 2.11) is exclusive to the Dark Edition Starter Packs. This trophy unlocks Kaos' signature vehicle, called the Doom Jet, as well as allows players to race as Kaos in special areas. You can buy the Kaos Trophy separately for $8 through major retailers and online.

Both the Standard and Dark Edition Starter Packs allow you to complete the game, so the main point of difference is in the collectability of the characters and the Kaos Trophy. Essentially, for the additional expense (an extra $25) for the Dark Edition Starter Pack, you will receive an extra vehicle (valued at $17) and the Kaos Trophy (valued at $8). The value added in bonus toys is ultimately the same as the extra cost, but the exclusivity of the Dark Edition toys gives them a higher intrinsic value in the long term.

FIGURE 2.11   Finally, the most evil Portal Master has been honored with his very own trophy! The Kaos Trophy is included in each Dark Edition Starter Pack, and opens up special racing gameplay and the ability to race as Kaos in his signature vehicle, the Doom Jet.

In addition to the Standard and Dark Starter Packs, some retailers also offer unique Skylander bundle packs after the initial promotional launch subsides, or they may offer bonus preorder incentives. You can find more information on current special offers and bonus packs from individual retailers.

NOTE

If you purchase second-hand characters online, you may need to remove the information stored on them from previous use. You can choose to reset the level and stats back to standard settings for a pre-loved character in the Manage settings of the Skylander info menu (see Figure 2.12).

FIGURE 2.12 Pre-owned characters often have coins, upgrades, trinkets, and hats already saved onto their RFID chip. Take them back to basics using the Reset option if you'd like a clean slate.

What You Need to Play

You'll find a huge assortment of character toys, vehicles, and special edition items available to buy from retailers, so if you're a collector, you have endless opportunity to expand and enhance your game. However, you don't need every SuperCharger and vehicle to complete the main story chapters. You can actually play the game through with just one SuperCharger and one land vehicle (which is included in the Starter Pack).

However, certain areas of the adventure are only accessible to vehicles of a matching element or type (land, sea, or sky). Likewise, Great Grizzo's

Elemental Gate challenges at Skylanders Academy can only be fully accessed by a vehicle of each element, in turn (you'll learn more about this in Chapter 8, "Great Grizzo's Elemental Challenges"). These areas contain collectibles or villains that allow you to complete 100% of the game. To access all of these additional areas, you'll need at least one Skylander, one vehicle of each type (air, water, and land), as well as or including one vehicle for each of the ten elemental types (Dark, Light, Air, Water, Life, Undead, Magic, Earth, Fire, and Tech).

Although there is a place in your new Portal of Power to hold a trap, these aren't necessary to complete the game. Inserting a trap into the portal with a villain inside (from your *Trap Team* game) will unlock a Skystone of that villain. This will increase your collection of cards for playing Skystones Overdrive. These villain cards have different health and attack values from those you have previously played in *Trap Team* (you can learn more about Skystones Overdrive by logging into the extra resources portal using the unique code in this book!). You can also insert a trap into your SuperChargers portal to receive a special ammunition boost for your vehicle, as discussed in the section called "Get Your Engines Burning" later in this chapter.

How the Game Works

The Nintendo-specific characters of Hammer Slam Bowser and Turbo Charge Donkey Kong, and their respective vehicles, the Clown Cruiser and Barrel Blaster, can only be played on the Wii, WiiU, and 3DS consoles and are not compatible with PlayStation and Xbox consoles.

Excluding this exception, however, all other character toys are compatible across all consoles, which opens the door to cooperative gaming with your friends no matter what game console they have! Each character toy is embedded with an RFID (radio frequency identification) card that contains the data for that particular character. This information connects to the card reader inside the Portal of Power, which interprets and displays the information (your character and vehicle) onscreen within the game. This RFID data constantly updates as you play, and new information (such as purchased upgrades, mods, and outfits) are resaved to the toy. Storing the character data inside the Skylander means it is completely transferrable across *SuperChargers* games—you can use your figurines on any portal (swapping across different platforms or taking them to a friend's house to play). The character will always retain his or her level, hats, and trinkets, gearbits/stardust/coins collected, powers and upgrades, and experience points. Therefore, you can constantly improve your SuperChargers' stats, no matter where you are playing. You can add a second player at any point in the game by putting another character toy on the portal and connecting a second controller to your game console. The SuperChargers Portal is compatible with all of the 337 previous and newly released Skylander figures, magic toys, and location toys, which is awesome news if you already have a collection from *Giants*, *Spyro's Adventure*, *Swap Force*, or *Trap Team*.

The new SuperChargers Portal was designed with space in mind. It's larger than the previous generations of portals, so you can comfortably fit two character toys, two vehicles, and magic items on it for multiplayer racing. However, you can actually use an earlier model portal for the *SuperChargers* game; therefore, if you wish to buy a digital version of the game through your console, an older portal will supplement your need for a retail Starter Pack. The SuperChargers toys themselves (and vehicles) are not backward compatible for previous Skylander games, including the reimagined versions of early series characters (because they have new attack moves and upgrade paths to the original versions of the same character), as shown in Figure 2.13.

FIGURE 2.13   Some characters are represented in multiple games as reposed figures with each version. All earlier versions will work in *SuperChargers*; however the new *SuperCharger* version is not backward compatible. From left to right, Gill Grunt (Series 1), Gill Grunt (Series 2), Anchors Away Gill Grunt (Series 3), Gill Runt (Mini), Tidal Wave Gill Grunt (Series 4), Eon's Elite Gill Grunt, and far right, new SuperChargers Deep Dive Gill Grunt.

The Skylands Honor Roll

Things have never been worse in Skylands! The most evil Portal Master Kaos has taken control of the portals and created a devastating base called the Doomstation of Ultimate Doomstruction! To make matters worse, the machine is eating the sky! Without the sky, well, Skylands is doomed!

Our brave mission leaders, Flynn, Cali, and Hugo, have been taken captive. They must be saved, but the worst is yet to come! Skylands' greatest leader, Master Eon, has been imprisoned in the Land of the Undead! You'll need all the help you can get to make it through to the end of this adventure to save the day! But before you begin your epic journey, let's meet the heroes and villains you'll find along the way.

Master Eon

Master Eon is not only the leader of the Skylanders, but also the greatest Portal Master that ever lived (see Figure 2.14). Over many years protecting Skylands from the terrible force of Darkness that threatened it, Master Eon recognized the need for an elite team of warriors that could fight off the constant surge of trouble. He assembled the Skylanders, a team of heroes that he could count on to rush in whenever things got tough.

One day while Master Eon was patrolling with his Skylanders Team, the evil Portal Master Kaos appeared, intent upon destroying the Core of Light and ruling over Skylands with Darkness as his ally. Although they fought bravely, the Skylanders were no match for the wicked Hydra that Kaos summoned to do his bidding. The Core of Light was smashed into pieces, and the Skylanders were banished to Earth. Master Eon himself was exiled between realms, never to appear in his true form again. As the newest Portal Master, you have the power to bring the Skylanders back home by placing their earthly "toy" forms onto the portal and bringing them to life in the realm of Skylands.

But the stakes have been raised again—Master Eon himself has been taken prisoner by Kaos and is being held captive in the Land of the Undead. A brand-new team of Skylanders called SuperChargers must roar into action on their specially modified vehicles to scour land, sky, and sea in the search for Eon.

FIGURE 2.14   Master Eon, the greatest Portal Master that ever lived, has been captured by Kaos and is being held prisoner in the Land of the Undead. It's going to take a super-charged team of heroes to save him!

A Helping Hand!

The task ahead may be intimidating, but remember, you'll have some powerful friends by your side (see Figure 2.15). There are many inhabitants across the thousands of islands in Skylands, but none more brave than the team at Skylanders Academy. After Kaos destroyed much of the academy, the hard-working Mabu have rebuilt it to ensure the SuperChargers have a safe place to train and learn new fighting skills.

As the Head of Security and Secret Ninja Commando Operations, Buzz has years of experience guiding new recruits through dangerous missions. He has set up a training arena in Skylanders Academy so SuperChargers can practice their attack moves in a safe environment. A giant Greeble Dispenser (bought from the Minions Monthly Catalog!) drops critters onto the arena to test your new skills on. With a little practice, you'll soon learn the ways of a true Skylander!

Hugo is Master Eon's assistant. He's an intellectual who loves reading and history, and so you'll often find him buried in a book. As it happens, he may just have a book that can save Skylands from the Doomstation of Ultimate Doomstruction! Master Eon has left a special message in that book just for you (and a smelly sock, too, which is, well... weird)!

If you have a thirst for adventure, Cali is the Mabu for you. She trains young Skylanders in the art of defense and navigation and is dynamite with her knowledge of explosives. Although she often gets caught by the nasty villains of Skylands for getting in their way, her tough determination and awesome fighting skills always see her through.

Flynn is the "best pilot in Skylands"—at least that's what *he* thinks! He's a Mabu with a heart of gold who is always trying (and failing!) to impress Cali. His healthy ego leads him to bend the truth in hilarious ways and take credit for the hard work of others, but he doesn't mean any harm by it. When all else fails, enchiladas are the surest way to keep him happy.

The flying fox, Tessa, may swoop in to bring down the bad guys while you are on your journey. On the back of her colorful bird Whiskers, Tessa is a brave leader and the best flyer around. You'll find Persephone, the fairy queen, in her garden to the right of the entrance of Skylanders Academy. She'll also appear somewhere on your adventure within each chapter to offer you upgrades, so you can improve your attacks on the go in exchange for gold coins (we'll discuss this more in the section "Power Up Your Heroes with Upgrades," later in this chapter).

FIGURE 2.15   With the hard-working heroes of Skylanders Academy by your side, your greatest mission is bound to be a success! Clockwise from left: Buzz, Flynn, Cali, Persephone, Pandergast, Sharpfin, Hugo, and Mags.

Kaos and Glumshanks

Uh, oh! Kaos is back again! This nasty little Portal Master has a long history of evildoing in Skylands, and his latest escapade is no exception. His bad attitude and desire to rule over Skylands had led to his worst weapon yet—the Doomstation of Ultimate Doomstruction! Now even Kaos can't control the machine from eating up the sky! His career in villainy began after he was expelled from the most expensive school of evilness for eating the gymnasium with his giant floating head (which kind of sounds awesome). Cast out onto the streets with his loyal servant Glumshanks, Kaos became furious and bitter. He soon discovered he had a propensity for magic and learned all he could to become a powerful Dark Portal Master (see Figure 2.16). Kaos takes delight in creating trouble for Master Eon and the Skylanders. His relentless efforts to become the evil overlord of Skylands rarely work in his favor, though—Eon's team of heroes is always ready to save the day!

FIGURE 2.16   Not again! Kaos is stirring up trouble in Skylands while the ever-suffering Glumshanks does his bidding. This time, though, Darkness is on his side.

SuperChargers

With the Doomstation of Ultimate Doomstruction threatening the once-peaceful realm and new villains causing havoc across Skylands, Master Eon knew a new type of hero was needed. These important Skylanders, called

SuperChargers, would be trained to drive specially modified vehicles into the furthest reaches of the sky, the darkest depths of the sea, and the wildest lands to track down the bad guys and foil their evil plans.

Desperate times call for the bravest champions, and none are more worthy than Master Eon's hand-picked team of heroes. Each one, like those pictured in Figure 2.17, has been especially chosen for his or her fighting skills, bravery, and magical powers. Every fighter is unique and draws power from one of the ten elements of Skylands: Earth, Fire, Air, Water, Life, Tech, Undead, Magic, Light, or Dark.

FIGURE 2.17 The newest team of champions to sweep across Skylands is the SuperChargers. When paired with their signature vehicle, their fighting performance is revved to the max!

With Master Eon taken prisoner and Kaos threating Skylands with destruction, it's up to the SuperChargers to track down trouble and ultimately save the day.

Each of the 20 new SuperChargers can drive and modify any vehicle; however, when paired with their unique vehicle match, they become a super-charged combination. When a SuperCharger is matched with his or her signature vehicle, the combination will unlock an exclusive mod to boost both the Skylander and the vehicle into hyper-performance mode. They can also open SuperCharger gates throughout Skylands, gaining access to additional playing areas.

Skylanders from previous adventures can also join the SuperChargers gameplay. Over 300 unique character toys are available from earlier games, which are categorized by the color of their base plate (you'll also find each Skylander's element on his or her base for quick reference). Skylanders from the original *Spyro's Adventure* game have a green base, those from *Giants* have an orange base, the character toys from *Swap Force* have a blue base, and *Trap Team* editions have a red base (see Figure 2.18). To jazz things up a bit, the newest *Skylanders SuperChargers* characters boast an "engine" base with their element printed on the front.

FIGURE 2.18 You can identify which game your characters belong to by the color and shape of their base plate: pictured here (left to right) are Stump Smash from *Spyro's Adventure* (green base), Thumpback from *Giants* (orange base), Blast Zone from *Swap Force* (blue base), Short Cut from *Trap Team* (red base), and Stormblade from *SuperChargers* (engine base).

Vehicles

Every SuperCharger has a unique vehicle pair to match. The vehicles are a new addition to the Skylanders collection, and most vehicles (but not all) have moving parts and decorative colors to encourage non-gaming play as a fun toy—don't put them in the bath though!

There are motorcycles, tanks, racing cars, boats and submarines, rafts, jets, planes, and helicopters, and other weird and wonderful machines, including all those pictured in Figure 2.19.

Each vehicle also belongs to a specific magical element (Air, Earth, Light, Dark, Magic, Undead, Life, Water, Fire, or Tech) and is suited to a particular terrain (land, sea, or sky). Their capabilities are powered by magical inventions called "Rift Engines" (which also form the base shape for the SuperCharger character toys). These engines power the vehicles and create portals between magical realms that the SuperChargers can use to travel throughout the Skylands Universe.

Each vehicle has a range of modifications ("mods") and weapon boosters that can be used to customize and improve its performance. Mods are unlocked when you find racing chests throughout your adventures in Skylands or when a vehicle is paired with its matching SuperCharger Skylander. You can increase the performance of your vehicle by trading gearbits with a team of mechanics (Fender, Socket, and Clyde) at Skylanders Academy. Collecting Winged Sapphires goes a long way to reducing your upgrade bills by providing you with a discount.

FIGURE 2.19   Fly, float, zoom, rev, and sail 20 new vehicles through Skylands on the trail to beat Kaos at his own game. With these incredible machines you can explore more of Skylands than ever before!

In-Game and Chase Variants

Certain character toys are released in retail outlets as variants. These toys usually hold the same abilities and stats as their original counterparts (but not always!) but have a different in-game color scheme or costume and have a "special" title that appears when they are placed on the portal (see Figure 2.20). They will often begin as Level 5 Skylanders and are preloaded with a small quantity of gold coins for buying upgrades.

A limited number of these variants is shipped to retail outlets to be sold through random distribution throughout the world, which means a collector will never know where or when they may turn up. (In other words, you have to "chase" them!) Variants may also be distributed through promotional giveaways. Typically, due to the rare nature of these unique toys, they tend to be highly sought after and can often be found in online resale sites such as eBay (usually at a much higher cost than retail).

FIGURE 2.20 From left: The new SuperCharger Fiesta has a special Halloween variant release called Frightful Fiesta, whereas the Nitro Stealth Stinger variant was released alongside the standard Stealth Stinger vehicle. Both variants appear in game with a decorative appearance and slightly higher stats compared to the original.

Core Skylanders

In previous installments of the game series, many of the character toys were released as "core" Skylanders. These same characters reappear in subsequent games with new outfits, poses, and a new variation on their attack moves (such as the new Wow Pow! attack). These are usually available in a limited release or through specific retailers and have an in-game variation of their name (similar to Chase Variants, discussed earlier). Each new Core Skylander begins as a Series 1 Skylander; the next variation of that same character will be a Series 2 Skylander, then Series 3, and so on.

Although you will recognize eight out of the 20 new SuperChargers as recurrent "core" characters, this time, these are not actually a continuation of the earlier series. They have been completely "reimagined" by the game designers. Each familiar character has a brand-new range of attack moves and upgrade paths and a new Soul Gem to find within the game (unlocking a super-strong attack move). This means that even if you weren't too impressed with the attacks or stats of a character you've played before, chances are, they now have a new set of skills to offer that you'll like.

Dark and Legendary Skylanders

Legendary Skylanders are special character releases in gold and dark blue coloring. They carry higher Critical Hit and/or Armor stats than their core counterparts, with the same standard upgrades available. In the highly competitive arenas where defensive training takes place, Skylanders have to out-do each other in a great contest of skill and strength. Only the very best fighters receive the honor of Legendary status. As a reward for his or her courage and ability, the winner gets immortalized in a golden statue that stands as guardian until such time as it is awakened by a Portal Master to defend Skylands. In *SuperChargers*, there are three new Legendary Skylanders: Legendary Astroblast, Legendary Bone Bash Roller Brawl, and Legendary Hurricane Jet-Vac.

NOTE

Dark Skylanders are different from Skylanders of the "Dark" element. This can be a little confusing. There are ten elements of Skylands, with the two newest being Light and Dark. Some Skylanders belong to the Dark element and so have elemental attacks relating to its power (such as dark energy attacks). On the other hand, a "Dark Skylander" is one included in the Dark Edition Starter Pack. It belongs to the same element as its "Standard" version and has identical attack moves, but sports black and silver coloring instead.

If you purchase a Dark Edition Starter Pack, you'll find your included character toys are black and silver variations of their *SuperChargers* pose (see Figure 2.21). These are "Dark Skylanders" and join the ranks of eight other Dark variation characters previously released.

The legend goes that Kaos experimented with Petrified Darkness made of Dark Traptanium, an evil substance that would help him dominate Skylands. Some brave Skylanders discovered Kaos' plot and attacked his lair, falling into his trap! They attacked the Petrified Darkness prison with their weapons and it exploded into a poisonous gas. The heroes had no choice but to take the Dark energy of the gas into their own bodies. Together they learned to use their Dark energy for good instead of evil, giving them an extra edge when fighting against villains. In the *SuperChargers* game, these characters include Dark Super Shot Stealth Elf, Dark Spitfire, Dark Hammer Slam Bowser, and Dark Turbo Charge Donkey Kong. The vehicles Dark Clown Cruiser, Dark Hot Streak, Dark Sea Shadow, and Dark Barrel Blaster were also released alongside them.

FIGURE 2.21   Dark SuperChargers are only available through the Dark Edition Starter Packs (or for resale individually online). These include (back left to right): Dark Super Shot Stealth Elf, Dark Turbo Charge Donkey Kong, Dark Hammer Slam Bowser, Dark Spitfire, and their vehicles.

Eon's Elite

Eon's Elite Skylanders rush in where even the bravest heroes fear to tread! No matter what terrible force threatens Skylands, this special team is always ready and willing to put their lives and weapons to the test. Due to their special status, these toys are available as a premium collector's edition with a gold base. They are sold in a clear presentation box with their name on front for you to proudly display. Eon's Elite characters are up to three times stronger than their standard counterparts. They're a fantastic way to bring down enemies fast in the big boss fights you'll inevitably face.

The Eon's Elite character toys, so far, are Whirlwind (Air), Terrafin (Earth), Spyro (Magic), Gill Grunt (Water), Chop Chop (Undead), Stealth Elf (Life), Trigger Happy (Tech), and Eruptor (Fire). *Skylanders SuperChargers* brings a new range of Eon's Elite character toys to the collection: Ghost Roaster (Undead), Dino-Rang (Earth), Boomer (Tech), Slam Bam (Water), Voodood (Magic), and Zook (Life).

Elements

Each Skylander and villain draws power from one of the ten main elements that make up the realms of Skylands (see Figure 2.22). They are all equally powerful, but are usually expressed in different ways through types of attack; for example, a Water elemental Skylander might use a water cannon or geyser to attack enemies, whereas an Earth character may throw boulders, create earthquakes, or burrow underground. In certain areas of the game, a Skylander of a particular element may be stronger than others. At that point, it's a good idea to interchange the Skylanders on your portal so you have the best chance of success while fighting your enemies.

FIGURE 2.22   The ten elements that make up the Skylands realms and the Core of Light (from left to right) are Magic, Water, Earth, Undead, Dark, Tech, Air, Life, Fire, and Light, plus the Kaos element (shown in the middle).

Back at Skylanders Academy, a Greeble caretaker called the Great Grizzo stands guard at an Elemental Gate, waiting to challenge you with some hair-raising quests to increase your Portal Master Rank. You can rescue twitterpillars, gather boulders, destroy turrets and tombstones, dodge lava and asteroids, catch sheep thieves, and a whole lot more!

The Great Grizzo will change the gate and challenge to match the element of the vehicle you take inside. There are ten elemental challenges to try (one for each element). We will explore this area more in Chapter 8, "Great Grizzo's Elemental Challenges."

NOTE

There is one additional element called Kaos, which is only associated with the evil Portal Master himself. This element can be used to harness the power of the other elements and use them against enemies, as well as summon Doom Sharks as an attack move.

The Traptanium Portal and Traps

The Traptanium Portal is your gateway to the Skylands Universe! As the new Portal Master, you can place your figurines on the Portal to bring the SuperCharger and his or her vehicle to life inside the game. The SuperChargers Portal was created with space in mind—with the addition of vehicles to the new game, earlier portals may get a little crowded (especially in multiplayer mode). At any one time you can have up to two SuperChargers (or Skylanders), two vehicles, and a magic item in play.

The SuperChargers Portal, like the one pictured in Figure 2.23, has a small slot in the "engine" control area, in which you can put a trap. Traps were introduced in *Skylanders: Trap Team* as a magical way to capture and store villains that were caught during adventure mode. They are sold separately as translucent traps for each particular element (so far, there is a retail collection of nearly 60 unique shapes, including the Kaos trap, which is specifically made for the evil Portal Master himself). Although traps were an important addition to the *Trap Team* game, their role in *SuperChargers* is fairly small.

Using a trap while playing SuperChargers will give your fighter an additional elemental weapon. In addition to this, if you place a trap in your SuperChargers portal with a trapped villain inside (carried over from your *Trap Team* game), you will unlock a Skystone of that villain for your Skystones Overdrive collection. Each trap is capable of holding a single villain at a time, but to swap one trapped villain for another you will have to visit the Villain Vault at Skylanders Academy in the *Trap Team* game (assuming you have it, of course). You can replace the villain inside a trap as many times as you like, but there is no way of completely emptying a trap once it has been used. Traps will only hold a villain of a matching element inside, so you will need at least one trap for each element to bring them all into *SuperChargers* from *Trap Team*. Because villains themselves are not transferred from traps into the *SuperChargers* game, the new portals don't have the flashing, multicolored lights or the speaker of the Trap Team portal.

FIGURE 2.23   Watch this space! The newest Portal of Power (on right) has extra space built in for vehicles, multiple character toys, traps, and racing trophies; however, any of the previously released portals will still work with *SuperChargers*.

Study Your Stats

As you fly, dive, and race your way through Skylands, you're going to be faced with some pretty tough competition. The more experience, health, and skill your SuperChargers have (see Figure 2.24), the better your chances of a swift victory! In this section, we have a look at the different ways you can enhance your SuperChargers to give you the greatest chance of success. For a quick reference guide to the new SuperChargers stats, see Table 2.1.

FIGURE 2.24 Every SuperCharger has a unique set of skills. These can be improved throughout the game via upgrades, XP points, hats, stardust, and emblems.

TABLE 2.1 Your Quick Reference Guide to SuperCharger Stats

SuperCharger	Element	Max. Health	Armor	Speed	Critical Hit
Astroblast	Light	180	18	35	6
Big Bubble Pop Fizz	Magic	300	24	43	4
Bone Bash Roller Brawl	Undead	220	12	50	6
Deep Dive Gill Grunt	Water	270	24	35	6
Dive-Clops	Water	250	30	35	4
Double Dare Trigger Happy	Tech	300	18	50	6
Fiesta	Undead	230	6	50	4
High Volt	Tech	260	24	50	2
Hurricane Jet-Vac	Air	240	12	43	6
Lava Lance Eruptor	Fire	290	24	35	8
Nightfall	Dark	230	6	43	10
Shark Shooter Terrafin	Earth	270	24	35	4
Smash Hit	Earth	350	24	35	2
Spitfire	Fire	200	18	50	8

SuperCharger	Element	Max. Health	Armor	Speed	Critical Hit
Splat	Magic	240	6	43	4
Stormblade	Air	220	6	50	6
Super Shot Stealth Elf	Life	190	12	50	6
Thrillipede	Life	250	12	50	8

Keep in mind that by combining the power of a SuperCharger with its unique signature vehicle, you'll improve its attack strength by 10% and increase its overall health. When you're playing a hard-to-beat powerful enemy, this can mean the difference between victory and breaking down.

Experience Orbs

As you defeat villains and minions in story mode, you'll notice they give up XP (experience) orbs (little balls of light that remain on the ground after your enemy disappears). Collect these orbs to increase your SuperCharger's individual experience levels (you can see how many XP orbs you have on the experience meter). When your experience (Level) meter is full, your Skylander will progress to the next level. Your Skylander's agility and strength will increase with each level jump up to a maximum of Level 20.

Health

Each time your Level meter fills, your Max Health meter will have the potential to increase even further. This displays how much damage your SuperCharger has taken while fighting—when your Max Health meter hits zero, you will need to take your SuperCharger off the portal and give him or her time to "rest" (until you begin the next level). You can use a different SuperCharger, and then another one, until you've run out of character toys and must begin that level again. In the case of more difficult levels, it helps to have a larger collection on hand to help fight your way through.

You can increase your health by picking up food you see on the ground.

Speed

The Speed meter tells you how fast your SuperCharger can move. You'll find some Skylanders move slower than others, although this is often offset by an improvement in another stat. You can increase your speed by wearing a magical hat that holds a speed boost (you will learn about magical hats in Chapter 5, "Cool Collectibles"). Some magic items can increase your speed for a short time (for example, the Winged Boot item that was released in the Dragon's Peak Adventure Pack for the *Spyro's Adventure* game).

Armor

Your Armor meter shows you the chance you have of deflecting an attack on your SuperCharger (that is, an enemy hit does no damage to your Skylander at all). Each SuperCharger has a specific Armor stat associated with that character. To calculate its usefulness, this stat is represented on the Armor meter as a percentage. The Armor level on the meter is calculated at a rate of 1% per three points of Armor stat.

For example, a SuperCharger character that has 30 Armor, such as Dive-Clops, has a 10% chance to deflect an attack, which is indicated on the Armor meter. A Skylander such as Hurricane Jet-Vac, who has an Armor stat of 12, has only a 4% chance of deflecting an attack entirely. Although the stats are initially set for each character, you can increase them in game through buying upgrades and wearing hats that have an Armor boost included.

Critical Hit

Critical hits are attack moves that create 150% of the regular damage level to an enemy—so of course, the higher the better. The percentage chance for scoring a critical hit is equal to their score on the Critical Hit meter. For example, a SuperCharger such as Spitfire with a Critical Hit of 8 has an 8% chance of scoring a critical hit against an enemy.

This stat can be increased by wearing hats and buying upgrades as well.

Elemental Power

Each SuperCharger begins with an Elemental Power of 25. The more Skylanders you collect of a particular element, the higher your overall elemental power will become.

You'll find that certain areas of Skylands also give bonus damage to SuperChargers of a particular element as you pass through the story chapters. This provides a great opportunity to switch up your playing characters to take advantage of additional strength against enemies. For example, if you use Dive-Clops (a water SuperCharger) with an Elemental Power stat of 25 points in a zone that favors Water Elemental Skylanders, you will increase his power by 1% damage per point. Therefore, Dive-Clops would receive an additional 25% bonus power in these areas. If you increase Dive-Clops' strength by adding more water Skylanders to your collection, to say 40%, then in these "water zones," you'll receive an additional 40% power to your punch.

Power Up Your Heroes with Upgrades

You now have your favorite SuperChargers revved up and you're zooming through the game—so what's next? The excitement of your character toys isn't just in their speed and stats—it's up to you to decide how you want them to perform. Every SuperCharger (even the reimagined ones from earlier games) has a completely unique fighting style and a choice of special abilities. In your main menu, you'll find a category called "My Team" where you can view all of your SuperChargers and their stats, attacks, and accessories. Choose your favorite, then look at the subcategory called "Upgrades" to find out what awesome fighting moves they can offer your gameplay.

Standard Upgrades

Each SuperCharger starts with two basic attack moves. You can upgrade each character further by purchasing upgrades with the gold coins you collect during the story chapters or during challenges at Skylanders Academy (see Figure 2.25). Remember that coins aren't transferrable—each SuperCharger collects his or her own coins, so you have to play with each one enough to collect the coins for his or her own upgrades.

You can upgrade your SuperChargers by visiting Persephone at Skylanders Academy or wherever you find her in the story chapters. To access the upgrades faster, you can collect Winged Sapphires that are hidden throughout the story chapters to earn a discount on upgrades (this discount applies for all SuperChargers). These are blue gems with wings attached. Each Winged Sapphire is worth 2%, and you can earn up to 20% off your upgrades by collecting them all. To begin, Persephone will offer your SuperCharger four new upgrades. Some of these may be prerequisites to later upgrade paths. Each of the four new upgrades cost gold coins:

Upgrade 1: 500 coins

Upgrade 2: 700 coins

Upgrade 3: 900 coins

Upgrade 4: 1200 coins

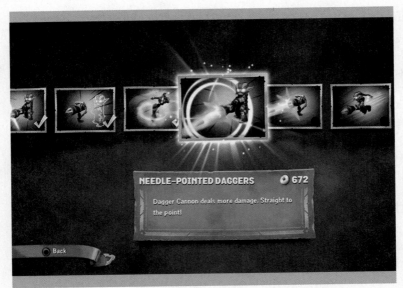

FIGURE 2.25   Every SuperCharger is gifted two basic attack moves to begin; from there on, you can buy upgrades from Persephone to improve and expand your fighting abilities.

Upgrade Paths

After you have bought the first four powers, you have a choice to take one of two further upgrade paths, consisting of three new powers each (see Figure 2.26). You must choose one path or the other to extend the capabilities of a specific attack move by the SuperCharger. Once you have chosen a particular attack path and bought the upgrades, you lose the ability to access the other path, unless you forgo the first path and its powers. Even still, this function won't be available to you unless you reach Portal Master Rank 74 and choose the Skylander Tutor Power (log in to your extra resources online for a full list of Portal Master Ranking Powers).

Upgrade 5: 1700 coins

Upgrade 6: 2200 coins

Upgrade 7: 3000 coins

FIGURE 2.26 Have a good think about which upgrade path to choose before you buy—it's difficult to change once you've decided and you'll waste coins doing it.

Soul Gem Abilities

Each SuperCharger (including reimagined characters) has a Soul Gem hidden somewhere in the game. When you collect this gem, you'll have access to another exciting attack move or ability from Persephone. This is usually their best and strongest attack, so it's worth hunting those Soul Gems down. You may receive the Soul Gem as a reward for your racing prowess with Pandergast, or you may find them throughout the story chapters in Epic Treasure Chests or hiding inside reward stashes. You can also purchase them at Skylanders Academy, from the shop or by throwing Wish Stones into the Wishing Well (this is a random reward—you may receive trinkets or other prizes instead). You'll need to collect the specific Soul Gem for your SuperCharger before you can upgrade with Persephone, at a cost of 4000 gold coins.

Portal Master Rankings

In previous Skylander games, the Portal Master Rank didn't contribute too much to your game playing, aside from unlocking new rewards as you leveled up. In *SuperChargers*, increasing your Portal Master Rank actually gives you some pretty nifty benefits.

To rank up (see Figure 2.27), you'll need to collect stardust. Essentially the more you play, and the higher your skill becomes, the more stardust you'll earn throughout the game. Stardust might be earned during story chapter mode or at Skylanders Academy as a reward for completing challenges and races, opening treasure chests and smashing piñatas and objects, completing quests and earning emblems (we'll look at emblems in the next section of this chapter).

There is a small number of rewards with each rank up, and the benefits and usefulness of these increase the higher up the food chain you climb. You'll begin on Level 1, and if you stick to your guns and play hard, you can make it up to the highest level of 75.

FIGURE 2.27   Earn stardust to increase your Portal Master Ranking for access to extra special powers.

You can activate one bonus power at a time, so pick the one you think will give you the best advantage from the Portal Master section of the main menu at Skylanders Academy. You'll find some rewards suit SuperChargers of a particular element or against a specific type of enemy, so each time you change your SuperCharger on the Portal, think ahead to what might be useful in your upcoming gameplay. You really are spoiled with choices here—there are heaps of fun rewards to take advantage of. For example, if you are about to begin a new adventure chapter, check what level rewards are available to you before you begin; you may have a power available that makes all Undead enemies weaker, or boosts the health of Life Skylanders, or perhaps even provides an Undead Skylander with an extra minion to help beat the bad guys. For a complete list of rewards you can access by levelling up and where you can use them, check online in the companion resources for this book using your unique login. (You first must register your book by going to quepublishing.com/register, and then create an account.)

Emblems

Emblems are a new addition to the *Skylanders* games. Essentially, whenever you hit a certain milestone during your game (by collecting items or completing challenges, such as those listed in Table 2.2), you'll be rewarded with a celebratory emblem that promotes your achievement, such as the one in Figure 2.28. This may be as simple as making it through all the chapters of story mode or playing with a friend, or as tricky as tracking down every collectable in the game. Don't worry, we'll make a lot of these challenges easier for you by giving you hints as to where to find Soul Gems, Legendary Treasure, Kaos Diaries, Skystones, mods, hats, and many more items in Chapter 5.

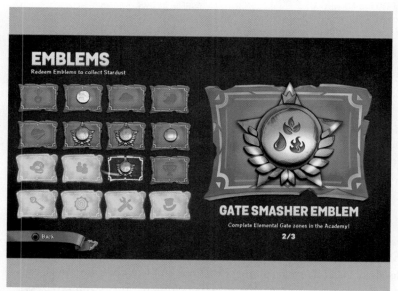

FIGURE 2.28 Play to win! To increase your Portal Master Rank, you need to collect stardust. The fastest way up is by collecting emblems for completing challenges.

TABLE 2.2 Earn Emblems by Completing Special Challenges

Emblem	Challenges to Complete	Milestones Achieved
Card Battler	Win Skystones Overdrive	1, 3, 5, 8, 11, 15
Gate Smasher	Complete Elemental Gate challenges at Skylanders Academy	1
Gemologist	Find all Soul Gems	1, 3, 5, 8, 11, 14, 18
Hero	Complete each level on any difficulty mode	All chapters over 13 levels
Locksmith	Collect three sparks in each Live Wire Lock	1, 3, 5, 8, 11, 15
Mad Hatter	Collect magical hats	4, 12, 24, 40, 60, 86, 118, 158, 206, 266
Relic Seeker	Collect Kaos Diaries, Skystones, and Legendary Treasures	4, 10, 20, 32, 44, 58, 74, 92, 116, 150
Seafarer	Earn stars in sea races	1, 5, 10, 25, 43
Shooting Star	Earn stars in missions	1, 3, 5, 8, 11, 14, 18, 22, 27, 33
Sky Pilot	Earn stars in sky races	1, 5, 10, 25, 43
Speed Racer	Join in online races	1, 3, 5, 8, 11, 15
Speedster	Earn stars in land races	1, 5, 10, 25, 43
Tag Team	Complete missions in Multiplayer mode	1, 3, 5, 8, 11, 15
Technician	Collect vehicle mods	4, 10, 20, 30, 42, 56, 72, 88, 106, 126
Treasure Hunter	Collect Epic Treasure Chests	3, 6, 10, 14, 19, 24, 31, 40, 50, 66
Warrior	Defeat enemies	50, 150, 300, 525, 825, 1200, 1650, 2200, 2900, 3750

If you earn a gold emblem, you can use it to gain stardust to increase your Portal Master Rank. Some emblems have a few rewards to offer as you hit higher levels of success, so keep an eye on your emblem collection page via the Portal Master menu to see what may be helpful to you as you progress through the game.

Get Your Engines Burning!

Of course, it's not all about the Skylanders in *SuperChargers*. You have a host of fantastic vehicles to upgrade as well. By upgrading both your SuperCharger and its vehicle with special abilities, you can create a fully customized fighting team that suits your style. There are two ways to upgrade your vehicles.

Gearbit Upgrades

First, you can buy upgrades from those masterful mechanics at Skylanders Academy; Sharpfin and his team of grease-monkeys (or should it be grease-sharkies?!) can improve your weapons and shields for you in exchange for the gearbits you collect as you play through the racing and story challenges (see Figure 2.29). There are five upgrades per section, giving you huge improvements in your vehicles stats. The cost for each vehicle to upgrade is different (see Chapter 3, "The Good Guys," for individual vehicle upgrades). You can earn a discount on buying your vehicle upgrades by collecting Winged Sapphires, to a total of 20%.

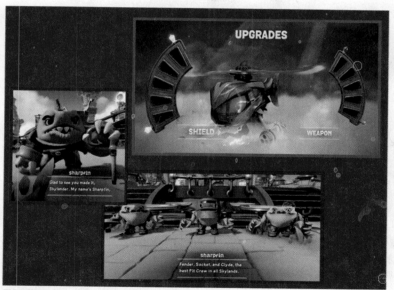

FIGURE 2.29 Visit Sharpfin and his toothy mechanic friends to improve your vehicle's abilities in exchange for collectable gearbits.

Mods

Second, you can also ask Sharpfin and his pit crew to exchange performance mods, specialty mods, and horns for you, or manage this yourself while you are in active vehicle sections of the story chapters. Each vehicle has a special set of interchangeable improvements, called "mods," that will alter a specific part of their performance, as shown in Figure 2.30. For example, the submarine Dive-Bomber might use its specialty mod called "Torpedo Buoys" in a race to increase its top speed by ten points. Mixing and matching the mods can really give you the edge to win a race. You can get a sneak-peek at the mods for your vehicle in the main menu via My Team and then Blueprint.

Mods will become available to your vehicle as you find them. They are hidden in red boxes called "Racing Chests" throughout the sky, sea, and land racing sections of the game and in the races with Pandergast at Skylanders Academy.

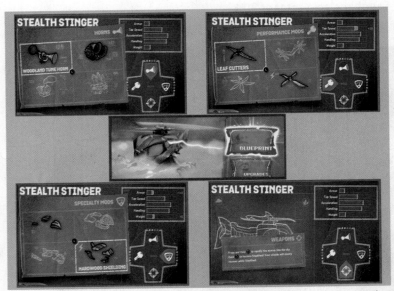

FIGURE 2.30   Interchange the mods of your vehicle as you earn them, to suit your racing style and the challenge ahead.

NOTE

Use Your Traps!

You'll notice your new Portal of Power has a slot in it for an elemental trap, like those you used to catch villains in for *Skylanders: Trap Team*. Sadly, no, you can't transfer villain characters into *SuperChargers* (that is what made *Trap Team* unique!), but the traps themselves can still be used (see Figure 2.31). Placing an elemental trap in the portal will bring a temporary but awesome new attack move for the vehicle you are currently driving. The attack will match the element of the trap, overriding your original weapon. You'll also get a major ammo boost and a shield to protect your vehicle. The clock is ticking though—when the ammo runs out, so does the trap weapon, and then you're back to your original settings.

FIGURE 2.31 Don't let your elemental traps collect dust—pop them into the portal to inject a special weapon and ammo boost to your vehicle!

Friends Online: Multiplayer Adventure Mode

Skylanders has always been a great game to play in multiplayer mode with a friend, by simply connecting a second controller and adding another Skylander to the portal. Now, though, you can go that extra step further. For the first time, *Skylanders* has a fully functional online player mode, so you can connect with your friends across the world.

Work through the adventures of the story chapters with a friend by adding them to your "Friend" folder on the main menu, and then sending them an invite to join you in play (see Figure 2.32). The only limitation to this is that your friend will need to be using the same type of console (for example, PS4 or Xbox One) as yourself.

FIGURE 2.32   Invite your friends to go an epic adventure with you! Chat online as you chase down evil villains, fight minions, and collect rewards!

Race Online: Multiplayer Racing Games

An exciting new era has hit *Skylanders* with the inclusion of racing games! Pandergast has plenty of races at Skylanders Academy. Choose either a sky, sea, or land race, then connect a second controller (see Figure 2.33). You can choose from three different multiplayer race options (with multiple tracks) to have twice as much fun with your friends!

FIGURE 2.33 Rev up the competition with awesome new multiplayer racing options!

Even better, you can even connect with up to three other online players (see Figure 2.34) and four AI-controlled players to make a racing team of eight!

If you are playing with a "recognized" friend through your console, you can also use the chat features as you play. If you're online, but not playing with people you know, the chat feature is disabled.

You can even defeat villains and then race as them in their unique vehicles when using the Racing Action Packs (such as Kaos and his Doom Jet!) and unlock extra racing challenges. You'll earn immediate-use power-ups as you race that can give you a power boost or slow down your opponents (you can't store power-ups for use at a strategic time), these will be hidden somewhere along the track for you to drive through and collect. When you finish, an online leaderboard is posted with all of your friends' best times listed for you to beat.

FIGURE 2.34 No friends nearby? Jump online to send an invite out or find new friends on-the-go to race against!

We'll look more at the racing component of *SuperChargers* in Chapter 9, "SuperCharged Racing."

Skylanders: BattleCast!

When you buy your Starter Pack, you'll notice that some collectible BattleCast cards are included. These cards are not part of your *SuperChargers* adventure, but they are definitely worth keeping.

BattleCast is an interactive card game for Android mobile devices and tablets as well as iPads and iPhones that's due for release by Activision in 2016 (powered by Vuforia). To get started with BattleCast, download the free BattleCast app off the App Store, Google Play, or Amazon Apps. Hold your cards still (flat on a table or upright in your hand, for example) and then scan them into the BattleCast app, as shown in Figure 2.35.

Whoa! The character jumps right out at you in a blaze of fire! Scan two at once to watch them battle each other with a tap of your finger!

You can collect BattleCast cards to build an unbeatable team of Skylanders to play with as well as battle against your friends online.

This mini-game looks absolutely brilliant and will be a fun addition to the Skylanders Universe, so keep your eye out for those collectible cards in retail stores soon.

FIGURE 2.35   Stand back! BattleCast cards will soon explode from the Skylanders Universe right onto your mobile device!

The Good Guys

What's the very best thing about an adventure? Of course, it's the brave and clever heroes who rush in where others fear to tread! With *Skylanders SuperChargers*, we got *super* lucky—there are 20 inspiring Skylanders to lead us into battle, and each one has his or her own unique, crazy, and powerful fighting abilities.

Alongside these feisty fighters, you can summon laser-sheep on flying meteors, shoot water cannons from giant eyeballs, paint with explosives, erupt volcanoes where you stand, surf tidal waves, and go completely berserk! (Just to name a few... phew!) Let your imagination go wild, fighting with this stellar new team of champions as you hunt down Kaos and his minions throughout Skylands.

Meet the New SuperChargers

In this chapter you'll meet each of the newest SuperChargers and find out why they were hand-picked for Eon's team of heroes, take a closer look at their attack moves, upgrades, strengths, and weaknesses, and learn all about their signature SuperCharged vehicles as well.

FIGURE 3.1 Twenty new characters are waiting to drive their SuperCharged vehicles into the Skylander history books. Get your portal ready!

SuperCharger Upgrades

As discussed in Chapter 2, "Start Your Engines," each Skylander can be upgraded by visiting Persephone at Skylanders Academy, or wherever else she pops up during the story chapters. All SuperChargers begin with two basic attacks, which can be improved upon until your Skylander is an all-powerful fighting machine. You can customize their abilities by choosing an attack path that suits your fighting style, as outlined in each character's biography in this chapter. Try to make sure you have a range of skills available across your collection for big boss fights—some melee, some long-range, and a few healing abilities. You'll need them when times get tough.

Vehicle Upgrades

Visit Sharpfin and his team at Skylanders Academy (they are also hiding somewhere in each chapter, usually near the vehicle challenges) to buy upgrades for your vehicles' shields and weapons. There are five levels of increasing defensive power to buy using the gearbits you collect as you play, as outlined in this chapter, although this cost can be reduced by collecting Winged Sapphires (see Chapter 5, "Cool Collectibles"). The costs for buying shield and weapon upgrades are different for each individual vehicle (as listed in the upcoming biographies).

Racing Chest Bonus Mods

Don't forget that upgrading your vehicles doesn't end with shields and weapons! You'll find special "mods" (modifications) to rev up your machine as you explore Skylands. The performance mods and specialty mods can be interchanged at any time to create an easier ride by improving your vehicle handling or to increase your acceleration and power (for the speed demons out there, like you!). You can even switch up your horns (just for fun!). There are four different kinds of horn mods (as shown in Figure 3.2), each of which has a different name and sound for each vehicle. You'll find mods in the vehicle challenges of the adventure chapters. These are also given as rewards for coming in first in race mode.

Upgrading your SuperChargers and vehicles will make a huge difference to your gameplay and really give you the edge over villains. Have a browse through this chapter to get up close and personal with your new team and their vehicles so you can plan ahead for upgrade paths and mod exchanges!

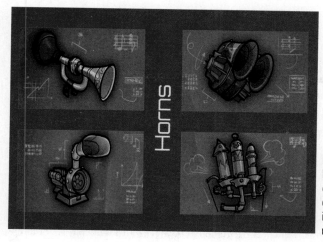

FIGURE 3.2 Choose between four different horns for each of your vehicles as interchangeable mods.

Shark Shooter Terrafin: "It's Feeding Time!"

FIGURE 3.3 Don't be fooled by this FIN-fighter's FANCY FOOTWORK, he's a real KNOCK-OUT!

TABLE 3.1 Shark Shooter Terrafin's Stats!

Element	Earth
SuperCharged Vehicle	Shark Tank
Max. Health	270
Armor	24
Speed	35
Critical Hit	4
Elemental Power	25

Although he grew up surfing the soil of the Dirt Seas, Terrafin never plays dirty! His bravery and epic boxing skills led him to become a champion fighter in his homeland, where he drew the attention of Master Eon. He was quickly recruited for the SuperChargers team. Behind his toothy grin is a fin-sharp mind; with one quick dive, he'll disappear underground, leaving a trail of rocky earth for his enemies to tumble over until—BAM!—Terrafin emerges shooting shark rockets right on target! This land shark is always ready to whip up a whirlpool of trouble for the bad guys.

Attack Moves:

Ballistic Frenzy: Press **Attack 1** to fire shark rockets that burrow into the ground.

Earth Swim Blast: Press **Attack 2** to burrow into the ground. Press **Attack 1** to emerge and shoot a rocket at the ground.

Soul Gem Ability: Sand Snare – 4000: During Earth Swim Blast, press **Jump** to create a sand whirlpool to trap enemies in.

Upgrades:

TABLE 3.2 Shark Shooter Terrafin's Upgrades!

Slam Support – 500: Press **Attack 3** to slam the gun on the ground and knock back nearby enemies. Press **Attack 3** during Earth Swim Blast to launch a shark ally that will attack nearby enemies.
Seek or Swim – 700: Ballistic Frenzy rockets do more damage to enemies.
Surface to Air to Surface Missiles – 900: Hold **Attack 3** to fire rockets into the ground that emerge and land on enemies. (Prerequisite- Slam Support.)
Seconds Please – 1200: Ballistic Frenzy rockets now hit enemies twice.

Shark Team Squadron Path: Gain more support from powerful shark allies!	**All Terrain Trooper Path:** Use advanced underground abilities to surprise and defeat enemies!
Three Best Fins – 1700 Press **Attack 3** during Earth Swim Blast to launch three sharks.	**Mentor Program – 1700** Press **Attack 3** during Earth Swim Blast to make a bigger shark ally that lasts longer, can hit enemies multiple times, and does more damage.
What Goes Up – 2200 S.A.S. missiles do more damage on the way up and on the way down.	**Finesse – 2200** Earth Swim Blast speed is increased and enemies are damaged by the fancy new fin.
Land Shark – 3000 Hold **Attack 1** and release to fire a mortar that summons a sand whirlpool and a large land shark.	**Mega Boomflop – 3000** During Earth Swim Blast, press **Attack 1** to fire rockets and perform a belly flop that knocks back enemies.

Shark Tank

FIGURE 3.4 Tear up the road with Shark Tank's UNDERGROUND NAVIGATION, and enemies will EAT YOUR DUST!

Watch your toes—this tank's got teeth! Shark Tank will blow enemies right off track with its all-terrain spiky tread. Its handling is good because Shark Tank is heavy and sticks to the road. This vehicle is a bit slow to get up to pace, but once there it's a fast ride. Upgrade its low value armor as soon as you can to make sure you don't come undone under enemy fire. Drilling underground in Street Swimming mode will help you get an enemy off your tail when racing or under attack. Keep your finger on the shark missiles to knock winners out of the water ahead of you with awesome aim so you can zoom by unscathed.

Upgrade Shark Tank's shields and weapons with Sharpfin and his crew:

Upgrade Level 1: 800 gearbits

Upgrade Level 2: 900 gearbits

Upgrade Level 3: 1000 gearbits

Upgrade Level 4: 1100 gearbits

Upgrade Level 5: 1200 gearbits

Weapons

Ballistic Drill Missile: Press **Attack 1** for shark missiles.

Street Swimming: Press **Attack 3** to enter Street Swimming mode!

Horns

- Quarry Clang Horn
- Bedrock Bop Horn
- Terrain Trumpet Horn
- Sand Shark Alarm Horn

Specialty Mods

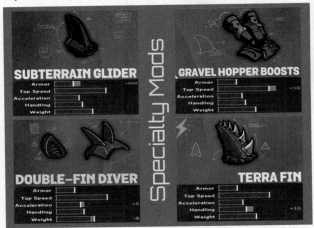

Performance Mods

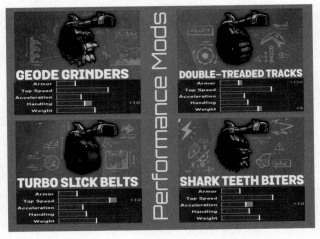

Smash Hit: "Let's Rock!"

FIGURE 3.5 Duck and cover! There's no HAZARD PAY if you're in the way when Smash Hit comes in with his WRECKING BALL!

TABLE 3.3 Smash Hit's Stats!

Element	Earth
SuperCharged Vehicle	Thump Truck
Max. Health	350
Armor	24
Speed	35
Critical Hit	2
Elemental Power	25

Looking for a sweet, little, furry bunny to play with? Well, you'd better keep looking! Despite his big, bright eyes and fuzzy face, Smash Hit is anything but snuggly—he's all about smashing! In his earlier life as a professional demolisher of all things Ancient Arkeyan, this mighty Warsupial was renowned for his ability to dismantle a giant Conquertron faster than anyone could strap their war helmet on! These days, Smash Hit just adores swinging his chained boulder around his head and laying waste to enemies that get in his way. Stand clear and let the smashing begin!

Attack Moves:

Demolisher: Press **Attack 1** repeatedly to swing the boulder around in a circle.

Crushinator: Press **Attack 2** to smash the boulder on the ground in front of you.

Soul Gem Ability: Down, Under – 4000: Hold **Attack 3** when connecting to the boulder to create a huge explosion underneath you!

Upgrades:

TABLE 3.4 Smash Hit's Upgrades!

Connect and Disconnect – 500: Press **Attack 3** to disconnect the boulder and gain unique chain attacks. Press **Attack 3** again to connect.

Junkyard Dog – 700: Boulder attacks deal more damage. Rock on!

Spikey Spinner – 900: Hold **Attack 3** for a short time to charge up the boulder and send it spinning at enemies. (Prerequisite: Connect and Disconnect.)

Junker – 1200: Chain attacks deal more damage. Chain time! (Prerequisite: Connect and Disconnect.)

Bolder Boulder Path: Gain more powerful boulder attacks.

Heap – 1700

Hold **Attack 2** for a short amount of time to charge your boulder. The next attack with the boulder will deal massive damage!

Better Together – 2200

Gain a large armor increase when connecting. Press **Attack 3** to disconnect the boulder; press **Attack 3** again to connect.

Catch! – 3000

Hold **Attack 1** while connected to throw your boulder at enemies!

Chain Champ Path: Gain more powerful long-range chain attacks.

G'Day! – 1700

Hold **Attack 1** while disconnected to pull yourself to enemies!

Cut Loose – 2200

The next attack will be a critical hit when disconnecting. Press **Attack 3** to disconnect the boulder; press **Attack 3** again to connect.

Earth Currents – 3000

Press **Attack 2** while disconnected to pull enemies into the spinning boulder.

Thump Truck

FIGURE 3.6   PACK a PUNCH with the land-racer that SLAMS enemies FISTS down!

This is a racer with a serious payoff to consider; if you're patient with the very l-o-n-g time it takes to get up to top speed, you're rewarded with a fast, solid vehicle that can really take a punch (and make one, for that matter!). Its weapons system champions one-on-one combat—you can annihilate enemies with a giant stone fist using the Under Punch attack, or take a whole tribe out by smashing into them with the Bush Booster move. Both of these are powerful attacks, but the downside is they're both front-on only, leaving you open to attacks from behind. (But keep this vulnerability in mind if you're racing against Thump Truck with Pandergast.) This vehicle has a really tight turning circle and is great for rounding up objects or attacking in small spaces. If you can upgrade your mods with the Rough Truck Grill and Fusion Mixer to put the gas on your acceleration, you'll have a star all-rounder on your hands.

Upgrade Thump Truck's shields and weapons with Sharpfin and his crew:

    Upgrade Level 1: 800 gearbits

    Upgrade Level 2: 900 gearbits

    Upgrade Level 3: 1000 gearbits

    Upgrade Level 4: 1100 gearbits

    Upgrade Level 5: 1200 gearbits

Weapons

Under Punch: Press **Attack 1** to uppercut enemies with a fist of solid rock!

Bush Booster: Hold **Attack 3** to become unstoppable and slam into enemies for mega damage!

Horns

    Mammoth Toot Horn

    Builder Boom Horn

    Hornfoolery Horn

    Wrecking Racket Horn

Specialty Mods

Performance Mods

Fiesta: "It's Party Time!"

FIGURE 3.7 DANCE to the TUNE of DESTRUCTION to really BRING DOWN THE HOUSE!

TABLE 3.5 Fiesta's Stats!

Element	Undead
SuperCharged Vehicle	Crypt Crusher
Max. Health	230
Armor	6
Speed	50
Critical Hit	4
Elemental Power	25

Grab your violin and vihuela, the master of mariachi is in town! With a shake and a shimmy, Fiesta is not only the coolest trumpet player in the history of the Undead, but his music is to die for... literally! Before he became a SuperCharger, Fiesta joined a team of Skylanders investigating dangerous rifts that were appearing around Skylands. His bravery saved his friends many times, culminating in a deadly battle against Dark Drows at the Whirlpool of Destiny. After their success, Fiesta upgraded his vehicle, the Crypt Crusher, with a SuperCharged Rift Engine, to enable him to fight for Master Eon permanently. Armed with Amigos that ensure an epic fighting finale, this is one Skylander who will never miss an after-party!

Attack Moves:

Trumpet Concord: Hold **Attack 1** to play a tune on the trumpet gun that damages nearby enemies.

Amigos: Press **Attack 2** to summon a friendly instrument-wielding amigo.

Soul Gem Ability: Family Fiesta – 4000: Hold **Attack 2** to summon a fiesta! The guest list is huge!

Upgrades:

TABLE 3.6   Fiesta's Upgrades!

Laid Low – 500: Press **Attack 3** to become partially hidden, taking reduced damage.
Macho Amigos – 700: Amigos now deal more damage. Those little guys pack a punch!
Solo – 900: Press **Attack 1** while playing trumpet to play a solo note that will home in and damage nearby enemies.
Encore – 1200: Playing five solo notes in a row will cause Amigos to stay longer. (Prerequisite: Solo.)

What Amigos Are For Path: Make a stronger bond with your Amigos, making them more powerful. Best Amigos Forever!	**Super Star! Path:** Become the star of the show and bewilder enemies with magnificent performances!
Take it away Amigos! – 1700 Press **Attack 1** while trumpeting to play a solo note; every fifth solo note played makes Amigos get a damage boost!	**Diva – 1700** After you play five solo notes, a spotlight appears around you that gives increased money, experience, and food.
Mucho Amigos – 2200 Press **Attack 2** to summon an Amigo. Now have up to five Amigos!	**Shot to the Heart – 2200** Press **Attack 1** while trumpeting to play a solo note; solo notes now pierce enemies.
Soul Jam – 3000 Press **Attack 3** to become Laid Low; Amigos move faster while Laid Low.	**Big Finish – 3000** Press **Attack 3** to become Laid Low; Amigos grow large and then explode after a short time while Laid Low.

Crypt Crusher

FIGURE 3.8 When the MUSIC begins, spin the WHEEL OF DOOM to RAISE THE ROOF!

Crypt Crusher is a rocking land vehicle that shoots musical notes from the four trumpet launchers on its coffin chassis. You're not the only one keen for a spin this time—a team of cheerful Amigos are riding shotgun, ready to throw themselves at the bad guys and wear them down with crazy-awesome cheerfulness! The Crypt Crusher isn't your standard Undead vehicle; it brings enemies down with a bang, crash, boom! Tight turns are tricky in Crypt Crusher compared to other vehicles because it needs a bit of room to move, but this land vehicle has great speed and a strong attack. Keep those musical notes firing to play a song of destruction for an immediate attack and let your Amigos help you out when you've got time to kill.

Upgrade Crypt Crusher's shields and weapons with Sharpfin and his crew:

Upgrade Level 1: 800 gearbits

Upgrade Level 2: 900 gearbits

Upgrade Level 3: 1000 gearbits

Upgrade Level 4: 1100 gearbits

Upgrade Level 5: 1200 gearbits

Weapons

Tune Up: Press **Attack 1** to shoot musical notes at enemies. Shoot more notes with more Amigos.

Amigo Amplitude: Press **Attack 3** to shoot Amigos that attach to enemies, damaging them over time.

Horns

Decomposition Horn

Cacoffiny Horn

Creepy Critter Call Horn

Honkoween Horn

Specialty Mods

Performance Mods

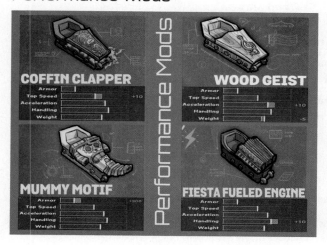

Bone Bash Roller Brawl: "Let's Roll!"

FIGURE 3.9 Send the KISS OF DEATH to Kaos, while you deliver some disastrous DERBY DAMAGE!

TABLE 3.7 Bone Bash Roller Brawl's Stats!

Element	Undead
SuperCharged Vehicle	Tomb Buggy
Max. Health	220
Armor	12
Speed	50
Critical Hit	6
Elemental Power	25

The roller-derby super-champion Bone Bash Roller Brawl must be the unluckiest vampire in the world! Why, you ask? Because she inadvertently won the undying love of the evilest of all Portal Masters—Kaos! That egocentric, bad-tempered little villain bent on world domination may have his charms (well, he's pretty funny!), but Roller Brawl was not impressed at all! She turned her back on the lovesick lunatic, and when her five brothers turned up to tussle, Kaos had them all kidnapped! Now Roller Brawl is on a deadly mission—to seek out the terrible Drow army and rescue her five vampire brothers while fighting Kaos every step of the way. You go, girl!

Attack Moves:

Derby Duke: Press **Attack 1** to slash nearby enemies with your Fang Blades.

Fangerang: Press **Attack 2** to extend your Fang Blades and throw them out at enemies. Press **Attack 1** while the Fang Blades are out to attack with your fists!

Soul Gem Ability: Brawling Bout! – 4000: Roller Brawl's rage grows over time. When she is at maximum rage, hold **Attack 2** to unleash her fury on nearby enemies.

Upgrades:

TABLE 3.8 Bone Bash Roller Brawl's Upgrades!

Love Bites – 500: Press **Attack 2** while Fangerangs are thrown to blow a fangy Vampire Kiss at enemies. Enemies hit by the kiss will be weakened and have some of their health drained.

Skaters Gonna Skate – 700: Press **Attack 3** to skate faster and extend your Fang Blades while doing so, which damages enemies that get in your way!

Derby Damage – 900: Derby Duke attacks now do more damage. All is fair in Derby!

Crossover Technique – 1200: Fangerangs seek out other targets after the first before returning.

Brawler Derby Path: Keep the enemy on their toes with aggressive upgrades that favor mobility!

Jam-Time – 1700

Hold **Attack 3** while skating to launch yourself like a missile, damaging any enemy in the way.

Serious Substitution – 2200

Fang Blades become more powerful and will do more damage to enemies.

Always Wear a Helmet – 3000

Hold **Attack 1** to do an explosive head-butt. That's using your head!

Waller Derby Path: Shrug off enemy attacks with upgrades that favor defense and range!

Eat Pavement – 1700

Hold **Attack 3** to tear up the pavement and damage all enemies in front of you.

Blocker Boutfit – 2200

Your armor bulks up and reduces enemy damage.

Contagious Kiss – 3000

When Love Bites connects, it will explode in smaller Vampire Kisses that can bite, weaken, and drain surrounding enemies.

Tomb Buggy

FIGURE 3.10 GRIND your enemies into BONE DUST with a BLAST of UNDEAD RAGE!

Tomb Buggy is a light vehicle with excellent handling, so hold on tight—you'll defy gravity in this machine to knock out the bad guys. It's a little slow to get started and not the fastest on the track, so build up your speed with mods and upgrades for a fully SuperCharged experience. Spread the Love is a great long-range weapon with a wide arc of destruction, but keep your finger on the attack longer to do permanent damage.

Upgrade Tomb Buggy's shields and weapons with Sharpfin and his crew:

Upgrade Level 1: 800 gearbits

Upgrade Level 2: 900 gearbits

Upgrade Level 3: 1000 gearbits

Upgrade Level 4: 1100 gearbits

Upgrade Level 5: 1200 gearbits

Weapons

Spread the Love: Tap **Attack 1** to blast a spread shot of Undead power at enemies.

Unfair Play: Hold **Attack 3** to grind nearby enemies with wheel energy.

Horns

Scream Screech Horn

Underworld Hum Horn

Spectral Spooker Horn

Organ Blast Horn

Specialty Mods

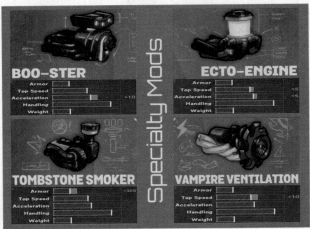

Performance Mods

Lava Lance Eruptor: "Born to Burn!"

FIGURE 3.11 Need to make a POINT? BURN the baddies with lashings of LAVA POWER!

TABLE 3.9 Lava Lance Eruptor's Stats!

Element	Fire
SuperCharger Vehicle	Burn-Cycle
Max. Health	290
Armor	24
Speed	35
Critical Hit	8
Elemental Power	25

Fancy a nice dip in a steaming pool of red-hot lava? Me neither! But to Lava Lance Eruptor, chillin' in a bubbling volcano is paradise! He never meant to be marooned on the surface of Skylands (his volcanic home *kind of* exploded everywhere!), but since he arrived he has put his magma-tic personality to good use chasing down evil and protecting his fiery clan. Eruptor's wicked lance attack moves will bring down close-range enemies easily. Treat the bad guys to a triad of exploding volcanoes with the Eruption Ruffian Path for a solid long-range attack. Just remember when you win, no high-fives (ouch!)

Attack Moves:

Lava Lancing: Rapidly press **Attack 1** to unleash a series of lance attacks.

Lance Legwork: Press **Attack 2** to spring forward with your lance out to damage enemies along the way.

Soul Gem Ability: Magma Chamber – 4000: Press **Attack 3** while in the air to cannon ball into the ground, creating a lava fountain. Rapidly tap **Attack 3** to stay on top of the fountain shooting hot magma all around you.

Upgrades:

TABLE 3.10 Lava Lance Eruptor's Upgrades!

Hot Spot – 500: Press **Attack 3** to spit a magma ball into the ground that burrows toward your enemies. It will create an active volcano that shoots fiery projectiles at nearby enemies.	
Lava Joust – 700: Hold **Attack 2** to dash for a longer amount of time, damaging enemies along your way.	
Lance Advanced – 900: Upgrade your lance with metal and do more damage.	
Lance Cannon – 1200: Hold **Attack 1** to charge up and throw a super lance that explodes on contact.	
Eruption Ruffian Path: Make the earth shake with this eruption-based path!	**Volcano Vaulter Path:** Joust through your foes and blow them away with your lava spike lance!
Hot Feat – 1700 Gain an uppercut explosion at the end of dash attacks.	**Volatile Volcanoes – 1700** Dashing over active volcanoes will boost you forward, causing extra damage and extending the dash and the active volcano's time.
Volcanic Rain – 2200 Using Hot Feat causes all active volcanoes to erupt, damaging and knocking nearby enemies up into the air.	**Eruption Conduction – 2200** While you are dashing, your lance grows extra spikes. Press **Attack 3** to shoot the spikes off your lance, causing them to form a volcano where they land.
Third Volcano's The Charm – 3000 Hold **Attack 3** and release to shoot out three magma balls that create three active volcanoes.	**Cannon Stop Me Now – 3000** Your Lance will now regrow spikes over time, allowing you to create volcanoes to boost over forever!

Burn-Cycle

Armor
Top Speed
Acceleration
Handling
Weight

BURN-CYCLE

FIGURE 3.12 Put your pedal to the metal and BURN, baby BURN!!!

Burn-Cycle is a red-hot speed demon but takes a bit of acceleration to get up there. Take advantage of speed boosters to rip through land tracks and cause a lot of damage along your way. This vehicle has a tight turning circle, which is great for rounding up spheres, magnets, and collecting rewards, but you'll need to watch your aim with the fireball attack because it has to be right on target to score. There's a bit of a fishtail when you spin out on turns, so be light on the direction control so you don't lose time straightening up. The blazing trail attack is a good way to leave trouble for enemies trailing you in a race, but fireballs are the way to go for maximum damage in a fight.

Upgrade Burn Cycle's shields and weapons with Sharpfin and his crew:

> Upgrade Level 1: 800 gearbits
>
> Upgrade Level 2: 900 gearbits
>
> Upgrade Level 3: 1000 gearbits
>
> Upgrade Level 4: 1100 gearbits
>
> Upgrade Level 5: 1200 gearbits

Weapons

Delayed Blast Pyreball: Tap **Attack 1** and stick your enemy with an exploding fire ball.

Releasing Fire: Press and hold **Attack 3** and blaze a fiery trail, damaging any enemy who passes through it.

Horns

Eruption Uproar Horn

Cinderinger Horn

Heat Beep Horn

Volcanic Volume Horn

Specialty Mods

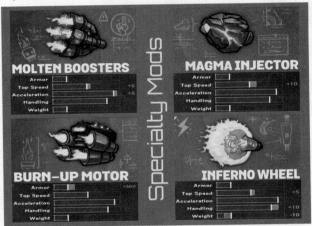

Performance Mods

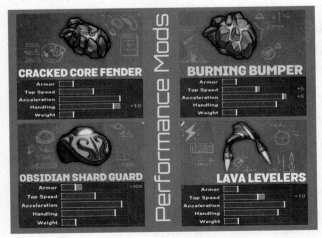

Hammer Slam Bowser (Nintendo Consoles Only)

FIGURE 3.13 The ultimate villain-turned-hero is out for revenge with his TROOP OF KOOPAS, CLAWS, and triple-hit HAMMER SLAM!

TABLE 3.11 Hammer Slam Bowser's Stats!

Element	Fire
SuperCharger Vehicle	Clown Cruiser
Max. Health	280
Armor	30
Speed	35
Critical Hit	6
Elemental Power	25

On his own far-away world across the rift divide, Bowser was the undisputed, tyrannical king of the Koopas. When evil Kaos created the Sky Eater and Skylands was plunged into impending doom, Mags sent out a distress call that crossed the breach between worlds where the Sky Eater had torn it apart. Bowser jumped through the rift to investigate the call. Suddenly faced with pirates on the boundary of Skylands, Bowser fought to save his own life and that of his mortal enemy Donkey Kong, and the two finally stood victorious together. SuperCharged with Rift Engines that they discovered nearby, and given a new fighting jet, the Clown Cruiser, to aid him, Hammer Slam Bowser agreed to keep fighting against The Darkness to prevent it from reaching his own world as well. Until Kaos is defeated and the war is won, enemies become friends. After that... who knows?

Attack Moves:

Hammer Slam: Press **Attack 1** to swing your hammer and attack nearby enemies.

Koopa Troopa!: Press **Attack 2** to call in a Koopa. Jump on Koopas to send them spinning around the level!

Soul Gem Ability: Molten Bones – 4000: Press **Attack 3** to turn into Molten Bowser. Turning into Molten Bowser transforms all active Koopas into Molten Bones, which do more damage to enemies!

Upgrades:

TABLE 3.12 Hammer Slam Bowser's Upgrades!

Molten Bowser – 500: Press **Attack 3** to become a fiery Bowser! Press **Attack 1** to swipe at enemies with fiery claws or press **Attack 2** to breathe out fire!

Shell Smash – 700: Press **Attack 1** to hit a nearby spinning Koopa, causing them to spin around faster and do more damage.

Red Koopa – 900: Press **Attack 2** to spawn a Red Koopa. Red Koopas home in on enemies while in their shell.

Royal Authority – 1200: Press **Attack 2** to spawn a Koopa. This will also cause nearby Koopas to stop spinning.

Koopa Commander Path: Use masterful battle tactics to cause your Koopas to do devastating damage to enemies.	**Molten Monstrosity:** Power up with new mighty lava attacks to make enemies feel the burn!
Warp Pipe – 1700	**Molten Hammer – 1700**
Hold **Attack 2** to summon a Warp Pipe that spawns Koopas.	Press **Attack 1** three times to do a massive lava slam attack.
Koopa Paratroopa – 2200	**Bowser Bomb – 2200**
Press **Attack 2** to summon a Koopa Paratroopa. Flying and Homing!	Press **Attack 3** to enter Molten Bowser mode, causing an explosion and massive damage to the enemies around you.
Super Koopa Spin – 3000	**Infinite Fire – 3000**
Press **Attack 1** to make nearby spinning Koopas spin even faster. You can now spin up Koopas even more, thus doing more damage to enemies!	Hold **Attack 2** while in Molten Bowser mode to deliver a continuous stream of fire.

Clown Cruiser (Nintendo Consoles Only)

FIGURE 3.14 Light up the sky with FIREBALLS of FURY; this JOKER just got serious!

The Clown Cruiser is a custom-made Air element jumbo jet with the Nintendo-familiar markings of Bowser's Amiibo Koopa Car. This is a reinforced armor-plated warplane made of Koopa shells with heavy ammunition. Interestingly, the armor still gets damaged pretty easily, so upgrade your shields with Sharpfin as you progress. Blow the bad guys out of the sky with its super firepower and tight barrel rolls. This plane is a little touchy on the controls, so be careful not to overshoot your target. The Bullet Bill has a pretty nifty homing device that helps keep you on track. Remember, the air practice range at Skylanders Academy is a great place to put your skills to the test. Clown Cruiser is quite slow to accelerate (this is a very heavy vehicle!) but offers a super-fast ride once you hit top speed, so boost your strength with the Dry Bone Basher and Steeled Bone mods to get there faster.

Upgrade Clown Cruiser's shields and weapons with Sharpfin and his crew:

Upgrade Level 1: 800 gearbits

Upgrade Level 2: 900 gearbits

Upgrade Level 3: 1000 gearbits

Upgrade Level 4: 1100 gearbits

Upgrade Level 5: 1200 gearbits

Weapons

Fireballs: Press **Attack 1** to fire a Red Shell Koopas.

Bullet Bill: Hold **Attack 2** to charge up a Bullet Bill. Release to fire!

Horns

Platform Horn

Pip Squeaker Horn

King's Bellower Horn

Sky Rage Horn

Specialty Mods

Performance Mods

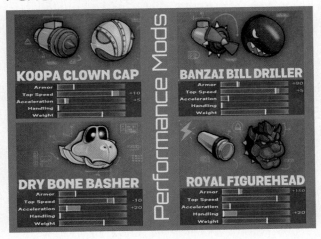

Spitfire: "Fuel the Fire!"

FIGURE 3.15 FUEL THE FIRE to FLAME and FORTUNE by unleashing the FLAMENADO!

TABLE 3.13 Spitfire's Stats!

Element	Fire
SuperCharger Vehicle	Hot Streak
Max. Health	200
Armor	18
Speed	50
Critical Hit	8
Elemental Power	25

Spitfire is a speedster flame spirit with moves as fast as lightning! In the Super Skylands Racing Circuit, his destiny seemed assured... that is, until he hit a bump in the road! Instead of seeking racing revenge on the naughty goblin that knocked him off course and made him lose the championship race, Spitfire is putting a hold on his hobby for a very good cause. He's valiantly leading the fight against Kaos and that terrifying Sky Eater! With minions of Kaos on the loose, it's a race against time. Upgrade Spitfire's flaming melee combos to create a homing fire attack that will have them running scared. Never fear—as soon as Skylands is safe again, Spitfire will be back on track at Skywinder Canyon, leaving competitors in the dust!

Attack Moves:

Butane Brawling: Press **Attack 1** rapidly to perform flaming melee combos.

Flash Fire: Press **Attack 2** to quickly dash forward in an explosive flash.

Soul Gem Ability: The Flamenadoing – 4000: Create a large explosion at the beginning of each Flamenado!

Upgrades:

TABLE 3.14 Spitfire's Upgrades!

Flamenado – 500: Press **Attack 3** to spin into the air and create a giant fire tornado!
Flamenado Chasers – 700: Tornadoes now home in on nearby enemies. (Prerequisite: Flamenado.)
Flame Fury – 900: Hold **Attack 2** to charge up and then quickly dash around hitting nearby foes.

Intensified Fury – 1200: Boost your melee combo with a flaming spin attack.

Speed Demon Path: Become the fastest Skylander around and blaze through Skylands!

Fusion Path: Master the ability to combine the strength of a storm and the heat of a torch!

Mega Marathon – 1700

Gain an even more powerful charge level when you hold **Attack 2**. Release to dash around the Skylands, damaging enemies in your way.

Fuel Injected Claws – 1700

You can now have up to two Flamenadoes out at any given time.

Volcanic Armor – 2200

Nitro Boost – 2200

Holding **Attack 2** while fully charged will cause you to move extra fast and take less damage!

Constant exposure to tornadoes has superheated your core, causing you to do more melee damage.

Volcanic Armor – 3000

Triathlete – 3000

Tap **Attack 2** after dashing around the world to dash around two extra times.

Become resistant to damage by having super tough, lava-like armor.

Hot Streak

FIGURE 3.16 STREAK ahead of your enemies with a NITRO BOOST that's OUT OF CONTROL!

Hot Streak is the quintessential racing vehicle, with superb handling and great speed. Acceleration is steady, but you can get up to super-speed, especially if you deploy the nitro boost attack. In a fight, this vehicle can hold its own, with a strong long-range attack of streaming fire to take out enemies in front. Upgrade Hot Streak for the ultimate ride.

Upgrade Hot Streak's shields and weapons with Sharpfin and his crew:

Upgrade Level 1: 800 gearbits

Upgrade Level 2: 900 gearbits

Upgrade Level 3: 1000 gearbits

Upgrade Level 4: 1100 gearbits

Upgrade Level 5: 1200 gearbits

Weapons

Fire Grill: Hold **Attack 1** to unleash a powerful stream of fire to heat up your enemies.

Nitro Blaze: Press **Attack 3** to boost forward in a nitro blaze of glory!

Horns

Searing Snarler Horn

Fire Crackle Horn

Semi Blaze Horn

Pop Snapper Horn

Specialty Mods

Performance Mods

High Volt: "Protect and Surge!"

FIGURE 3.17 Make LIGHT WORK of villains! This Commander will AMP UP and re-FUSE to let evil SHORT CIRCUIT Skylands!

TABLE 3.15 High Volt's Stats!

Element	Tech
SuperCharger Vehicle	Shield Striker
Max. Health	260
Armor	24
Speed	50
Critical Hit	2
Elemental Power	25

There's no one keeping a closer eye on the comings and goings of Kaos' minions than Commander High Volt. From the Shockspire Tower Security HQ, he was the first to discover the Doom Station of Ultimate Destruction as it was being built, and gave up his post to alert Master Eon. Now as a tactical leader in the SuperChargers, High Volt uses his military training and vast knowledge of machinery to uphold the law. His electrically charged Static Spear and Shock-It Shield are powerful in melee attacks and can hold off an army of Trolls. Upgrade to cause an electrical explosion to black out even the most hardened criminals.

Attack Moves:

Static Spear: Press **Attack 1** rapidly to perform melee attacks with your Static Spear.

Shock-It Shield: Hold **Attack 2** to block attacks. Gain charges when hit, and release **Attack 2** to issue the charges in a big blast that damages nearby enemies.

Soul Gem Ability: Re-Fused – 4000: Restore some health when you block and have low health.

Upgrades:

TABLE 3.16 High Volt's Upgrades!

Traveling Light – 500: Hold **Attack 3** to throw your Static Spear and create an electric beam that damages enemies caught between you and the spear.

Quick Currents – 700: While using Traveling Light, you will gain a huge movement increase!

Insulated Iron – 900: Upgrade your armor to help against enemy attacks!

Amped Lamp – 1200: Hold **Attack 1** to charge up your spear; release to cause a huge electric explosion that damages nearby enemies.

Light Fighter Path: Use powerful electric close-range attacks to stun and defeat your enemies!	Light in Shining Armor Path: Defeat enemies with a powered-up electric beam!
Bring into Light – 1700	**Bright Idea – 1700**
Enemies caught inside your electric beam will be drawn to you when the spear returns to you.	Hold **Attack 3** to throw your Static Spear and create a more powerful electric beam that does more damage to enemies caught in it.
Stun Shocked – 2200	
Hold **Attack 3** to throw your Static Spear and create an electric beam. After your spear returns, your next melee attack will damage and stun nearby enemies.	**Everything is Relative – 2200**
	Hold **Attack 3** to throw your Static Spear and create an electric beam that now also slows enemies caught in it.
Black Out – 3000	**Unbreakable – 3000**
Increases critical hit chance.	Stay in the fight longer with more health! Ample room for error!

Shield Striker

FIGURE 3.18 This super-SURGED land vehicle will ZAP an ELECTRIC CURRENT to blow the FUSE of evil!

Shock other racers with weapons that burn! Shield Striker boasts a double hit of defensive action with an electrical current to shoot enemies long-range as well as an electromagnetic shield to protect against counterattacks up close. The Doomproof Forcefield shield is super tough and can handle a lot of damage. The Crowd Control stream of electricity is super strong and will follow enemies as you move. This vehicle looks like a futuristic steam train with epic interlocking gears as wheels. It's a little hard to handle, slower than most land vehicles, and has a wide turning circle. But what it lacks in handling, it makes up in weapons. Upgrade your speed and acceleration with the High Speed Pursuer and Lightning Striker mods to balance out your ride.

Upgrade Shield Striker's shields and weapons with Sharpfin and his crew:

Upgrade Level 1: 800 gearbits

Upgrade Level 2: 900 gearbits

Upgrade Level 3: 1000 gearbits

Upgrade Level 4: 1100 gearbits

Upgrade Level 5: 1200 gearbits

Weapons

Crowd Control: Hold **Attack 1** to shoot a steady stream of electricity.

Doomproof Forcefield: Press and hold **Attack 3** to protect yourself with an electromagnetic shield and collect far-away gearbits. Release to explode the shield and damage nearby enemies.

Horns

Redirectors Horn

Shield Sirens Horn

Grinding Gears Horn

Battery Buzz Horn

Specialty Mods

Performance Mods

Double Dare Trigger Happy: "No Gold, No Glory!"

FIGURE 3.19 Let the GUN-SLINGING GREMLIN with the GOLDEN TOUCH super-charge your PISTOLS!

TABLE 3.17 Double Dare Trigger Happy's Stats!

Element	Tech
SuperCharger Vehicle	Gold Rusher
Max. Health	300
Armor	18
Speed	50
Critical Hit	6
Elemental Power	25

Watch out! There's a giddy gremlin on the loose and he's got a gleam in his eye for shiny gold! Trigger Happy just can't keep still when he's chasing down trouble—or in fact, any time at all! He's not hopping mad—he's hopping crazy! He loves to fire himself into the fray—from a cannon! With his tongue lolling, a mad grin, and peals of laughter wherever he goes, Trigger Happy will set fireworks (and his enemies!) shooting across the sky. Prepare to launch him from a blazing ring of fire or explode from his safe in a shower of gold. This is one SuperCharger that won't be left out of a fight and brings more than the usual coin rewards!

Attack Moves:

Fire Cracker: Press **Attack 1** rapidly to shoot your Fire Cracker.

Crowd Pleaser: Press **Attack 2** to shoot off pyrotechnics and damage enemies around you.

Soul Gem Ability: He's Safe! – 4000: Once only, Trigger Happy can revive after being defeated and jump out of a huge safe!

Upgrades:

TABLE 3.18 Double Dare Trigger Happy's Upgrades!

Breaking Cannon – 500: Press **Attack 3** to shoot yourself out of a cannon! Enemies in the way will be damaged by the force of impact.

Hoop 'n Holler – 700: Hold **Attack 1** to charge up and shoot out a fire hoop. Jumping or shooting yourself through it causes it to explode!

Just Warming Up – 900: Ignite your weapons, making them cause more damage to enemies.

Can On and On – 1200: Press **Attack 3** to shoot yourself out of a cannon over a greater distance! Enemies in the way will be damaged by the force of impact. (Prerequisite: Breaking Cannon.)

Spontaneous Performer Path: Upgrade your hoops and cause spectacular explosions!

Made for the Spotlight Path: Shoot to the top and defeat enemies along the way with this path!

Hot Feet Hoop – 1700

Hold **Attack 1** to charge up and shoot out a fire hoop. Jumping or shooting yourself through it causes it to explode and will cause you to gain increased movement speed.

Cannon Crash – 1700

Press **Attack 2** while charging your cannon to shoot up into the air and do a large amount of damage to nearby enemies when landing.

Pay Day! – 2200

Press **Attack 2** to damage enemies around you and pull in coins and food drops.

Acrobatic – 2200

Hold **Attack 1** while jumping to charge up your fire ring and jump through it.

Fire and Forget – 3000

When you charge up your canon, you'll shoot out a fire ring in front of you to burst through immediately.

Making it Rain – 3000

Hold **Attack 1** while jumping to unleash a gun barrage on your enemies below!

Gold Rusher

FIGURE 3.20 It's PAY DAY! Drown your enemies in a GOLDEN HORDE to die for!

Triggered Happy Mines are a clever to way to knock out your enemies while you're on the move. Drop them behind you as you spin down a race track or push your way through a field of enemies to slow your opposition. This is a solid long-range attack that can work well. The Currency Cannon isn't as useful because you need to shoot seriously heavy fire to take down your enemy. Upgrade your armor as soon as you can (the Pop and Sparkers mod or Gearwork Kit mod will help you there) because Gold Rusher is susceptible to damage.

Upgrade Gold Rusher's shields and weapons with Sharpfin and his crew:

Upgrade Level 1: 800 gearbits

Upgrade Level 2: 900 gearbits

Upgrade Level 3: 1000 gearbits

Upgrade Level 4: 1100 gearbits

Upgrade Level 5: 1200 gearbits

Weapons

Currency Cannon: Press **Attack 1** to rapidly destroy your enemies with sweet, sweet gold!

Triggered Happy Mines: Tap **Attack 3** to drop Triggered Happy Mines.

Horns

Clink Clankers Horn

Gilded Gizmo Horn

Honkamajig Horn

Widget Whir Horn

Specialty Mods

Performance Mods

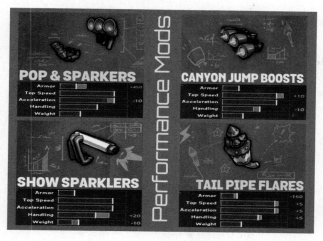

Performance Mods

POP & SPARKERS

Armor		
Top Speed		
Acceleration		-10
Handling		
Weight		

(Armor +450)

CANYON JUMP BOOSTS

Armor		
Top Speed		+10
Acceleration		
Handling		
Weight		-10

SHOW SPARKLERS

Armor		
Top Speed		
Acceleration		
Handling		+20
Weight		-10

TAIL PIPE FLARES

Armor		-150
Top Speed		+5
Acceleration		+5
Handling		+5
Weight		

Stormblade: "Feather the Storm!"

FIGURE 3.21 SPREAD YOUR WINGS and BREAK THE SOUND BARRIER, there's a STORM blowing your way!

TABLE 3.19 Stormblade's Stats!

Element	Air
SuperCharger Vehicle	Sky Slicer
Max. Health	220
Armor	6
Speed	50
Critical Hit	6
Elemental Power	25

Curiosity may have killed the cat, but it sure never hurt Stormblade! As a fledgling lark, she dove straight out of her nest in search of the furthest boundaries of Skylands. She wanted to discover what lay in the worlds beyond, but was dismayed to find Skylands had no end! Her bold and inquisitive nature led her to Know-It-All Island on a special mission for Master Eon, where she helped the Skylanders battle the evil Drow army and retrieve the Rift Engines from the depths of the Swirling Sea. Her heroic deeds won her a place as a SuperCharger, where she chases down evil in her custom-made vehicle, the Sky Slicer.

Attack Moves:

Feather Blade Throw: Press **Attack 1** to throw a feathered blade at an enemy.

Steeled Winds: Press **Attack 2** to perform a twirling blade dash forward, damaging enemies in your path. Hold **Attack 2** to continue dashing.

Soul Gem Ability: Feather Weather – 4000: Hold **Attack 1** while in the air to create a blade storm and rain down hundreds of blades on nearby enemies.

Upgrades:

TABLE 3.20 Stormblade's Upgrades!

Cyclone Surge – 500: Press **Attack 3** to jump into the air and damage nearby enemies.	
Storm Dive – 700: Press **Attack 2** while in the air to dive down and damage enemies underneath you.	
Fan of Feathers – 900: Press **Attack 3** to jump into the air and throw a spread of feather blades at nearby enemies. (Prerequisite: Cyclone Surge.)	
Feather Barrage – 1200: Hold **Attack 1** until fully charged and then release to throw multiple feather blades out in front of you.	
Wind Warrior Path: Use the power of the wind to defend against enemy onslaughts!	**Blade Dancer Path:** Hone your skill using feather blades!
Wind Wall – 1700	**Fist Full of Feathers – 1700**
Steeled Winds and Cyclone Surge now destroy projectiles. Wind powered!	Press **Attack 1**, **Attack 1**, **Attack 1** while in the air to throw out feather blades at enemies below you.
Sharpened Winds – 2200	**Storm Sais – 2200**
Steeled Winds now does more damage.	Feather blades become upgraded Storm Sais that do more damage!
Down Draft – 3000	**Feather the Storm – 3000**
Steeled Winds now slows enemies that are hit with it.	Tap **Attack 3** repeatedly to cause a hurricane underneath you that damages nearby enemies.

Sky Slicer

FIGURE 3.22 Send a TRIPLE MISSILE HIT to the tail of enemies to deliver a DOWN DRAFT of DAMAGE!

Sky Slicer has a slow, wide arc to turn and average acceleration in the skies, but its Pigeon Lock Missiles make this fighter a jet to remember. The feather spears are great up close for haphazard close-range shooting and can do some damage, but they're tricky on fast-moving targets. If you can set your crosshairs on a distant enemy with a definite lock (even just for the split-second you need to hit that attack button), then you can leave the missiles to do their work while you turn away in search of your next victim. Your score will shoot right up.

Upgrade Sky Slicer's shields and weapons with Sharpfin and his crew:

Upgrade Level 1: 200 gearbits

Upgrade Level 2: 250 gearbits

Upgrade Level 3: 300 gearbits

Upgrade Level 4: 350 gearbits

Upgrade Level 5: 400 gearbits

Weapons

Feather Fury: Tap **Attack 1** to shoot out feathered spears.

Pigeon Flock Missiles: Press and hold **Attack 3** to lock on and shoot out Pigeon Flock homing missiles.

Horns

Cloud Reverberator Horn

Radar Resonator Horn

Sky Call Horn

Electro Listener Horn

Specialty Mods

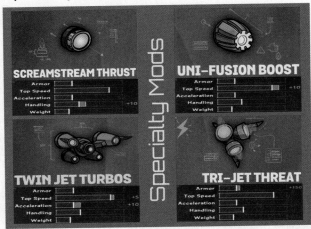

Performance Mods

Hurricane Jet-Vac: "Hawk and Awe!"

FIGURE 3.23 Descend on evil with a TALON of terror and a FLURRY of FEATHERED FURY. The SKY'S the LIMIT!

TABLE 3.21 Hurricane Jet-Vac's Stats!

Element	Air
SuperCharger Vehicle	Jet Stream
Max. Health	240
Armor	12
Speed	43
Critical Hit	6
Elemental Power	25

Jet-Vac is a famous Sky Baron and well known to be the bravest flyer in Windham. His melee skills are swift and powerful—he can slice through multiple enemies with fan blades or suck them into a vacuum of pain! When he showed true honor by sacrificing his magical wings to help a mother bird save her children in a terrifying raid, Master Eon was super-impressed. As a reward for his bravery and loss, Jet-Vac now flies using a SuperCharged vacuum jetpack strapped to his body, protecting Skylands and blasting enemies out of the sky!

Attack Moves:

Shooting the Breeze: Press **Attack 1** to shoot a fan blade that can bounce off multiple enemies.

Jet Turbine Vacuum: Press and hold **Attack 2** to suck in enemies. Press **Attack 2** again to shoot the enemy out.

Soul Gem Ability: Having a Blast! – 4000: Hold **Attack 2** to vacuum in enemies; release to shoot enemies as projectiles, which will bounce and hit other enemies. When an enemy has low health, they will be launched with extreme force!

Upgrades:

TABLE 3.22 Hurricane Jet-Vac's Upgrades!

Somer-Assault – 500: Press **Attack 3** to dash forward. Enemies in the way will get kicked and damaged.

Better Blade Bounces – 700: Fans bounce more times.

Hurricane Hurrah – 900: Hold **Attack 1** to charge up a hurricane; release to unleash it and damage any enemies in its path.

Make Them Sore – 1200: Somer-Assault attacks do more damage. Kicking and screaming! (Prerequisite: Somer-Assault)

Blade-Vac Path: Use your Jet Turbine Vacuum to create powerful vortexes.

Category Pain – 1700

Hold **Attack 1** and release it to create a hurricane. Press **Attack 1** repeatedly to shoot blades into the hurricane.

Hurricano – 2200

Hold **Attack 1** and release to create a hurricane. Hurricanes now explode once they are over and damage enemies inside and around the hurricane.

Splitting Air – 3000

Press **Attack 1** to shoot a bouncing blade while holding an enemy.

Hurricane Hawk Path: Use improved wind power to clear a path through enemies.

Turbulent Turbine – 1700

Press **Attack 3** to dash forward. Enemies behind you when the dash is started take more damage.

Talon Take Off – 2200

Enemies hit at the end of a Somer-Assault are knocked back further and take more damage.

Double Flip – 3000

Press **Attack 3** twice to give Somer-Assault another boost to travel further. Press **Attack 3** after performing the Double Flip to perform another on the same enemy.

Jet Stream

FIGURE 3.24 Fight fists with FEATHERS to clear the decks! CATEGORY PAIN is BLASTING into action.

The Avian Razors weapon is a strong long-range attack with pretty solid aim; leaving heavy damage, so is fantastic in an air strike. The Vacuum Bomb is a bit tricky to use and doesn't last long. Use it when there are so many enemies around you that they're likely to fly into it to give you a bit of breathing room. You'll need good aim to Razor the Tornado on the go, and you may not see its effectiveness as you fly off.

Upgrade Jet Stream's shields and weapons with Sharpfin and his crew:

Upgrade Level 1: 200 gearbits

Upgrade Level 2: 250 gearbits

Upgrade Level 3: 300 gearbits

Upgrade Level 4: 350 gearbits

Upgrade Level 5: 400 gearbits

Weapons

Avian Razors: Tap **Attack 1** to fire Avian Razors.

Vacuum Bomb: Tap **Attack 3** to create a tornado. Fire Avian Razors into it to charge it up!

Horns

Turbine Trumpet Horn

Avian Sirens Horn

Mallard Quacker Horn

Air Horn

Specialty Mods

Performance Mods

Super Shot Stealth Elf: "Silent but Deadly!"

FIGURE 3.25 Feel a shiver but no one's there? NOW YOU SEE HER, NOW YOU DON'T!!

TABLE 3.23 Super Shot Stealth Elf's Stats!

Element	Life
SuperCharger Vehicle	Stealth Stinger
Max. Health	190
Armor	12
Speed	50
Critical Hit	6
Elemental Power	25

A mysterious elf child with no family or memory—wherever did she come from? No one knows, including Stealth Elf herself! She awoke alone in a hollow tree one morning with no recollection of how she came to be there. A kind forest beast raised her and taught her to defend herself, until she finally decided to join the Skylanders team. Despite ever searching for her own true identity, this little green ninja knows who she is deep down—a warrior worthy of Eon's Elite. Stealth Elf sneaks up on enemies unawares, then with a swift move, slashes through their ranks with her blade cannons and deadly aim. She's an acrobatic ninja with melee moves to kill. For a strong long-range attack, follow the Stealth Saboteur path to enhance a decoy turret that explodes to maximize damage to enemies after Stealth Elf has safely snuck away.

Attack Moves:

Danger Cannon: Press **Attack 1** and hold to lock onto enemies and shoot daggers at them. Yes, it's a gun that shoots daggers.

Say Hello: Press **Attack 2** to disappear and create a turret that distracts enemies.

Soul Gem Ability: Health Elf – 4000: After injury and after defeating an enemy, a familiar face appears and brings a health bonus!

Upgrades:

TABLE 3.24 **Super Shot Stealth Elf's Upgrades!**

Circle Slash – 500: Press **Attack 3** to perform an acrobatic spin that hits and knocks back enemies nearby.	
Needle-Pointed Daggers – 700: Dagger Cannon deals more damage. Straight to the point!	
To My Little Friend – 900: The turret now shoots enemies in front of it.	
Speed of the Spin – 1200: Gain increased movement speed for a short time after using Circle Slash. (Prerequisite: Circle Slash.)	
Heavy Gunner Path: Focus on powerful ranged attacks with the Dagger Cannon.	**Stealth Saboteur:** Use deceitful tactics to disappear and attack enemies without them ever knowing what hit them!
Smog Slash – 1700	**Distraction Destruction – 1700**
Create a poison cloud when you exit stealth mode.	On expiration, the turret explodes and damages nearby enemies.
All Wound Up – 2200	**Acquisition Intelligence Mode – 2200**
Dagger Cannon projectiles do more damage the longer **Attack 1** is held.	The turret now aims at nearby enemies and does more damage.
Splinter Shells – 3000	**Spin to Win! – 3000**
Dagger Cannon projectiles splinter off enemies and hit nearby enemies.	Circle Slash does more damage and knocks enemies further away.

Stealth Stinger

FIGURE 3.26 It's quick, it's camouflaged, it's the CANOPY PIERCER that's a CUT ABOVE!

Stealth Stinger is a good speed vehicle but lacks in armor, so make upgrading your shields a priority. A barrage of acorns will take down an enemy ship pretty quickly (and those close by), but individual acorns don't do much damage, so keep the ammo coming to make an impact. A tight turning circle makes for good handling, so it's a great vehicle for weaving through obstacles and picking up cargo. Conserve your ammo by using the Forest Fog stealth mode sparingly, or you'll quickly run out of steam.

Upgrade Stealth Stinger's shields and weapons with Sharpfin and his crew:

Upgrade Level 1: 200 gearbits

Upgrade Level 2: 250 gearbits

Upgrade Level 3: 300 gearbits

Upgrade Level 4: 350 gearbits

Upgrade Level 5: 400 gearbits

Weapons

Canopy Piercer: Press and hold **Attack 1** to rapidly fire acorns into the sky.

Forest Fog: Hold **Attack 3** to become stealthed! Your shields will slowly recover while stealthed.

Horns

Woodland Tune Horn

Timber Wailer Horn

Grove Groover Horn

Bramble Blare Horn

Specialty Mods

Performance Mods

Turbo Charge Donkey Kong (Nintendo Consoles Only)

FIGURE 3.27 BLASTING BONGOS are BARRELING your way from the playful PRIMATE with a powerful PUNCH!

TABLE 3.25 Turbo Charge Donkey Kong's Stats!

Element	Life
SuperCharger Vehicle	Barrel Blaster
Max. Health	370
Armor	12
Speed	50
Critical Hit	2
Elemental Power	25

Everybody's favorite happy-go-lucky hero is back with his Bongo Barrel, bananas, and nephew Diddy Kong to save the day! You can always trust Donkey Kong to barrel into a fight with no regard for his own safety. His inquisitive nature led him to explore the open rift that appeared between worlds, when Kaos' evil Sky Eater was created. When he heard Mags' distress signal cross the breach, he leapt at the chance for adventure. Donkey Kong fell into Skylands, ready to lend a hand fighting evil to keep all worlds safe. Alongside his arch-enemy Hammer Slam Bowser, Donkey Kong was given a new Rift Engine SuperCharged vehicle called Barrel Blaster, to aid him in their cause. This hairy hero has a brilliant suite of melee moves that is sure to bring down the house. Explosions, spikey barrels, falling ladders, and a help-ing hand from Diddy Kong on his jetpack will see the bad guys flee in terror! Follow the Pointy Preparations Path to heal yourself while in Super Donkey Kong mode, to keep your strength up in a tough fight.

Attack Moves:

Primate Punch: Press **Attack 1** rapidly to perform melee attacks.

Barrel Toss: Press **Attack 2** to throw your barrels at nearby enemies. If they get too close, you'll smash them with the barrels instead.

Soul Gem Ability: Diddy you call? – 4000: Press **Attack 3** to build up a power meter. When it's filled, you will call in Diddy Kong to fly around on his jetpack and attack nearby enemies!

Upgrades:

TABLE 3.26 Turbo Charge Donkey Kong's Upgrades!

Bongo Barrel – 500: Press **Attack 3** rapidly to slam your barrel down and use it as a bongo. Use your bongos to damage nearby enemies. When you stop, your bongo will continue to play for a short time.

Super Donkey Kong – 700: Hold **Attack 1** to enter Super Donkey Kong mode. When in Super Donkey Kong mode, press **Attack 3** to stomp and **Attack 1** to do a barrel roll!

Barrels of Fun – 900: Charge up **Attack 2** and release to be put into an arrow barrel. While in the barrel you'll be able to aim around the level and shoot yourself, causing an explosion where you land.

Old School – 1200: Tap **Attack 3** in Super Donkey Kong mode to cause ladders and girders to fall from the sky.

Powder Keg Power Path: Bring in some explosive tactics to help defeat enemies!	Pointy Preparations Path: Upgrade all of your barrels with metal spikes to roll over enemies!
Boom Barrels – 1700	**Spikey Barrels – 1700**
Tapping **Attack 2** will now throw explosive barrels!	Tapping **Attack 2** will now throw spikey barrels! Also, Super Donkey Kong mode will use spiked barrels to attack enemies!
Explosive Landing – 2200	
Charge up **Attack 2** and release to be shot around in a barrel. At the end of the move you'll trigger a big explosion.	**Barrel Rolled – 2200**
	Hold **Attack 1** to enter Super Donkey Kong mode. Press **Attack 2** to roll over nearby enemies in a huge spiked barrel.
Bongo Blast – 3000	
Press **Attack 3** rapidly to start playing the bongos that are left behind. They will explode!	**Healthy Kong – 3000**
	Regenerate health while in Super Donkey Kong mode.

Barrel Blaster (Nintendo Consoles Only)

FIGURE 3.28 Spin out in the BARREL of ACROBATIC AWESOMENESS to EXPLODE the opposition!

Always forest-conscious (recycled wood!), this tech element speedster was built from Donkey Kong's famous mine cart and barrels! With a Rift Engine under the hood, there's nothing stopping this stunt car from sliding to success. Barrel Cannons are a powerful hit and have a built-in homing device, so your aim doesn't have to be spot on. It's a fast vehicle with tight turning but super touchy steering, so keep light on your directional controller. Spiked Barrel Mines are a great defensive shield that circles the vehicle while you're on the move and explode as they hit enemies. After a short time, they'll all detonate and you'll need to reboot for that extra layer of protection. SuperCharge by adding TurboCharge Donkey Kong to get Diddy Kong riding shotgun for extra mayhem on the road!

Upgrade Barrel Blaster's shields and weapons with Sharpfin and his crew:

Upgrade Level 1: 800 gearbits

Upgrade Level 2: 900 gearbits

Upgrade Level 3: 1000 gearbits

Upgrade Level 4: 1100 gearbits

Upgrade Level 5: 1200 gearbits

Weapons

Barrel Cannon: Press **Attack 1** to blast your enemies with a heavy-duty Barrel Cannon.

Spiked Barrel Mines: Hold **Attack 2** to surround yourself with Spiked Barrel Mines.

Horns

Howling Horn

Tree Top Whistle Horn

Old School Sound Horn

Factory Valve Horn

Specialty Mods

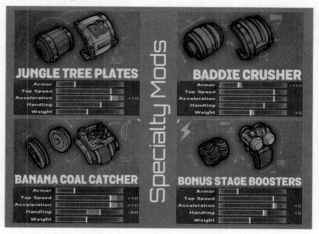

Performance Mods

Thrillipede: "All Hands on Deck!"

FIGURE 3.29   MANY HANDS make light work, especially when you're a MILLIPEDE with GRENADES!

TABLE 3.27   Thrillipede's Stats!

Element	Life
SuperCharger Vehicle	Buzz Wing
Max. Health	250
Armor	12
Speed	50
Critical Hit	8
Elemental Power	25

Thrillipede is famous among the Skylanders, and not only because he is the most celebrated pilot hero of the Great Greeble War. He is more famous because he beat the great Captain Flynn (the best pilot in all of Skylands... according to himself) at every flying challenge set for them to prove their skills at Thrillipede's home town of Flutter Bay. Flynn accepted the defeat graciously. (Well, to the crowd at least. Flynn later declared he'd let Thrillipede win to save him from embarrassment. Hmmm... do you believe him?) Follow Thrillipede's Insistent Insect Upgrade Path to create a dreadfully damaging swarm of insects to surround long-range enemies and wear down their health over time. Throwing a bug bomb into the fray causes collateral damage that amplifies its impact, making Thrillipede a little bug with a big bite.

Attack Moves:

Bug Bomb: Press **Attack 1** to throw cocoon grenades at your enemies, slowing them down in a cloud of bugs.

Bug Brawl: Press **Attack 2** to use those arms and punch nearby enemies in your way.

Soul Gem Ability: Beautiflies – 4000: When Sticky Grenades blow up, they will release butterflies that heal you when caught.

Upgrades:

TABLE 3.28   Thrillipede's Upgrades!

Cocooned – 500: Hold **Attack 3** to wrap yourself in a cocoon, protecting yourself from damage. Release to explode out and damage nearby enemies.

Bug n' Cover – 700: Press **Attack 1** to throw a grenade into a swarm of dragonflies, which slows enemy movement.

Mind Your Beeswax – 900: Hold **Attack 2** to prepare four sticky grenades that you can place as a trap in the ground or directly onto an enemy!

Cocooties – 1200: Hold **Attack 3** to wrap yourself in a cocoon, protecting yourself from damage. Release to explode out, which damages and slows nearby enemies. (Prerequisite: Cocooned.)

Mighty-Morphosis Path: Transform into a flying fighting machine with this path!

Insistent Insect Path: Use insect swarms to hinder and damage your enemies!

Better Fly – 1700

Hold **Attack 3** to wrap yourself in a cocoon protecting yourself from damage. Release to explode out and grow wings! While flying, hold **Attack 1** to bombard enemies with Bug Bombs!

Gnawing Gnats – 1700

Bug Bombs now cause a swarm of tiny insects to appear and do damage over time. Hitting targets again with Bug Bombs will remove the swarm and cause extra damage.

Bugging Out – 2200

Increase damage of all thrown grenade projectiles.

Nesting Gnats – 2200

The damage over time caused by the swarming insects can stack up to five times, doubling its damage.

Tick It To 'Em – 3000

Pressing **Attack 2** while jumping will toss sticky grenades below you.

Insect Epidemic – 3000

Targets affected by the damage over time from the swarm explode, spreading the swarm to nearby enemies.

Buzz Wing

FIGURE 3.30 Have you heard THE BUZZ? There's a new KING BEE on the BREEZE!

The Insect Strikes Back! A long time ago, in a galaxy far, far away (actually just nearby in Flutter Bay) is a vehicle so fast that it stings! Buzz Wing draws on the life element to bring a barrage of butterflies to attack enemies *en masse*.

Buzz Wing has zippy handling, acceleration, and speed, making it one of the fastest fighters in the sky. A few good knocks by the bad guys can knock it out, though, so try Beetle Shell Blast Plates and Beetle Tune-up to harden your shell. You'll need a bit of time to charge your long-range attack with Swarm Trail, but when you get it sorted, enemies will be falling from the sky.

Upgrade Buzz Wing's shields and weapons with Sharpfin and his crew:

Upgrade Level 1: 200 gearbits

Upgrade Level 2: 250 gearbits

Upgrade Level 3: 300 gearbits

Upgrade Level 4: 350 gearbits

Upgrade Level 5: 400 gearbits

Weapons

Insect Swarmer: Tap **Attack 1** to blast a barrage of butterflies.

Swarm Trail: Press and hold **Attack 3** to charge a swarm of friends. Release to fire the swarm!

Horns

Cricket Crackler Horn

Grasshopper Honker Horn

Ant Alarm Horn

Mantis Clack Horn

Specialty Mods

Performance Mods

Performance Mods

MONARCH LIFTERS
Armor
Top Speed
Acceleration
Handling +10
Weight

FOREST PATCHED WINGS
Armor
Top Speed
Acceleration
Handling +10
Weight

BEETLE SHELL BLAST PLATES
Armor +300
Top Speed
Acceleration
Handling
Weight

BUMBLE BUZZERS
Armor
Top Speed +10
Acceleration
Handling
Weight

Dive-Clops: "Look Out Below!"

FIGURE 3.31 Keep your EYE ON THE PRIZE and DIVE RIGHT IN to victory! This star PUPIL will make the bad guys CRY!

TABLE 3.29 Dive-Clops' Stats!

Element	Water
SuperCharger Vehicle	Dive Bomber
Max. Health	250
Armor	30
Speed	35
Critical Hit	4
Elemental Power	25

It turns out that one of our favorite Skylander Giants, Eye Brawl, has a twin brother who disappeared for thousands of years underneath the sea in the enigmatic Whirlpool of Destiny. Now reemerged in his custom-made diving suit (created by the Jelly Dwarves who once saved his life), he has joined his brother as a Skylander, working for Master Eon. Teamed up with his torpedo-shooting SuperCharger vehicle, the Dive Bomber, this giant eyeball doesn't miss a thing. Drown enemies with a torpedo of water shot from his eyeball using the Put the Eye in Geyser and Power of the Pupil upgrades, and don't forget to *mined* your manners ("excuse me!" and "sorry bad guys!") when you shoot Waterpedo mines for enemies to stumble over behind you. Dive-Clops is great on the ground with a combo of close-range moves that are sure to hit their target.

Attack Moves:

Waterpedo: Press **Attack 1** to shoot a Waterpedo that creates a mine that damages enemies close to it and explodes when hit with Sonar.

Sonar: Press **Attack 2** to create a sonar ping that damages enemies around you and causes Waterpedo mines to explode.

Soul Gem Ability: Depth of Field – 4000: Hold **Attack 1** and release to shoot a huge cluster of Waterpedo mines. If you couldn't "sea" mines, you will now!

Upgrades:

TABLE 3.30 Dive-Clops' Upgrades!

Put the Eye in Geyser – 500: Press **Attack 3** to unleash a geyser that pushes enemies back. Press **Attack 3** again to end the geyser.
Echo Enhancers – 700: Increases the range and damage of Sonar.
Power of the Pupil – 900: While using Geyser, press **Attack 1** or **Attack 2** to perform special attacks. (Prerequisite: Put the Eye in Geyser.)
Ping – 1200: Hold **Attack 2** and release to shoot existing Waterpedoes and mines upon the targeted enemy or location.

Tidal Torpedoes Path: Use lost deep-sea technology to increase the power of Waterpedo!	Dowsing Dowser Path: Learn more powerful Sonar abilities to defeat large groups of enemies!
Torpeslow – 1700 Press **Attack 1** to fire Waterpedoes that create mines that slow the movement of enemies close to the mines.	**Counter Measures – 1700** Enemies hit with Sonar take more damage from Waterpedoes for a short amount of time.
Mark II Waterpedo – 2200 Waterpedoes and Waterpedo mines do more damage. Mined your step!	**Hatch Off To You – 2200** Automatically send out a small Sonar pulse when hit that will damage nearby enemies.
Neato Waterpedo – 3000 Every other torpedo is a super Waterpedo that does more damage.	**Depth of Field – 3000** Geyser does more damage and can be used longer. Tear it up!

Dive Bomber

Armor
Top Speed
Acceleration
Handling
Weight

FIGURE 3.32
TORPEDOES on
your TAIL? DIVE the
murky depths in an
AQUATIC BATTLE-
TANK that BLOWS
ENEMIES out of the
water!

Dive Bomber is a nightmare to control (low handling) and easy to destroy
(low armor), but has some pretty nifty attack moves that are excellent for
exploration and searching out enemies at low speed. Use the second attack,
Deep Sea Sonar, to track down hidden bad guys underwater in the sonar
range, which will appear with a yellow target around them. The target is
a homing device. Now send off your Twin Torpedo Tubes (**Attack 1**) and
they'll do the hard work for you! This is a really fantastic weapons system,
but is best used at low speed so you don't spin off track. Try pulling in the
Power Propeller and Flex Floaties mods to improve your handling. Visit
Sharpfin to give your shields a boost, and then this submarine will be a
serious asset to your artillery.

Upgrade Dive Bomber's shields and weapons with Sharpfin and his crew:

Upgrade Level 1: 300 gearbits

Upgrade Level 2: 350 gearbits

Upgrade Level 3: 400 gearbits

Upgrade Level 4: 450 gearbits

Upgrade Level 5: 500 gearbits

Weapons

Twin Torpedo Tubes: Tap **Attack 1** to launch torpedoes.

Deep Sea Sonar: Tap **Attack 3** to mark enemies with a sonar ping.
Torpedoes seek out marked targets.

Horns

Dolphin Disorienter Horn

Blaring Seahorn

High Pressure Whistle Horn

Lost at Sea Signal Horn

Specialty Mods

Performance Mods

Deep Dive Gill Grunt: "Fear the Fish!"

FIGURE 3.33 Don't boil over, let the FINS OF FURY get you OUT OF HOT WATER... fast!

TABLE 3.31 Deep Dive Gill Grunt's Stats!

Element	Water
SuperCharger Vehicle	Reef Ripper
Max. Health	270
Armor	24
Speed	35
Critical Hit	6
Elemental Power	25

Gill Grunt may look a bit fishy, but he's really a hopeless romantic at heart. One sad day at sea, he lost his mermaid love after she was captured by a swarmy band of sea pirates. He has been searching for her ever since. Gill Grunt likes to sing love ballads (plug your ears!) while he travels around Skylands, courageously fighting Kaos' nasty minions. His heroic deeds are legendary. Once he travelled to Deep Water Wasteland in search of a missing fragment of the Mask of Power. After a barreling bar brawl with a Cloud Kraken and the pirate crew of the Fearsome Fang, Gill Grunt pretended he was entranced like the brainwashed merpeople of the village. He followed them to the secret cavern of Captain Grimslobber, where he fought for their freedom and recovered the missing fragment to save Skylands from the return of Darkness. What a hero! Deep Dive Gill Grunt can harness the power of lightning to bring down enemies from above and amp it up to shocking levels. Boost your impact with the jetpack by creating a water explosion with the Torrent Tamer Path and ride massive tidal waves to victory!

Attack Moves:

Trident Thrust: Press **Attack 1** to attack enemies with your trident.

Power of the Seas: Press **Attack 2** to attack enemies with a long-range lightning attack.

Soul Gem Ability: Storm of the Seas – 4000: Hold down **Attack 2** while not using the jetpack to summon a powerful lightning storm!

Upgrades:

TABLE 3.32 Deep Dive Gill Grunt's Upgrades!

Typhoon Turbine Jetpack – 500: Press **Attack 3** to begin hovering with your jetpack. Press **Attack 1** to dash forward or press **Attack 2** to send out a tidal wave. Press **Attack 3** again to land on the ground.

Trident True – 700: Hold **Attack 1** when not using the jetpack to rapidly attack nearby enemies.

Wild Whirlpool – 900: Hold **Attack 2** while using the jetpack to create a large whirlpool that damages nearby enemies. (Prerequisite: Typhoon Turbine Jetpack.)

Trident Unleashed – 1200: Trident attacks do more damage. Unleash the Trident!

Torrent Tamer Path: Learn how to ride on massive waves and damage enemies in your way!	**Storm Summoner Path:** Channel the power of the storms of the sea and electrify your attacks!
Wave Jumper – 1700 Press **Attack 3** to begin hovering with your jetpack. Press **Attack 3** again to land on the ground. Entering or exiting Jetpack mode causes a water explosion that damages nearby enemies.	**Lightning Strikes – 1700** Hold **Attack 1** while not using the jetpack to rapidly attack nearby enemies with lightning.
Tubular Tidal Wave – 2200 Press **Attack 2** to shoot out three large waves in Jetpack mode.	**Shocking Transition – 2200** Press **Attack 3** to begin hovering with your jetpack. Press **Attack 3** again to land on the ground. Entering Jetpack mode causes a lightning explosion that damages nearby enemies.
Drive the Wave – 3000 Hold **Attack 1** in Jetpack mode to ride a huge tidal wave!	**Lightning Build-Up – 3000** Lightning attacks do more damage. Storm powered!

Reef Ripper

FIGURE 3.34 Swish and flick! ELECTRIFY your enemies with a ZAP of lightning to CHARGE ahead of the pack.

Fancy floating like a fish? Gill Grunt's latest vehicle has the best underwater moves. The Reef Ripper has major maneuverability and handling but tends to spin out at the tail, so you've got to stay light-handed on the directional controller—a little movement makes a big difference. This sea vehicle has a powerful long-range trident, but it's very specific direction-wise, so you'll need top-notch aim to hit your target. If you're up close and personal or surrounded by bad guys, a quick electrical snap will get them off your case.

Upgrade Reef Ripper's shields and weapons with Sharpfin and his crew:

Upgrade Level 1: 300 gearbits

Upgrade Level 2: 350 gearbits

Upgrade Level 3: 400 gearbits

Upgrade Level 4: 450 gearbits

Upgrade Level 5: 500 gearbits

Weapons

Ocean Upheaval: Tap **Attack 1** to shoot a trident at enemies.

Electrify the Tail: Tap **Attack 3** to electrify nearby enemies.

Horns

Revving Gurgler Horn

Ocean Buzz Horn

Thumpback Call Horn

High-Tide Honker Horn

Specialty Mods

Performance Mods

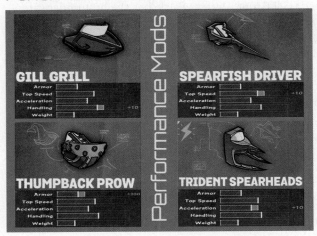

Splat: "The Art of War!"

FIGURE 3.35 Prove the BRUSH is mightier than the sword as you FLING INK with creative abandon and PAINT YOUR ENEMIES into a corner!

TABLE 3.33 Splat's Stats!

Element	Magic
SuperCharger Vehicle	Splatter Splasher
Max. Health	240
Armor	6
Speed	43
Critical Hit	4
Elemental Power	25

With a double-ended paint brush and a host of Inkling minions at her fingertips, Splat is a master artist on a mission! Although the other fauns in her village enjoyed coloring inside the lines and never making waves, Splat was far too creative to be contained. She secretly let her creative streak run wild and taught herself free-form fighting skills using her imagination and magic paint brush. It was lucky she followed her heart, because one day, Splat had to put her skills to use when a Drow army attacked her village. Of course, her heroic heart had all the right moves, and she was finally celebrated for the unique individual she'd kept hidden for so long. Splat can take on the baddies melee-style by spinning and smashing them with her paint brush like a ninja staff. She has a strong hit, especially when her Inklings upgrade and gain strength. If you're after a long-range attack move that really leaves its mark, try the Abstract Designer Path to paint an Inkling to remember! Bigger and better than ever, this horned helper will trample enemies and clear a path through the fray.

Attack Moves:

Artisan Arts: Press **Attack 1** to pummel enemies with your brush staff.

Heave Hue!: Press **Attack 2** to fling an explosive ink blob at enemies.

Soul Gem Ability: Bringing the Stain – 4000: Enemies hit with ink attacks are now slowed!

Upgrades:

TABLE 3.34 Splat's Upgrades!

Have an Inkling – 500: Press **Attack 3** to send an Inkling charging forward, leaving damaging ink pools behind and hitting enemies in the way!

Dye Hard – 700: Melee attacks do more damage to enemies. The sparkly bits make it hurt more!

Broad Strokes – 900: Press **Attack 2** to fling an even larger explosive ink blob at enemies.

Scape-Goat – 1200: Press **Attack 3** to summon a more powerful Inkling that leaves behind longer lasting ink pools. (Prerequisite: Have an Inkling.)

Prolific Painter Path: Create ink pools and more powerful ink creatures with this path.	**Abstract Designer Path:** Brush up on your doodling skills to make your Inklings even more powerful!
Wet Paint – 1700	**Running Colors – 1700**
Hold **Attack 2** and release to throw a huge explosive ink blob that leaves a pool of damaging ink on the ground.	Inkling creatures now charge a further distance to hit enemies.
Canvas the Area – 2200	**Stroke of Genius – 2200**
Ink pools created by Wet Paint are now larger.	Inklings and ink pools left behind by Inklings will now explode!
Shades of Pain – 3000	**Graffiti Gruff – 3000**
Hold **Attack 2** and release to throw a huge explosive ink blob that creates a large angry ink monster that attacks nearby enemies.	Hold **Attack 3** even longer and release to draw a huge Inkling that will trample enemies in front of you.

Splatter Splasher

🌊 **SPLATTER SPLASHER** 🌊

FIGURE 3.36 Make an impression with the hyper-color hydro-craft that paints the town red... and purple and orange and green!

If you need a strong arm in a water fight, try Splatter Splasher's second attack move. The vehicle shoots a muscle-bound fawn fighter called an "Inkling" to hit enemies out of your way (they look a bit like rainbow-colored goat-genies; super sweet, but... ouch!). This one is a strong long-range attack, with the bonus of Inklings staying around to fight enemies after you've continued on. (Leave them to distract enemies in a race so you can get ahead!) Splatter Splasher also has a solid melee attack called Oiled Ink, which shoots paint balls at your target like a missile. This is a fun vehicle with good speed, but it gets a bit hard to control underwater, so improve its handling with the Modern Hydo and Paint Palette Wheel mods. It doesn't take much to knock this boat out of the water, so upgrade your shields as soon as you can.

Upgrade Splatter Splasher's shields and weapons with Sharpfin and his crew:

Upgrade Level 1: 300 gearbits

Upgrade Level 2: 350 gearbits

Upgrade Level 3: 400 gearbits

Upgrade Level 4: 450 gearbits

Upgrade Level 5: 500 gearbits

Weapons

Oiled Ink: Tap **Attack 1** to paint your targets.

Inkling Interceptor: Tap **Attack 3** to fire a paint bomb that leaves an Inkling that attacks nearby enemies.

Horns

Bristle Whistle Horn

Airbrush Horn

Hue Tone Horn

Graffiti Clamor Horn

Specialty Mods

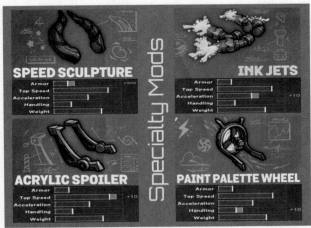

Performance Mods

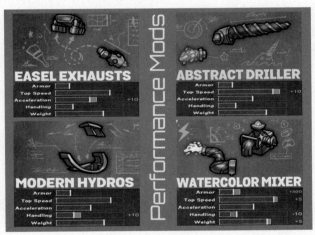

Big Bubble Pop Fizz: "The Motion of the Potion!"

FIGURE 3.37 Our favorite alchemist is BUBBLING with excitement for his new invention—it's TIME TO POP some bad guys! Chemistry's never been so fun!

TABLE 3.35 Big Bubble Pop Fizz's Stats!

Element	Magic
SuperCharger Vehicle	Soda Skimmer
Max. Health	300
Armor	24
Speed	43
Critical Hit	4
Elemental Power	25

If you want to bring a bonanza of bubbles and wild attack moves into your fight, call Big Bubble Pop Fizz, the crazy alchemist! Pop Fizz is always on the edge of creating catastrophe with his experiments, but he's perfectly happy to keep it that way. He blows humungous bubbles at his enemies that bounce around and cause damage to everything in their path. But even better, his secret weapon is his own awesome crazy spell—his second attack turns Pop Fizz totally berserk! This cute, furry little bubble-blower transforms into his own alter ego: a maniac rage-monster that scratches and smashes his way through bad guys like butter. No one is safe when Big Bubble Pop Fizz is bubbling with energy and blowing through Skylands!

Attack Moves:

Bubble Blast: Press **Attack 1** to blow bubbles that bounce on their way to enemies.

Bubbling Beast Form: Press **Attack 2** to transform into a beast. Press **Attack 1** to attack nearby enemies with claws.

Soul Gem Ability: Spiked Punch– 4000: While in Beast Mode, hold and release **Attack 1** to pound the ground and knock all enemies in the area up!

Upgrades:

TABLE 3.36 Big Bubble Pop Fizz's Upgrades!

Mixture Modifier – 500: Press **Attack 3** to cause a chemical reaction and transform the color and effects of liquid attacks.

Know Your Bases – 700: All base liquid attacks do more damage.

Genetic Engineering – 900: Press **Attack 3** while in Beast Mode to perform new attacks depending on the current liquid color. (Prerequisite: Mixture Modifier.)

Side Effects – 1200: After reverting to normal Pop Fizz mode, gain a temporary defense boost.

Alchemic Maestro Path: Master your Potion Creation Station!	Brass Of The Beast Path: Unlock the potential of the Beast!
Larger Lungs – 1700 Hold **Attack 1** to perform improved liquid attacks depending on the current color.	**Better Beast – 1700** Hold **Attack 3** to perform enhanced and longer versions of unique beast attacks.
For Science! – 2200 Hold **Attack 3** while in normal form to constantly spew liquids that damage enemies in the nearby area.	**Juiced Up! – 2200** Melee attacks in Beast Mode do more damage. I'm a monster, RAWR!
Follow the Formula – 3000 Mixture Modifier gains additional effects depending upon the liquid color.	**Feed the Beast – 3000** In Beast Mode, hold **Attack 3** to perform Better Beast attacks. Press **Attack 1** after using a Better Beast attack to do more damage with your claws.

Soda Skimmer

FIGURE 3.38 SHAKE UP the competition with a BUBBLE, POP, FIZZ frenzy on the foam! What a RUSH!

Soda Skimmer is easy to handle and speeds along well, but can easily take a hit. Booming Bubbles and Fizzy Floating will help you get a handle on hard times by boosting your armor. An array of crazy weapons give this vehicle a kick, but they're unpredictable in a fight. Shake and Change will mix you a new long-range weapon each time (on rotation), which could be lasers, missiles, or exploding spheres (look for the circling symbols to determine which one is up). It isn't always easy to adjust your aim to suit different styles on-the-fly, so your best bet is to use this in a fight with lots of room to move and just go crazy with it—the way Pop Fizz does best! Increase your firepower with Sharpfin and the gang to really make the magic happen.

Upgrade Soda Skimmer's shields and weapons with Sharpfin and his crew:

Upgrade Level 1: 300 gearbits

Upgrade Level 2: 350 gearbits

Upgrade Level 3: 400 gearbits

Upgrade Level 4: 450 gearbits

Upgrade Level 5: 500 gearbits

Weapons

Alchemic Admixture: Tap **Attack 1** to launch a crazy potion.

Shake and Change: Tap **Attack 3** to mix up a new crazy potion.

Horns

Pressure Blare Horn

Fizzled Foghorn

Caffeinated Jitter Horn

Party Pop Horn!

Specialty Mods

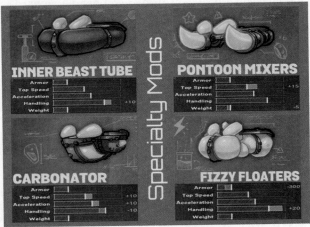

Performance Mods

Nightfall: "Dark and Dangerous!"

FIGURE 3.39 Beware of the lure of flowing black locks—she'll HOOK you in and leave you with WHIPLASH!

TABLE 3.37 Nightfall's Stats!

Element	Dark
SuperCharger Vehicle	Sea Shadow
Max. Health	230
Armor	6
Speed	43
Critical Hit	10
Elemental Power	25

Nightfall is a Dreadwalker who carries a brooding shadow of darkness over her like a veil. Her natural instinct to avoid others is constantly challenged by her courageous need to keep Skylands safe, no matter the cost. For many years, she dove alone into the abyss of the Poison Sea to hunt lurking monsters of Darkness. This led to an epic one-on-one battle against an enormous Leviathan that saved her people from a terrible fate. Nightfall wants to see justice served and hates to be underestimated. After a successful mission to find an Elite team of Skylanders for Buzz in Motleyville, Nightfall finally left her post on Fogshadow Tower and joined the SuperChargers with her customized deep-sea vehicle, Sea Shadow. Her devastating close-combat moves use dark energy attacks and metal hooks to cause damage in combat.

Attack Moves:

Handy Hooks: Press **Attack 1** to perform a flurry of right and left hooks.

Ambrush: Press **Attack 2** to dash forward or behind enemies.

Soul Gem Ability: Bad Hair Day – 4000: Tap **Attack 3** repeatedly to knock all enemies into the air in an area. Continue tapping **Attack 3** to increase the area and knock all enemies down to the ground.

Upgrades:

TABLE 3.38 Nightfall's Upgrades!

Whip Lash – 500: Press **Attack 3** to unleash a strand of dark energy that whips enemies and knocks them into the air. Using Whip Lash in the air knocks enemies down.

Split Hook Ends – 700: New hooks cause melee attacks to do more damage.

Hair Today, Gone Now – 900: Damage enemies at the start of Ambrush and move faster during it.

Layered Lunge– 1200: The first hook melee attack after an Ambrush is guaranteed to critically strike.

Master Angler Path: Master the power of your super sharp hooks.	**Dread Head Path:** Master the use of your dark energy attacks!
Splitting Hairs – 1700	**Ambrush Rush – 1700**
Hold **Attack 1** and release to unleash a devastating combo of hook and dark energy attacks.	Hold **Attack 2** to Ambrush and shoot strands of dark energy toward enemies.
Comb-O – 2200	**Up-Sweep – 2200**
Every fourth attack in the basic melee combo does more damage.	Knock enemies into the air at the end of Ambrush.
Playing Hooky – 3000	**Vast Volume – 3000**
Press **Attack 1** during Ambrush to deal more damage in a larger area on exit.	Press **Attack 3** to send three strands of dark energy out to knock more enemies into the air during Whip Lash.

Sea Shadow

FIGURE 3.40 CAST A SHADOW to make evil SHUDDER in the DEEP-SEA DIVER of darkness!

The Sea Shadow is an uber-cool vehicle with smooth sailing at top speed and strong acceleration to get you there. Its weaknesses are a wide turning circle (tricky in tight spots) and minimal armor, which makes it easy to blast in a race (try bolstering your shields and using the Deep Sea Denture mod so the bad guys don't sink their teeth into it). Alluring Lures is a stand-out specialty mod that increases your speed to maximum and looks brilliant underwater, like the glowing, bioluminescent lure of an anglerfish. A double-hit weapons system lets you create a Darkness Vortex to capture long-range enemies and then pummel the vortex with short-range attack orbs to increase the damage output. What could be better?

Upgrade Sea Shadow's shields and weapons with Sharpfin and his crew:

    Upgrade Level 1: 300 gearbits

    Upgrade Level 2: 350 gearbits

    Upgrade Level 3: 400 gearbits

    Upgrade Level 4: 450 gearbits

    Upgrade Level 5: 500 gearbits

Weapons

Abyss Cannon: Tap **Attack 1** to fire Darkness Orbs that track your enemies.

Luminescent Launcher: Tap **Attack 3** to launch a Darkness Vortex. Shoot it with Darkness Orbs to make it pulse with damage!

Horns

    Night Time Tuner Horn

    Abyssal Emitter Horn

    Sea Floor Horn

    Manta Music Horn

Specialty Mods

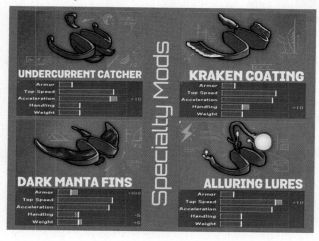

Performance Mods

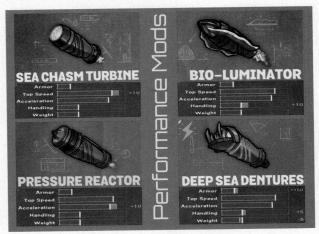

Astroblast: "Ready, Set, Glow!"

FIGURE 3.41 MOONWALK your way to victory with LASER weapons that are LIGHT YEARS ahead!

TABLE 3.39 Astroblast's Stats!

Element	Light
SuperCharger Vehicle	Sun Runner
Max. Health	180
Armor	18
Speed	35
Critical Hit	6
Elemental Power	25

Before he became a SuperCharger, Astroblast was already a super-secret spy. In his travels, he discovered a long-lost Rift Engine. His timing couldn't have been better, because trouble was on the way! Astroblast's epic bravery and laser skills cut through the bad guys as he single-handedly fought off an epic Troll army attack to stop the engine from being stolen and used for terrible purposes. With the Rift Engine saved, he flew it to Skylanders Academy and was greeted with a hero's welcome. Astroblast realized there was a greater cause to champion—saving the Rift Engines from the clutches of Kaos and his minions. He's a sharp shooter with a crystal clear goal: to rise against the power of the darkness to destroy evil.

Attack Moves:

Solar Flair: Press **Attack 1** to fire condensed sunlight, which bounces off walls.

Asteroid Belt: Press **Attack 2** to lob a prismatic space rock. Press **Attack 1** to shoot the prism, creating an area of lasers that damage enemies in the area.

Soul Gem Ability: Wool Encounters – 4000: Hold **Attack 3** to bring down a space rock inhabited by a creature with its own laser gun set to Blaaaaast!

Upgrades:

TABLE 3.40 Astroblast's Stats!

Starsault – 500: Press **Attack 3** to kick close enemies and knock them away.

Solar Field – 700: Fast-moving light particles around you protect your suit, improving your armor. Additionally, Life elemental Skylanders near you regenerate health.

Solar Powered – 900: Hold **Attack 1** to charge up Solar Flair with the light of hotter and hotter suns. Release to shoot a high powered laser at enemies.

Space Rocks! – 1200: Hold **Attack 3** to bring down an explosive space rock. (Prerequisite: Starsault.)

Cosmic Technology Path: Gain stronger laser abilities with powered-up gear!	Nova Hopper Path: Bring down huge rocks from space onto your enemies!
Surface of the Sun – 1700 Your Solar Field heats up and does damage to enemies that get too close.	**Meteor Shower – 1700** Hold **Attack 2** and release to lob multiple space rocks.
Meatier Meteors – 2200 Hold **Attack 3** down longer to bring down a bigger (more explosive) space rock.	**Full Spectrum – 2200** When you shoot a space rock, the dust will last longer.
Star Light, Star Bright – 3000 Rapidly press **Attack 1** to fire Solar Flairs at its currently charged level. The charge will slowly diminish over time.	**Supernova – 3000** Once before you lose your last hit point, you will go supernova and gain half health.

Sun Runner

FIGURE 3.42 SHINE LIGHT on your enemies' weakness then BLAST them into ATOMS with your laser-precision heat!

The Space Age has begun! You're about to be blinded by the light of a galaxy-class ship sporting a killer laser beam. The Satellite Support attack is very helpful to identify the health of your enemies in-flight, and you can use it to prioritize your attacks by taking out the strongest fighters first. Sun Runner has a great weapons system and a solid hit, but don't expect to hit light speed as you chase down enemies in the sky. This vehicle is actually pretty slow to fly. In one sense, that helps because you have lots of time to get your aim right, but on the other hand, it's not very helpful in a race. Add the Meteor Crux and Crystalline Cover mods to rev up your acceleration and boost your speed. If Sun Runner is racing against you, be sure to dodge its laser beam as you run rings around it on the course.

Upgrade Sun Runner's shields and weapons with Sharpfin and his crew:

Upgrade Level 1: 200 gearbits

Upgrade Level 2: 250 gearbits

Upgrade Level 3: 300 gearbits

Upgrade Level 4: 350 gearbits

Upgrade Level 5: 400 gearbits

Weapons

Light-Matter Laser: Tap **Attack 1** to fire a laser as hot as a thousand suns!

Satellite Support: Tap **Attack 3** to perform a laser sweep that reveals the health of all enemies.

Horns

Noisy Nebulizer Horn

Anti-Grav Vibration Horn

Interface Blips Horn

The Little Bang Horn

Specialty Mods

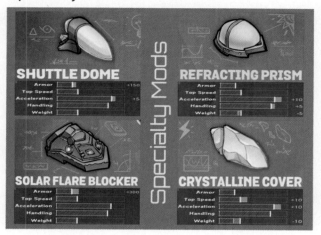

Performance Mods

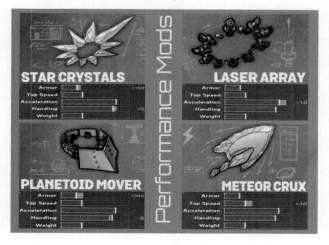

The Bad Guys

Beware the sea and skies! Lord Kaos isn't the only evil mastermind in Skylands—there are plenty of other villains waiting in the wings to take you down! As you play through the adventure chapters, you'll meet some crazy criminals lurking on each new island (see Figure 4.1). They'll throw obstacles and minions in your path until you finally have to battle it out and teach them who's boss. Think it sounds easy? It isn't over yet! These rascals like to rock the boat... literally!

Once you've defeated them, each of these villains will be ready to race you at Pandergast's racing challenges on a sea, sky, or land track. You'll have to outwit them first by earning a star in a Single Race at their home island (you'll learn more about Pandergast's challenges in Chapter 9, "SuperCharged Racing"). After you've won a Single Race, you can challenge them to a Boss Pursuit at the same location to show those troublemakers who's the fastest hero in town.

Wolfgang the rock-star Werewolf is slashing his guitar in Time Town, where you'll need to time-travel to save the future from his ego-centric interference. Captain Frightbeard and his scurvy crew are stashing loot and wrecking ships in Tropic Plunder, hoping you'll dare to drop by for a tussle. A storm of trouble is brewing at the Cloud Factory where Stratosfear is spinning hurricanes with his bad temper! There's no end to the trouble these scoundrels cause, and of course it's up to you as the newest Portal Master to make sure your SuperChargers teach them a lesson they won't forget!

Once you've beaten them in a one-to-one Boss Pursuit race, you can commandeer their vehicles and race *as* these villains! Each of them has a signature vehicle with set stats and weapons (no upgrading necessary). They're fully charged and ready to race.

You've got your work cut out for you! It's time to hunt down some bad guys.

Chef Pepper Jack

Capn' Cluck

Wolfgang

Stratosfear

Dragon Hunter

Chompy Mage

Kaos

Glumshanks

Count Moneybone

Mesmeralda

Golden Queen

Spellslamzer

Captain Frightbeard

FIGURE 4.1 What would Skylands be without the troublemakers that make victory so sweet? Track down these baddies for a battle of wits and strength, then challenge them to a race at Skylanders Academy!

Sea Villains

Earn your sea legs in a swashbuckling challenge on the water. None of these sea villains are wet behind the ears—they've got years of fighting experience under their belts and an ocean of experience between them. They'll chase you down with missiles and launchers, dive deep, ride rapids, fire cannons, and throw swords across the waves. Hold on tight and set sail. You're in for some serious splashing to stop their strife on the seas!

Mesmeralda & Wave Singer

There's a diving diva on the stage and she does *not* want to share the limelight! Mesmeralda isn't happy that you're on her case; the only thing this singing starlet wants chasing her down the racing track are paparazzi! Grab some upgrades or you'll be hanging by a string as she strikes with the puppet curse in her signature vehicle, the Wave Singer (shown in Figure 4.2). Mesmeralda is ready to teach you why she's the star of the sea in an action-packed performance on the waves. Go on, give her a hand!

Cursed Puppet: Press **Attack 1** to shoot a puppet that leaves a curse on its victim!

Hands of a Puppeteer: Press **Attack 3** to gain a speed boost! Pays to be a puppeteer!

Racing against Mesmeralda: The Wave Singer is a fast vehicle that can attack racers in front of it and beside it, but she is vulnerable to attack from behind. Keep a little bit of distance (about the length of your vehicle), so you won't get damaged if she pulls out the Hands of a Puppeteer attack against you. She's a tricky one to hit because she spends a lot of time ducking underneath the water where your ammo won't work. Choose a particularly strong attack, such as Sea Shadow's Luminescent Launcher (Darkness Orbs shot into a Darkness Vortex), to really knock her health (of 950 points) down. Top up your ammo—you're gonna need it!

Racing as Mesmeralda: The Cursed Puppet attack needs a solid lock on your target to hit, so wait until you get a clear shot so you don't waste precious ammo. It takes a few seconds to recharge and will leave some damaging aftershocks after the hit. If enemies are closing in, use the Hands of a Puppeteer attack to smack them away (they need to be right next to you). You'll get a bonus speed boost that pushes you forward.

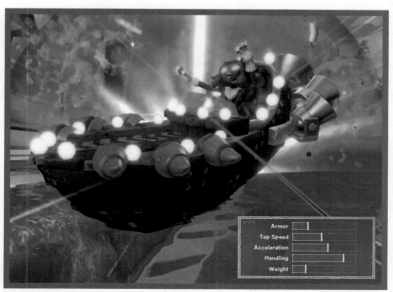

FIGURE 4.2 Mesmeralda loves to be center stage! Knock her off her pedestal with some classic moves on the ice.

Spellslamzer & Rune Slider

A mystical magician is on your tail with some evil tricks up his sleeve! Spellslamzer reaches high speeds with ease. He's causing trouble at the Mystical Vault, where nothing is as it seems. A quick turning circle and heavy weight mean his vehicle, the Rune Slider (shown in Figure 4.3), is hard to knock off track. Psych up for a mind-bending ride over and under the waves where this black-cloaked mystery man might just spell the end of you!

Runes: Press **Attack 1** to fire multiple runes at enemies.

Purple Electricity: Press **Attack 3** to shock enemies with a dose of purple electricity.

Racing against Spellslamzer: Don't get too close to Rune Slider on the track; its Purple Electricity attack will zap everyone around and knock them off Spellslamzer's trail. The Rune Slider is a tough one to beat up close, so stay behind and hit it from long range. If it gets in front of you, the Runes attack will inflict damage from multiple rune hits at once, so move around a lot to keep it off your tail. Spellslamzer has 1150 health points to knock off before he runs out of gas.

Racing as Spellslamzer: This isn't the easiest vehicle to handle and takes a hit easily because it has low armor, but the weapons make it a great choice if you have a high-health opponent. Runes have a homing ability, so they'll track down your enemy long range on a tricky, windy path, as long as you get a quick target on them first. Zap off your competitors when they get too close using the Purple Electricity attack. It has a limited range in front of the Rune Slider (you'll see a light sphere form over the middle of the vehicle at its reach-limit) so it's most useful for enemies immediately touching or behind you.

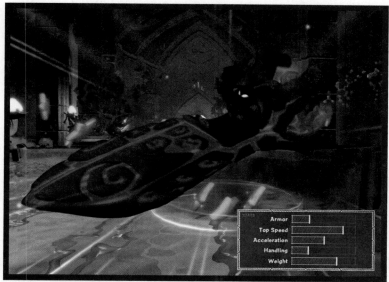

FIGURE 4.3 Homing runes are on your case, so step back and work your long-range magic to bring down this evil trickster!

Golden Queen & Glitter Glider

A trail of glittering gold falling from the sky can only mean one thing—the Golden Queen is on your tail! From the throne of her Glitter Glider, this evil royal beauty is determined to prove that she doesn't bow to anybody! The Golden Queen has a lot of health to get through (1000 points). You'll need to keep your pedal to the metal over the full three laps to wear her down in her vehicle, the Glitter Glider (shown in Figure 4.4).

Golden Scarab: Press **Attack 1** to shoot a mighty golden scarab!

Glitter Shield: Press **Attack 3** to gain a speed boost and a glitter shield.

Racing against Golden Queen: The Golden Queen doesn't have a defensive attack from the back of the vehicle, so you're safe to follow and attack closely from behind. If she has the Glitter Shield up, you'll have a tough job of knocking her out as long as there is ammo to spare, so race in front and pick it all up yourself before she gets her golden hands on it. She can't use both the shield and scarab missile at once, so you're bound to get an opportunity to strike. Cut her off by taking shortcuts if possible to catch her unawares!

Racing as Golden Queen: With the Glitter Shield attack, you've got it made. Use your special bonus shield to deflect enemy attack while you zoom ahead of the pack—they'll be eating gold dust for dinner! This attack chews through the ammo though, so make sure your ammo bar stays full. If you're racing at the Golden Temple, track down the Powered Pods at the top of the giant boulder fall. The Golden Scarab is a useful missile, but doesn't do as much damage as other weapons. You can only use one attack at a time, so spend your ammo wisely. Glitter Glider turns easily but can be slow to accelerate into a good speed, so getting knocked out by obstacles will make a big dent on your time performance.

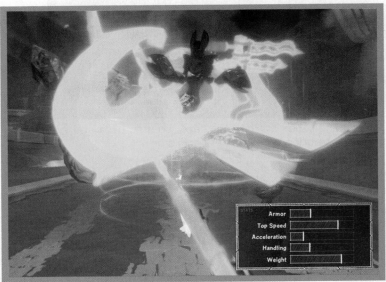

FIGURE 4.4 The Royal Queen is dreadfully displeased that you want to steal her racing crown!

Captain Frightbeard & Lil' Phantom Tide

Captain Frightbeard is an old seadog with a strong health bar (1250 points). He's convinced that you don't belong in the sea and he'll do anything to spin you out of his territory. His pirate pals drop him at Tropic Plunder (while firing snapping chompies from ship cannons!). Track him down there in his pirate ship, the Lil' Phantom Tide (shown in Figure 4.5) for an outrageous adventure!

Elemental Swords: Press **Attack 1** to shoot elemental swords! Yarr!

Phantom Tide Cannon: Press **Attack 3** to fire the Phantom Tide's cannons!

Racing against Captain Frightbeard: The Phantom Tide cannon attack will only damage you if you are right up close, so as long as you keep a vehicle's length behind Frightbeard, you're safe. Keep your firepower locked on him any chance you get; you'll need a concerted effort during all three laps to wear his health right down and win. On your first lap through Tropic Plunder to capture Frightbeard, take the right path around the volcano and steer right to find a little cave with a Magic Box—this is a Powered Pod and will keep your ammo up for the entire race. It's worth losing a few seconds to pick it up because Frightbeard has a high health score and is hard to get a target lock on while racing due to the high number of obstacles, turns, and alternate paths. With a full ammo bar, you can fire him down without losing time to recharge.

Racing as Captain Frightbeard: You'll be able to pick up a surprising amount of speed with this vehicle, but if you spin out it takes a long time to get back on track. The acceleration for the Lil' Phantom Tide is minimal, and it has a wide turning circle, making it difficult to maneuver in tight spaces. Your strongest attack is the Elemental Swords, which will home in on an enemy as long as you had a target lock on them when you fired. The Phantom Tide Cannon is much more powerful, but will only affect racers that are right up next to you when you use it, making it less useful at high speed.

FIGURE 4.5   Practice your sword-shooting with the scurviest sailor on the Skylands seas!

Sky Villains

Take to the sky in an air battle to remember! Each of the sky villains is at home in the clouds and boasts a full-throttled vehicle of missiles, energy bombs, explosions, or electricity. Grab your sky SuperChargers and hit the big blue to teach them that it's better to straighten up and fly right!

Chef Pepper Jack & Toaster Bomber

He's the meanest hot-and-spicy vegetable this side of Calamity Canyon! Chef Pepper Jack has the crowd in an uproar, throwing peppers and tomatoes across the racecourse to knock you out of the sky. He's hot under the collar to teach you who the king of the kitchen is (him, of course!) so you'd better fire up your weapons, and get ready for a showdown! The Toaster Bomber (see Figure 4.6) is a super-fast vehicle with a blazing burner behind it so don't get caught on its grill!

Pepper Sauce: Press **Attack 1** to fire homing peppers full of hot sauce!

After Burners: Press **Attack 3** to gain a speed boost and leave a hazard behind!

Racing against Chef Pepper Jack: The Pepper Sauce attack is a strong weapon that can knock an enemy off its tracks, but your advantage is that Pepper Jack is slow to respond and maneuver. If you're in a zippy little aircraft, keep on the move because his missiles have a homing device. It's easier to bring the Toaster Bomber down from behind. Stay a safe distance behind him to avoid the fire blaze of After Burners and keep your target locked on with a rapid-fire missile so you can use a continuous stream of ammo to knock out his huge 1500 health points. Remember to pick up ammo pods as you pass them so you don't run out. If you're at Calamity Canyon, look for Powered Pods at the left-side path split in the canyon.

Racing as Chef Pepper Jack: This is a really heavy vehicle that is, strangely, a little touchy when you first begin to fly. It's super-fast, though, so it's fantastic in a race. The After Burners will clear the competitors from directly behind you, keeping you safe from short-range attacks. Pepper Sauce missiles do heavy damage, and the homing device is great to make short work of enemies.

FIGURE 4.6 Chef Pepper Jack is raging hot and ready to race!

Wolfgang & Sub Woofer

Like a true rock star, Wolfgang's passion for music led him to the heights of fame—he put on the greatest show Time Town had ever seen! Of course, he had to destroy the island's entire future to do so. Using his epic guitar-playing skills, Wolfgang split apart Time Town to create a giant molten space-rock connected by musical laser tunnels and asteroid belts. He's a fun villain to chase down, with 1050 health points to plow through and a super-fast sky vehicle called the Sub Woofer (shown in Figure 4.7). It's time to pull the plug on his musical mischief!

Musical Strike: Press **Attack 1** to fire a homing musical strike!

Big Bad Speaker: Press **Attack 3** to drop a big bad speaker that will damage enemies! That'll show 'em!

Racing against Wolfgang: This werewolf is quick behind the wheel, so you'll need to take as many boost gates to bring him down as you can manage. This will be easier in the longer straights of old Time Town. Keep your firepower up during the entire chase to wear him down. There will be times obstacles get in your way, so lock targets any time you can. Pick up the Powered Pod just after the first right-side path in future Time Town for extra ammo. He'll often drop a speaker using the Big Bad Speaker attack, which falls directly behind his flight path, so keep clear of that space. You can still knock him out from behind if you are constant on the trigger.

Racing as Wolfgang: The Sub Woofer has two strong, useful attack moves—one for enemies in front, and one to trail behind you. The Big Bad Speaker will keep competitors off your tail and give anyone in the way an energy shock. Musical Strike will take out your target with a homing device, as well as anyone who happens to be on either side of it at the time. This is a great attack for clearing the path ahead because you get multiple damage hits for minimal ammo.

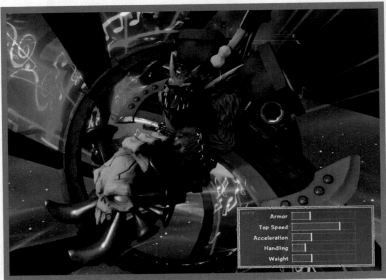

FIGURE 4.7 Wolfgang has a nose for trouble. (He's usually the one causing it!) Amp up your game to catch this fearsome felon and put him behind bars!

Stratosfear & Storm Striker

Lord Stratosfear is the meanest, crankiest aristocrat you've ever seen, turning his nose up at all of your attempts to knock him off his perch. You'll find him at his home base, the Cloud Factory (see Figure 4.8). He has stolen evil winged boots that give him a flying edge on the racecourse, so you'll need to up your game to catch up and shoot him down. Stratosfear has lower health than most other villains, at 975 points. Storm Striker has two attacks, one from the front and one from behind, which is really useful if you're racing it against stronger competitors.

Electrical Staff: Press **Attack 1** to fire an exploding electrical staff.

Orbs of Light: Press **Attack 3** to drop orbs of light that will damage enemies on impact.

Racing against Stratosfear: Electrical Staff is a close-range attack that sends a strike of electricity ahead of the Storm Striker to knock other racers off course. If you are racing against Stratosfear in a Boss Pursuit, the hit is pretty localized. Unless you're directly in front of Stratosfear while racing, you're generally safe. Try to keep slightly off center from him at all times, and take your hits on an angle. Use your firepower as much as possible when you are about to take a sharp turn so his Orbs of Light aren't in your trajectory as you do. The five orbs are shaped like a cross, so stick to one of the four corners where they aren't going to trail into you. Be relentless with your artillery, and if possible use a vehicle with a continuous ammo stream such as Stealth Stinger.

Racing as Stratosfear: This is a pretty fast racer but can get easily knocked off course and damaged. The Electrical Staff is a great way to clear the path ahead, creating a small sphere of collateral damage. Only the vehicle in your crosshairs will be put off course by a direct hit, though. The Orbs of Light attack is Storm Striker's strongest and the one you'll want to get your hands on. Five large orbs fly directly out from behind the vehicle and cause a lot of damage to anyone in their path. Get in front of the pack and let the orbs do their work.

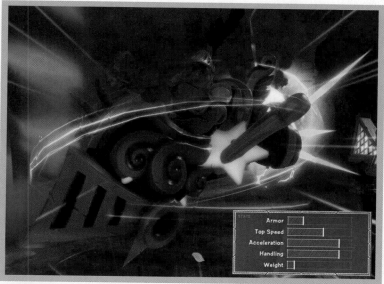

FIGURE 4.8 Stratosfear is sending a tornado of trouble your way in his Storm Striker!

Cap'n Cluck & Sky Scrambler

Cap'n Cluck is no spring chicken—he's a wise-cracking veteran of the skies with some pretty swift moves! The Sky Scrambler (see Figure 4.9) has a super-tight turning circle and moves quickly, with a solid 910 health points to crack away at. Pick a vehicle with great speed and handling for this race. (A souped-up Stealth Stinger does an egg-cellent job!)

Egg Blast: Press **Attack 1** to fire an egg that will scramble enemies!

Egg Missile: Press **Attack 3** to fire a big egg missile!

Racing against Cap'n Cluck: The Sky Scrambler is light on the armor, but has good speed, so you'll need to stay on your toes. It has no weapon to protect it from behind, so this is your best spot to wear down Cluck's health at a safe distance. Beware the blue energy field that appears when an Egg Missile hits its target—this can affect others nearby as well. You'll have to be directly in front of the Sky Scrambler to get hit by the egg missiles because they don't move with their target. The Egg Blast, on the other hand, has a homing device and will track you down. There is no rapid fire (one egg at a time), with a couple of seconds between shots for recovery. Grab the Powered Pods at Cuckoo Nest at the top-right side of the Chicken Shed to keep your ammo full and stay on his tail.

Racing as Cap'n Cluck: Use the Egg Missile attack when you need to deal collateral damage to your competitors or to stop them from picking up ammo ahead of you. Egg Blast is a great attack and will seek out the target as long as you fire when locked onto it. This attack will damage one vehicle at a time, but can be used consistently and is great for tight turns and tricky tracks.

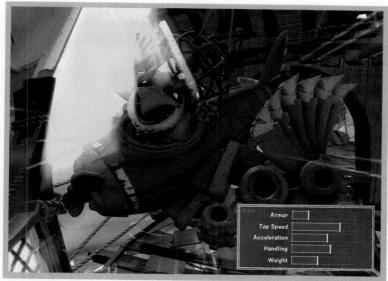

FIGURE 4.9 Cap'n Cluck is all cracked up! Chase him down at the Cuckoo Nest for a scramble to the end of the hen house.

Kaos & the Doom Jet

The evilest Portal Master in Skylands wants to teach you a thing or two about racing, and he's not going to play nice! Chase down Kaos (pictured in Figure 4.10) on any of the tracks or put the Kaos Trophy on your portal to race as him. Kaos has the highest health of all the villains, at 1600 points. It takes a lot of ammo to beat him. The Doom Jet has good handling, but the weapons are a little tricky to use. You'll get a burst of speed with the Invincible Doom Dash, which can shoot you ahead of the pack.

> **Doom Energy Ball of DOOM:** Press **Attack 1** to fire a Doom Energy Ball. Hold **Attack 1** to charge your DOOM!

> **Invincible Doom Dash of DOOM:** Press **Attack 3** to enter an ultimate DOOM dash and be invincible for a while!

> **Racing against Kaos:** The Doom Jet is a nifty vehicle with good handling and some strong weapons, but you can outsmart it by moving around a lot. It needs a good lock on its target to hit straight, especially if the Energy Ball is triple-charged. These often go to waste if the target shifts, so your best bet to beat Kaos is by catching every boost gate you can to keep up and shooting him from behind. He has no trailing weapon, so you're safe from damage. Kaos does have a massive amount of health, though (the highest of all villains), so you'll want to pick up lots of ammo and Powered Pods to sustain your firepower in a race.

Racing as Kaos: Use the Invincible Doom Dash to break away from enemy fire and to smash through objects that would normally cause you damage, such as asteroids, fire, and ice. Your speed boost only lasts a few seconds, but it's usually enough to get you out of trouble. It will take a bit of time to recharge. Hold the **Attack 1** button to charge your Doom Energy Balls up before firing. They'll change from blue (normal damage) to purple (double damage) and then red (triple damage). Then fire. This is brilliant in a boss fight, where your priority is damage, not speed. Save this attack for straight sections of the course, though, because it's easy to lose a moving target and waste your efforts and ammo.

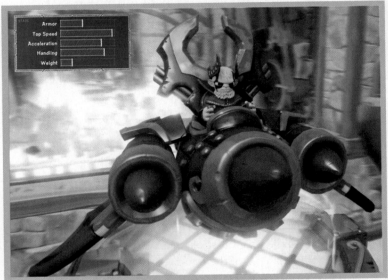

FIGURE 4.10   The Greatest Dark Portal Master that ever lived has some evil new tricks up his magic sleeve! Triple damage hits and invincibility are just the beginning....

Land Villains

There's nothing better than tearing up the track on wheels to claim gold and glory in a race, especially if you get to show these villains who's boss! They'll try to throw you off your game with lava missiles, damaging bones, junk mines, purple fire, and bad attitudes! Keep your eyes and ammo on the bad guys and get ready to swerve, drift, and jump your way to victory.

Chompy Mage & Chompy Buster

Deep in the over-grown Chompy Gardens, all the critters are cheering! Their brave and questionably insane leader is ready to race you. This crazy character asks his own hand puppet for advice, and even lets it drive the Chompy Buster! Chompy Mage is a bit of a tease and a very bad loser, as you can see in Figure 4.11. He'll taunt you on the track, but don't let it get you down—just get even! Keep him in your crosshairs, and take advantage of his low armor with some weapons upgrades on your racing vehicle for a quick win.

Chompy Bola: Press **Attack 1** to fire a Chompy Bola that bounces between enemies!

Chompy Ball: Press **Attack 3** to fire big Chompy Balls! Chompy POWER!

Racing against Chompy Mage: The Chompy Buster is a zippy little vehicle with solid speed but low armor. You can bring his 950 points of health down easily enough with most weapons—if you can catch hold of him long enough to lock your target! The Chompy Buster has the highest acceleration of any vehicle; and when you're chasing it down, he swerves and dodges like a professional. Your best bet is to boost your weapons before you ride to make sure that any hit you get is going to make a big impact. You're safe driving behind Chompy Mage as he has only front-end weaponry; but beware of getting too close. He'll knock you out spinning if you get caught alongside in a Chompy Ball explosion.

Racing as Chompy Mage: The Chompy Buster is easy to handle and quick to take off, but the weapons are a bit tricky to use. Chompy Bola is a strong hit, but you need to be right on target and keep your steering straight while you fire. It doesn't take much to nudge this one off course. The Chompy Ball is a heavy hitter, but only good for clusters of competitors. The aim is poor; and if it falls short, it won't have any effect at all. Save it for big groups of racers in your way or blasting through obstacles.

FIGURE 4.11 Chompy Mage is nimble on the track and super-fast. Use a strong, long-range homing weapon for your best chance of success.

Count Moneybone & Spirit Dragster

This fancy bag of bones has been partying hard! Find him at The After Party to give him a time-out in his coffin car. Count Moneybone has 900 health points to get through before defeat, which isn't the highest of the villains; but the tricky part is keeping him in your crosshairs long enough to hit him! Spirit Dragster is a zippy coffin on wheels that could outrun a stampede of skeletons! It has great handling but is low on armor, so choose a hard-hitting weapon to bury Moneybone fast (see Figure 4.12).

Machinegun: Press **Attack 1** to fire the Count's special machine gun!

Ghostly Explosions: Press **Attack 3** to cause massive explosions around your vehicle!

Racing against Count Moneybone: This creepy villain has strong acceleration and can zip ahead a lot quicker than most land vehicles. His weapons are forward firing and can take out a competitor right alongside, but you're safe if you stay a vehicle-length distance behind to sustain a constant stream of fire power. The hard part of bringing down Moneybone is keeping up with him on those tight turns at The After Party—Spirit Dragster has great handling and can lose you in an instant. Use a constant stream of firepower over the full three laps to wear him down.

Racing as Count Moneybone: Spirit Dragster has great handling and enough acceleration to maintain a steady pace, but the weapons aren't too crash hot. The Machinegun weapon is an individual fire, long-range hit that only causes about 18 points of damage per hit—so, it will take a long time and spot-on targeting to take anyone down on that alone. The Ghostly Explosions weapon is stronger and causes decent damage, but you need to be right alongside your competitors to make a dent. Hit every boost pad you can to keep up with other racers, and save your ammo for when Ghostly Explosions will give you the biggest effect.

FIGURE 4.12   Rattle some funny bones at The After Party as you slip, slide, and salsa through a fiesta of fun! (Watch out for slime under your wheels!)

Dragon Hunter & Scale Biter

The Dragon Hunter has a high health load at 1250 points, so choose a strong vehicle to last the distance. His vehicle, Scale Biter, is like the spikiest, purple pet dog you've ever seen, and he has the bone to prove it! Dragon Hunter throws the bone ahead of him as he drives, damaging enemies that run over it. Use it for an extra speed boost, or just zoom ahead of the pack and stay there for a swift win. This dragon racer and his barking best friend are a powerful team, as shown in Figure 4.13.

Purple Fire: Hold **Attack 1** to shoot powerful purple fire!

Dragon Bone: Press **Attack 3** to throw your vehicle a bone and gain a speed boost! Don't forget to pick it up.

Racing against Dragon Hunter: Dragon Hunter has everything on his side—except armor. Strike him in his weak spot by pulling in the big guns (literally) to knock him out. His trailing weapon is to drop Dragon Bones on the track, which can be hard to miss if you're directly behind. But don't worry—each one will damage your health without spinning you out. Run over them if it means keeping a solid target on Dragon Hunter's back. Take advantage of straight runs where you can fire continually.

Racing as Dragon Hunter: The weapons are a bit confusing, so take this one for a test run first. The Purple Fire attack creates a solid stream of damage, but you really do need to hold the button down and keep it on target the whole time to be effective. This is great for a straight course like Dragon Spine where you can follow without too many twists and turns. Keep about two vehicle lengths behind so that your arc of fire hits its mark. The Dragon Bone weapon is a little hit or miss. If you throw a bone (it is thrown ahead of you onto the track), and then deliberately run over it yourself, you'll gain a little speed boost (not as much as a boost pad, though). If you leave the bones behind for competitors to hit, they'll cause damage, but not enough to spin a racer out. Where the bone lands on the track is a little unpredictable, so it's quantity, not quality, with this attack to get results. Weapons aside, if you're aiming for speed and maneuverability, Scale Biter is the vehicle/dragon/dog racer for you!

FIGURE 4.13 Throw your dog a bone and watch racers collide over it! Dragon Hunter is a super-speedy racer that's hard to out-run on the track.

Glumshanks & Steam Roller

No more Mr. Nice Guy! Glumshanks has thrown off his shackles and jumped behind the wheel of a fire-powered dragster! Bring him down in a no-holds-barred race at the Temple of Arkus, as shown in Figure 4.14. Although he seems a little reluctant to race, make no mistake—Glumshanks is a tough troll to beat. His high health (1400 points) and the double-ended weaponry of Steam Roller make him a worthy opponent to test your skill on the track.

Big Missile: Press **Attack 1** to fire a big missile! Better watch out!

Junk Mine: Press **Attack 3** to drop a junk mine that'll explode on contact!

Racing against Glumshanks: Be prepared to swerve and dodge as the Steam Roller drops lava-style mines behind it while Glumshanks zooms ahead. This vehicle is very fast and takes a few laps to bring down, mostly due to time wasted dodging mines. The mines explode and disappear after about two seconds; but if you are right behind Glumshanks, you'll hit them and knock your health bar down very quickly. Try zig-zagging to avoid the mines, and keep your finger on the ammo to fire every time the Steam Roller gets in your radar. There are plenty of turns on the Temple of Arkus track to hit him from a safe angle and wear him down. You'll run out of ammo quickly here, so pick up the Powered Pod for extra help. A vehicle with a constant stream of firepower, like Gold Rusher, gives you the best chance of hitting your target.

Racing as Glumshanks: Single missiles leave solid damage, but your aim needs to be right on the money. Missiles only home in on their target if you have it in your crosshairs precisely when you fire—even a tiny bit off the mark will miss by far. This is a fast vehicle, but heavy, so it feels a little sluggish to accelerate and takes a few seconds to reach high speed. Changing direction is slower than usual to react. Use speed boosts to get ahead and make the most of Steam Roller by fully utilizing its awesome weapons. As soon as you get ahead of the pack, leave a trail of mines to slow the racers behind you.

FIGURE 4.14   Glumshanks is in top form on the racetrack, so watch out! Avoid his blistering trail of trouble by following on an angle—not directly behind.

Cool Collectibles

Skylanders SuperChargers isn't just all about fighting baddies and spinning off onto crazy adventures (although that's why we love it!). There are plenty of hidden rewards to search for as you play, to fill your piggy bank and buy upgrades or special items from Ari at the Academy Store. After all, you might like to show off a fancy new hat that makes the wearer super-strong (and really ridiculously good-looking too!). Perhaps you need as many Wish Stones as you can find to fling into the Wishing Well and make all your dreams come true! Or maybe you're a serious tactical fighter who covets Soul Gems that will bestow your Skylanders with epic new attack moves!

There is plenty of loot up for grabs in *SuperChargers*, if you know where to look. As you explore, keep your eyes peeled (or "eye," if you happen to be a Cyclops!) for treasure chests overflowing with golden coins, gleaming gems, goblets, and trinkets.

Rainbow piñatas are stashed away in dark places and behind puzzle doors, just waiting for you to come and smash them open. If you've got a funny bone, perhaps you're a collector of Kaos Diaries, those insane little ramblings from the most evil, hilarious dark Portal Master that ever (badly) ruled Skylands!

Collectibles can be tracked by viewing the "Stats" section of the Portal Master menu. With the exception of Magic Item Toys, which are brought to *Skylanders SuperChargers* from earlier versions of the game, and Wish Stones, which are found in specific locations, all other collectibles can be found as random rewards throughout your adventure. You can win them in races, find them while completing challenges such as SuperCharger Gates, behind Live Wire Locks, and in Epic Treasure Chests and piñatas. It's a lucky dip—just like Dive-Clops, shown in Figure 5.1, with the spoils of his exploration in The Fuel's Errand. You never know what you're going to get!

In this chapter, we're not only going to find out about the incredible riches you can score on your journey through Skylands, but also what you can use them for once collected. Let's get to it!

FIGURE 5.1 Piñatas, magic hats, gems, and jewels; Dive-Clops has his eye on the prize!

Legendary Treasure

Legendary Treasure items are fantastic. You can collect and interact with them in special ways (each one is different), but they can only be placed in Skylanders Academy. They're not particularly useful but are ornamental instead—that's part of their charm. Decorate Skylanders Academy and play with them for a bit of relaxation when you need a break from battling bad guys. A full list of Legendary Treasure to hunt down can be found in Table 5.1.

TABLE 5.1 Legendary Treasures

Icon	Treasure	How It Works
	Beach Ball	Just for fun, give it a kick.
	Bioluminescent Mushroom	Jump onto it and bounce forever!
	Black Hole	Opens a mini-game of coins.

Icon	Treasure	How It Works
	Blue Goal	Matches the Red Goal—kick a ball in!
	Boom Box	Fancy a dance?
	Chompy Ball	Super-cute! You have a new pet!
	Elemental Flower Pot	The flower color matches your Skylander's element.
	Elemental Gem	Pretty! The gem color matches your Skylander's element.
	Elemental Torch	The fire color matches your Skylander's element.
	Eon Statue	A word of advice from the master....
	Food Stand	Attack it when you're hungry!
	Kaos Punching Bag	A good spot to take out your frustrations!
	Live Wire Lock	Pick a lock.
	Red Goal	Matches the Blue Goal—kick a ball in!

Icon	Treasure	How It Works
	Sheep Ball	That's one very tolerant sheep!
	Shrink Ray	Hilarious! Become a mini-me!
	Snap Shot Doll	Did you miss the joke?
	Spitfire Doll	The laugh's on you....
	SuperChargers Rug	Time to decorate.
	Toy Boat Racetrack	Jump in for a spin with Reef Ripper.
	Toy Car Racetrack	Mini Hot Streak streaking past.
	Toy Plane Racetrack	Sky Slicer zooming overhead.
	Trampoline	Keep on jumping!
	Traptanium Crystal	Music time!
	Tree Rex Doll	Laugh it up!

Icon	Treasure	How It Works
	Trigger Happy Doll	That's a crazy laugh!
	Wash Buckler Doll	Hmm, a bit scary....
	Water Fountain	A pretty spot to watch the birds.
	Zen Rake	Watch your step—OUCH!

Magic Items

Many magic items have been introduced in earlier games of *Skylanders*, and each performs a special function in its corresponding game (see Figure 5.2). Although these don't all work in *SuperChargers* as you are used to, they can still be used at the Academy to help you earn some extra money or to give you a temporary boost in power. Most of them can be attacked like training dummies to add a shiny reward to your fighting practice, although many only allow a single visit per day. Visit the online bonus resources to this book using your unique login, to find a complete table describing which magic items can be brought into *SuperChargers* from earlier Skylanders games and find out how to use them to help you pay for those important upgrades with Persephone.

FIGURE 5.2 Bring your old magic items from *Spyro's Adventure*, *Giants*, *Swap Force*, and *Trap Team* into *SuperChargers* for daily rewards!

Wish Stones

When you wish upon a star—or a stone—you might just be rewarded with something extra special! Gather Wish Stones as you explore the deepest, darkest hiding places in Skylands, then cash them in at the Wishing Well near Persephone's courtyard for a random reward, just like lucky Spitfire in Figure 5.3. You may get a new magic hat, a Skystones Overdrive card, Legendary Treasure, or a heap of gold!

One or two Wish Stones are hidden in secret locations throughout most of the adventure chapters. We'll track them down in Chapter 10, "Gear Up for Adventure."

FIGURE 5.3 Close your eyes and make a wish! Bring Wish Stones back to Skylanders Academy for your reward.

Epic Treasure Chests

Have you discovered an Epic Treasure Chest in your travels? BOOMSTICKS!! Open it up and frolic in the shower of sparkling gold! Then gather it all up! Epic Treasure Chests are a super way of boosting your pocket money to buy upgrades from Persephone. Each chest will contain gold coins, jewelry, rings, crowns, gems, and/or goblets, like the one pictured in Figure 5.4. There are up to eight Epic Treasure Chests in most sections of the story, each filled to the brim with goodies. Keep a sharp eye out as you explore, and read Chapter 10 for more detail on their individual locations to help track them down.

FIGURE 5.4 It's raining treasure for Dive-Clops in his crazy Shark hat—he can't believe his eye!

Kaos Diaries

Dear Diary... of DOOM!!

My goodness, what is that crazy little Portal Master up to now?

Every time you discover a secret entry of Kaos' Diary, like the one shown in Figure 5.5, you'll gain some hilarious insights into his ultimate evil plan for victory. Kaos describes his incomparable genius for you in his own words, and we all know how modest he is! You'll want to listen to his monologues more than once, so luckily for you, you can! Just visit the gramophone in the Games Room at Skylanders Academy to re-live the wisdom of the Illustrious Emperor Kaos (the First!).

He is such a magnificent wannabe conqueror of all the insufferable "Skylosers" that it's a treat to get inside his twisted little mind. He even promised his loyal followers a sequel autobiography, "Evil – and Other Four Letter Words," available in future evil gift shops everywhere. Now, that's got to be a bestseller!

The grapeness

Hello, future friends. Now that I - Kaos - am poised on the edge of my complete and utter domination of all Skylands, I feel it is my duty to make sure that my supreme glory is captured for all time so that future generations of evil will marvel at my awesome grapeness!

FIGURE 5.5 Get ready to giggle as you hear Kaos' innermost thoughts and evil plans come to life—but not quite how he imagines them!

Soul Gems

There is one collectible Soul Gem for every SuperCharger hidden somewhere throughout the adventure. Alternatively, you may be gifted one from the Wishing Well, or you can buy one from Ari's shop. Once you have collected the Soul Gem for a specific Skylander, take it to Persephone to buy a new attack move or ability for that Skylander, just like Stormblade in Figure 5.6. You'll need to spend 4000 gold coins for the upgrade. Each Skylander's Soul Gem ability is included in his or her biography in Chapter 3, "The Good Guys."

FIGURE 5.6 You have 18 Soul Gems to find in *SuperChargers* (20 if you are playing on a Nintendo console, to include Bowser and Donkey Kong). Collect them all to master epic new fighting upgrades for your heroes.

Winged Sapphires

Now, here's a collectible you'll really want to get your Skylander's hands on! Winged Sapphires are blue gems adorned with butterfly wings (see Figure 5.7). They are hidden throughout the adventure chapters, sometimes in plain sight, but you may have to crack a puzzle or treasure chest to reach it. You may also receive one as a Wishing Well reward at Skylanders Academy.

Every Winged Sapphire you find is worth a 2% discount on buying upgrades from Persephone. Not just once, but for all of the SuperChargers, as well as their vehicles (with Sharpfin), in your collection. The more you collect, the greater the discount—up to 20% off your upgrades (this is the maximum). There are ten to collect, and Winged Sapphires go a long way to helping your Skylanders become the best fighters they can be. They're worth their weight in gold (literally!), so start hunting!

Winged Sapphire

You get a 2% discount on Upgrades!

FIGURE 5.7 Fully upgrading a SuperCharger will cost 14,200 coins each—that's a lot of treasure hunting! Collect Winged Sapphires to save time and gold.

Magic Hats

Magic hats are really the ultimate collectible to find! Why, you ask? Because these special items don't just look fabulous, they're super-helpful too! Every magic hat is imbued with powers to boost your Skylander's stats. Hats can help your Skylander run faster, hit harder, shield better, and fight longer. Each hat is unique, a little zany, and a lot awesome! There have been many hats introduced throughout the earlier editions of Skylanders games (266 so far!), which can be added to your inventory (see Figure 5.8). Many of these earlier hats are rewarded again in *SuperChargers*, gifted from the Wishing Well, or can be bought from the Academy shop. For those you can't find, you may need to carry them across from one game (for example *Trap Team*) into *SuperChargers* on the head of a Skylander if you really want them in your new inventory. That could take a while if you're a long-time player! Table 5.2 details all new hats introduced in the *SuperChargers* game.

FIGURE 5.8 Just like Spitfire, who is modeling the trendy Candy Cane Hat here, you can swap your Skylander's hat at any time by visiting the My Team menu and choosing Hats.

TABLE 5.2 Boost Your SuperChargers Stats with a Magic Hat

Hat	Critical Hit %	Speed	Elemental Power	Max. Health	Armor
Burn-Cycle Header	7		25		
Buzz Wing Hat	15	4	10		
Crypt Crusher Cap	10		10	30	
Dive Bomber Hat				40	15
Eon's Helm			15	30	15
Gold Rusher Cog Cap		9	15		
Hot Streak Headpiece		6	10		10
Jet Stream Helmet	7	6			15
Kaos Krown	15	9		30	
Mags Hat	15		15	30	
Reef Ripper Helmet	15				15

Hat	Critical Hit %	Speed	Elemental Power	Max. Health	Armor
Sea Shadow Hat		9	7		10
Shark Tank Topper		6		20	15
Shield Striker Helmet				20	25
Sky Slicer Hat		15			7
Soda Skimmer Shower Cap	15		7		10
Splatter Splasher Spires		6		30	10
Stealth Stinger Beanie	15		15		
Sun Runner Spikes	10		10		10
Thump Trucker's Hat				60	7
Tomb Buggy Skullcap	25				7

Explore Skylanders Academy

Skylanders Academy was almost completely destroyed at the hands of Kaos and his terrible sky-eating machine! Luckily for us, the ingenious inventor Mags has managed to salvage the very best parts—and converted it into an enormous training arena pulled by Flynn's ship, as shown in Figure 6.1. With so many villains willing to do Kaos' bidding, it's best to keep on the move!

In this chapter, we'll look at some of the fantastic new features of Skylanders Academy. After each adventure with your SuperChargers, you'll return to the academy for some rest and relaxation and to explore new areas that open up. There are plenty of great rebuilds to check out, including mini-games, upgrade stations, quests, and scene replays. Challenge Kaos to a game of Skystones Overdrive in his tower, take on some target practice under the giant bubble-gum ball dispenser (oops, I mean, the Greeble dispenser!), and dare to undertake an online racing challenge with Pandergast.

FIGURE 6.1 Leap from Flynn's ship over to Skylanders Academy to expand your adventure.

Eon's Academy

After you rescue Master Eon from the Land of the Undead, he takes up residence at the academy and offers advice as you take on new adventures. This is an easy place to visit to keep track of your progress in the game. You can redeem emblems here and place Legendary Treasure items that you find on your journey. The element panels on the wall behind Eon keep track of how many Skylanders are in your collection. Like Elite Voodood in Figure 6.2, make sure you stop by often to chat with Eon and get some helpful tips.

FIGURE 6.2 The most wise and powerful Portal Master, Eon, is waiting to offer you advice in Skylanders Academy.

Kaos' Tower

Just to the right of Master Eon, in the entrance to the main hall, is a ledge with a bounce pad and trail of gold coins. Hop on for a ride up to visit Kaos' Tower. The door on the right leads to his living quarters. You might even run into poor Glumshanks doing the housework and keeping a close eye on his wayward master. This new area will become available after you have completed the adventure chapters. After you defeat Kaos (spoiler alert!), that crazy, little ego-maniac decides to change his evil ways (have we heard that one before?!) and live at Skylanders Academy to become its "Ultimate Evil Consultant of Ultimate Evil," which is possibly the best job description in the world.

This is a fun area to explore, gather coins, and place your Legendary Treasure (see Figure 6.3). You can also defeat Kaos at a game of Skystones Overdrive to complete the Kaos' Crown quest and earn a special reward.

FIGURE 6.3 Bounce up to Kaos to battle him in a game of Skystones Overdrive to win his crown.

The Games Room

The most interactive new addition to Skylanders Academy is the Games Room, as shown in Figure 6.4 by Elite Slam Bam, who loves jumping on tables! Interact with the giant gramophone on the left to hear Kaos Diary entries that you find during story chapters (we discussed these more in Chapter 5, "Cool Collectibles"). You can have a lesson in Skystones Overdrive on the table in the center, or best of all, re-watch special scenes from the adventure on the Theatre Screen at the back of the room.

FIGURE 6.4 Settle back to be entertained in the Game Room or challenge your opponent with a game of Skystones Overdrive.

Sharpfin and His Pit Crew

Before you take off on another adventure with Flynn, Cali, and the gang, visit Sharpfin outside the central staircase at Skylanders Academy to upgrade your vehicle's shields and weapons (see Figure 6.5). Each upgrade will cost you gearbits, which you collect by competing in races, participating in training exercises, and throughout vehicle zones in the story chapters. Minimize the cost of your upgrades by collecting Winged Sapphires as you play (you learn more about these in Chapter 5) for a maximum 20% discount. You can learn more about vehicle upgrades in Chapter 2, "Start Your Engines."

Every vehicle has unique capabilities and limitations with regard to their weapons and defensive shields, so it's worth boosting them up with upgrades to make sure they are the best they can be. You'll appreciate having a fully charged shield and super-strong weapons when you reach the big boss fights toward the end of the game.

FIGURE 6.5 Sharpfin and his pit crew (Fender, Socket, and Clyde) are the best in the business! Keep your vehicle in tip-top shape by exchanging gearbits for upgrades.

Persephone's Courtyard

To the right of Cali's control center and down some stairs, Persephone the fairy is floating around, willing to offer upgrades for your Skylanders (see Figure 6.6). Spend gold coins to buy new Skylander attacks and choose one of the two upgrade paths to further specialize your fighting skills. You can also spend 4000 gold coins to buy each Skylander's special Soul Gem attack move, once you have found their Soul Gem during the adventure chapters (you'll learn more about Soul Gems in Chapter 5). Gather Winged Sapphires for a discount on buying your upgrades. Persephone, like Sharpfin, will also appear in each adventure chapter to offer you upgrades on-the-go.

FIGURE 6.6   Increase the strength of your attacks and buy new ones by chatting with Persephone wherever you find her.

The Wishing Well

On the front-right side of Persephone's courtyard is a magical wishing well. Find Wish Stones as you travel through the adventure chapters, or earn them by winning races. Throw them into the Wishing Well at Skylanders Academy after you finish each adventure chapter. Just like Nightfall in his jaunty Leprechaun hat in Figure 6.7, you'll be rewarded with a new treasure such as a magical hat that boosts your stats and makes you the talk of the town. You might also score a Skystones Overdrive card or Legendary Treasure item (we discuss these in Chapter 5).

FIGURE 6.7 Fingers crossed? Make a wish at the well near Persephone to try your luck!

Training Dummies

Practice new attack moves using the training dummies (like SuperCharger Splat, in Figure 6.8) to test their capabilities and learn their attacks. The amount of damage you inflict on an enemy is unique to each character and type of attack. Some characters are stronger than others, so it's a good idea to learn a Skylander's strengths and weaknesses before you throw yourself into the fray. Another bonus to using a training dummy for practice is that your health won't be decreased by fighting. Quite a few of the magic items from previous *Skylanders* games can also be used as training dummies in Skylanders Academy. You can find a complete list of these older magic items and their uses at Skylanders Academy by visiting the bonus online resources to this book. (You first must register your book by going to quepublishing. com/register, and then create an account.

The Food Stand Legendary Treasure item is another fun way to practice your attacks. Each time you hit it, the stand will release food items that you can eat to replenish your health. Place it somewhere accessible at Skylanders Academy to visit whenever you return from a challenge for an all-you-can-eat take-out health boost! Legendary Treasure will also be covered in Chapter 5.

FIGURE 6.8 Get a feel for the capabilities and the strength of new upgrade abilities using the training dummies and Food Stand in Persephone's courtyard.

The Storage Room

After you return from an adventure, make sure you take time to explore Flynn's ship before you bounce over to the academy. Behind your starting spot, to the right side, you can drop over the edge of the ship to the lower deck and enter a glowing golden door. A treasure-filled room awaits you, restocked each time you visit with shiny coins. (Lava Lance Eruptor has scored a jackpot in Figure 6.9!) Bounce back up to the top deck to continue on your way.

FIGURE 6.9 You'll return to Flynn's ship after each adventure. Make sure you fill your coffers down below before you take the leap again!

Vehicle Training Zones

If you're after a bit of practice with the SuperCharger vehicles without the worry of being blown to bits by bad guys, check out the Land, Sea, and Sky training areas at the academy (shown in Figure 6.10). The course will change daily, so you won't get tired of running the same path. Test out your weapons and get used to hitting a moving target in new vehicles with different handling abilities. Enemies will attack you, but can't damage your health, although you can shoot them down. All courses have a few tricky areas to navigate as well as puzzles and mini-challenges to complete, which make them a fun challenge to hone your skills. Collect trails of gearbits to use for vehicle upgrades with Sharpfin. The Sky Training Zone is just on the left of Hugo (in front of the Games Room). The Water Zone is at the left side of the platform in front of Sharpfin's pit crew station, and the Land Zone is to the right of Sharpfin.

FIGURE 6.10 Take a spin in your new wheels! Vehicle Zones are a super fun way to grab some extra gearbits when you're looking to upgrade.

Academy Shop

Just across the bridge, on your way to visit Pandergast, is a little house with a glowing golden door. Enter to visit Ari in the Academy Shop to find a range of useful objects to buy in exchange for gold coins (see Figure 6.11). You'll find Skystone Overdrive cards to add to your deck, or magical hats that bestow the wearer with a boost in stats. You might also be lucky enough to find a special trinket, Legendary Treasure, or gem.

FIGURE 6.11 Missile-Tow Dive-Clops couldn't believe his eye when he found a fancy Peacock hat at the Academy Store! A perfect match!

Buzz's Training Arena

Just above Persephone's courtyard, Buzz is waiting for you in a small arena. As the Head of Secret Ninja Commando Operations, it's his important role to prepare you for the onslaught of villainous types in your search for Kaos. To aid this, he has bought a giant Greeble dispenser from the Minions Monthly Catalog (at a bargain price!) for you to practice your impressive fighting moves on. Interact with the dispenser, and a critter will fall out, just like candy from an enormous bubble-gum ball machine (see Figure 6.12). If you change your mind and want to step away from a fight, jump off the platform, and the Greeble will be vacuum-sucked back up into the bowl.

Buzz and his helper, Agent 11 3/5ths, also have individual quests for each Skylander to undertake. We'll look at these challenges individually in Chapter 7, "Questing with Tessa, Hugo, and Buzz."

FIGURE 6.12 Those Greebles go straight for your noggin with their rubber mallets... OUCH! Get them before they get you!

Statues and Maps

As you wander around Skylanders Academy, you'll notice additional objects such as statues and signposts that you can interact with. Each one offers you a bit more information about your adventure. Visit the signposts for an update on available quests and racing challenges, and whom you should visit to begin them. There is a signpost behind Sharpfin, another near Pandergast, and one in Persephone's courtyard, just like the sign that Elite Zook has found in Figure 6.13. Some of these challenges will expire after a short time, so don't forget to check back often so you don't miss out.

FIGURE 6.13 Ready for a quest? Signposts will show you the way to greatness!

The Boom5000 robot is standing on a platform near Pandergast selling Bonus Racing Kits for your vehicles, as shown in Figure 6.14. In exchange for gearbits, you'll score new defensive powers that you can interchange for your existing vehicle weapons.

FIGURE 6.14 Soup up your ride with some extra firepower from Boom5000!

There are two glowing statues outside the main entrance of Skylanders Academy (see Figure 6.15). On the right side, a statue of Spitfire brings up a display of your Skylander collection, categorized by element type. This includes any earlier Skylanders you bring into the SuperChargers game, so make sure you pop them on the portal at some point. Remember, the more Skylanders you have of any particular element, the stronger your elemental power will be. You can also play promotional videos for new characters through this screen.

On the left side, interact with a statue of Hot Streak to show a list of all your collected vehicles, including the option of viewing their blueprints, weapons, and available mods.

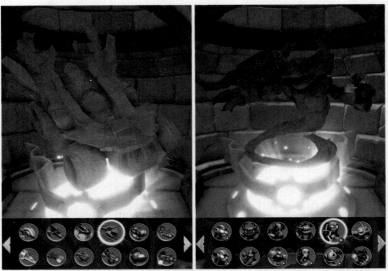

FIGURE 6.15 Keep track of your collection by visiting the Spitfire and Hot Streak statues near the main entrance.

Skystones Overdrive

Skystones is back! In this edition, our favorite mini-game is even better—it has been revved into OVERDRIVE! Skystones Overdrive essentially plays by the same rules as standard Skystones from previous *Skylanders* games, but this time, an awesome new type of stone has been added to the deck—Vehicle Skystones! These souped-up Skystones feature the famous land, sea, and sky vehicles of the SuperChargers, and each one holds a special bonus ability to either help or hinder you in your game. But there's a catch—you have to charge them up!

You will be playing Skystones Overdrive against characters from the story, such as Guss, a very bored local of the Cloud Kingdom (see Figure 6.16). You can also play at Skylanders Academy in the Games Room, or against Kaos in his tower after you have completed all of the adventure chapters. Sometimes winning the game will open a special locked area for you to explore or may instead give you a reward or a new Skystone for your collection.

FIGURE 6.16 Find Guss waiting impatiently behind the Live Wire Lock in the Cloud Kingdom. If you beat him, he'll grant you a Calliope Skystone to add to your deck.

You can build up your deck of Skystones by collecting them during the adventure chapters as rewards or by winning Skystones Overdrive games, or they may be rewarded to you from the Wishing Well. You'll be asked if you'd like to customize your own deck before you play. Some stones have bonus power attacks that can give you an advantage, so make sure you choose those to be included in your 20-stone deck before you play. If you don't wish to build your own deck, a random deck will be selected for you from your collection.

Visit your bonus online companion to this book for rules and tips on how to play (and win!) Skystones Overdrive, including a full list of Skystones to collect in adventure mode.

Questing with Tessa, Hugo, and Buzz

When it's time for rest and relaxation from fighting the forces of evil, why not take a quick quest to discover even more about magical Skylands? Tessa, Hugo and Buzz are waiting at the Academy with unique challenges for each SuperCharger and their vehicle to test their skills in racing, combat, and puzzle-solving. You might be challenged to replay a star in the adventure chapters to achieve a new reward or perhaps to race against the clock, dodging flying peppers and washing lines at Calamity Canyon. Perhaps you'll capture jewel thieves, gobble bananas, or blow the wool off sheep instead! You can even win treasure in a nail-biting game of Skystones Overdrive or prove your mettle against a tide of Bitning Bugs. There's always something crazy and new in Skylands—are you up for the challenge?

Tessa's Quests

Tessa will be waiting for you on the steps outside the main entrance to Skylanders Academy after Adventure Chapter 37 (Titanopolis) to offer you a host of exciting new quests (listed in Table 7.1). You will only be allowed to complete three per day, so you'll need to check back with her each time you play to see what's new. Once you have completed your challenge, you do not need to continue through the story chapter (although you can). Simply use your Main Menu map to navigate back to Tessa at Skylanders Academy to collect your reward (which will be a random prize of stardust, coins, or collectibles) and then continue exploring, like Lava Lance Eruptor in Figure 7.1.

FIGURE 7.1 Visit Tessa to win great rewards by completing mini-challenges within the adventure chapters.

TABLE 7.1 Visit Tessa for Daily Challenge Quests

Find Your Quest	Complete Your Challenge
The Bandit Train	
Fill 'er Up	Get the fuel supply.
For the Birds	Rescue the gold beak birds.
Poor Glumshanks	Rescue Glumshanks' prized possession.
That belongs in a museum	Recover the priceless art.
To the rescue	Rescue Toppins.
Speeding Train	Get the blusterbomb.
Super-secret mission	Grab the plans.
Battlebrawl Island	
Bad Breath Boris	Defeat the villain.
Bone Head Brutes	Defeat the villain.
Captain Thump Tusk	Defeat the villain.
The Barnyard Rejects	Defeat the villain.
The Crawler Co.	Defeat the villain.
Ridepocalypse Demo Derby Quests	
A new challenger	Win the derby.
Crashing and bashing	Win the derby.

Find Your Quest	Complete Your Challenge
Defend your title	Win the derby.
Demolition time	Win the derby.
One true champ	Win the derby.
Tough contenders	Win the derby.
Level Replays	
Cap'n Clucks Chicken HQ	Squish eight enemies with their own acorns.
Gadfly Glades	Squish 13 squash.
Land of the Undead	Shoot down 12 flying enemies.
Monstrous Isles	Destroy 50 buildings and trees.
Spell Punk Library	Defeat eight glass enemies by jumping on them.
The Cloud Kingdom	Deflate five enlarged Inflatrators.
The Cloudbreather's Crag	Destroy 50 tents.
The Rift to Skylands	Defeat 45 chompies.
Vault of the Ancients	Make ten mines collide with each other.
Other Quests	
Card Shark	Play a game of Skystones Overdrive.
Dealer's Choice	Play a game of Skystones Overdrive.
The Wishing Well	Throw three Wishing Stones in the wishing well.

Hugo's Quests

You can complete another three quests per day by visiting Hugo at Skylanders Academy (see Figure 7.2). He'll only offer quests once you have completed Adventure Chapter 45 (Highway Robbery), but by visiting him you'll get the opportunity to relive some of the best challenges of the game directly (no need to navigate through the entire chapter again to find them). Once you have completed the challenge, simply use the map in the Main Menu to navigate back to Hugo at Skylanders Academy to receive your reward! There are also a few opportunities to complete quests at Skylanders Academy itself, and occasionally Eve will fill in for Hugo when he's off exploring. You'll find Eve waiting at the steps near Persephone. All of Hugo and Eve's quests are listed in Table 7.2.

FIGURE 7.2 Visit Hugo up to three times per day to relive some of the best challenges of the adventure story and win rewards for your efforts!

TABLE 7.2 Visit Hugo for Daily Replay Challenges

Find Your Quest	Complete Your Challenge
Adventure Chapter Replays	
The Rift to Skylands	Land Star (Ch. 2: Save the Pit Crew)
	Sea Star (Ch. 3: Destroy the Catalytic Cyclotron)
	Sky Star (Ch. 4: Save the Escape Pods)
The Cloudbreather's Crag	Land Star (Ch. 6: Ring the Dragon Gong)
	Sea Star (Ch. 7: Destroy the Blockages)
	Sky Star (Ch. 9: Save the Temple)
	SuperCharger Gate (Ch. 9: Temple of the Cloudbreather)
The Cloud Kingdom	SuperCharger Gate (Ch. 11: The Brewing Storm)
	Sky Star (Ch. 11: Destroy the Transport Ships)
	Sea Star (Ch. 13: Destroy the Storm Sequencer)
	Land Star (Ch. 14: Catch Lord Stratosfear)
Land of the Undead	SuperCharger Gate (Ch. 17: Upside, Downstairs, Overtheres)
	Sky Star (Ch. 17: Help Prisoners Escape)
	Sea Star (Ch. 18: Destroy Blockage)
	Land Star (Ch. 19: Defeat Moneybone)

Find Your Quest	Complete Your Challenge
Spell Punk Library	SuperCharger Gate (Ch. 23: The Spell Punk Library)
	Sky Star (Ch. 23: Destroy the Mothership)
	Sea Star (Ch. 23: Get to the Bottom)
	Land Star (Ch. 23: Defeat the Darkness)
Gadfly Glades	SuperCharger Gate (Ch. 26: Fungi Funhouse)
	Sea Star (Ch. 26: Save the Twitterpillars)
	Sky Star (Ch. 27: Shut Off the Water)
	Land Star (Ch. 27: Rescue Pomfrey)
Cap'n Clucks Chicken HQ	Sea Star (Ch. 30: Drop Feed in Water Supply)
	Land Star (Ch. 30: Chicken Shoot)
	SuperCharger Gate (Ch. 31: Cuckoo's Nest)
	Sky Star (Ch. 31: Defeat Cockadoodle Doom)
Monstrous Isles	Sky Star (Ch. 35: Destroy Clam Bunkers)
	Sea Star (Ch. 36: Catch Beachcomber)
	SuperCharger Gate (Ch. 37: Titanopolis)
	Land Star (Ch. 37: Destroy Sandcastles)
Ridepocalypse Demo Derby	SuperCharger Gate (Ch. 39: Win, Lose, or Glumshanks)
Vault of the Ancients	Land Star (Ch. 41: Restore Sentry Statues)
	Sky Star (Ch. 42: Ring the Chimes)
	SuperCharger Gate (Ch. 43: Slumbering Spires)
	Sea Gate (Ch. 43: Power the Core)
The Sky Eater	Sky Star (Ch. 47: Infiltrate Sky Eater)
	Land Star (Ch. 48: Get Past Kaos' Defenses)
	Sea Gate (Ch. 49: Hunt and Destroy the Hydra)
	SuperCharger Gate (Ch. 49: Darkest Goo)

Grizzo's Element Gate Challenges

Air Zone	Defeat 40 enemies.
Dark Zone	Rescue five sheep.
Earth Zone	Collect 12 boulders in the air-vacuums.
Fire Zone	Complete the challenge quickly.
Life Zone	Rescue 12 twitterpillars from spider webs.

Find Your Quest	Complete Your Challenge
Light Zone	Destroy 25 enemy ships.
Magic Zone	Rescue 12 Mabu underwater.
Tech Zone	Rescue five sheep from thieves.
Undead Zone	Destroy 55 bugs.
Water Zone	Help the scuba sheep through obstacles.
Other Challenges	
Chompy Garden	Win a race.
Cloud Factory	Win a race.
Co-Pilot	Collect gearbits in multiplayer mode.
Friendly Game	Complete a multiplayer Skystones Overdrive game.
Fun and Games	Play Skystones Overdrive at Skylanders Academy.
Skystones Winner	Win a game of Skystones Overdrive.
Challenges from Eve	
Land Training Zone	Collect gearbits on the track.
Sea Training Zone	Collect gearbits on the track.
Sky Training Zone	Collect gearbits on the track.

Buzz and Agent 11 3/5th

There are special quests for each SuperCharger and vehicle. You can discover these by talking to Buzz near his Greeble Arena at Skylanders Academy (see Figure 7.3). The first quest is a simple challenge whereby your Skylander needs to use a particular attack move to defeat enemies within the arena. Use the Greeble dispenser to drop enemies from the sky as you progress, and you'll get it done in no time at all. Your reward is a permanent boost in stats for your Skylander, which is always handy in a fight.

The second quest from Buzz is the challenge to use a particular attack move while in your vehicle. The reward will be gifted to your vehicle (not the Skylander driving it). The vehicle must be SuperCharged (that is, paired with its matching SuperCharger Skylander) at the time it completes the challenge to win the prize. The stat boost reward is only applied to your vehicle when your SuperCharger and its paired vehicle are on the portal together. You can complete this challenge on a training track or in adventure mode. Make sure you check back with Buzz to claim your reward. Each of these quests is unique to the Skylander and its vehicle undertaking the challenge. These are listed in the individual SuperCharger quest challenges in the remainder of the chapter.

The third quest can be undertaken by visiting Agent 11 3/5ᵗʰ (who is waiting to the right of Buzz's arena). These are the "SuperCharged Challenges." Again, each challenge is specific to the Skylander undertaking it. You'll receive your reward when you return to Skylanders Academy after the challenge, from a treasure chest next to Pandergast. Use the individual descriptions provided in the following sections to get some tips and tricks on how to complete all the quests from Buzz and Agent 11 3/5ᵗʰ successfully.

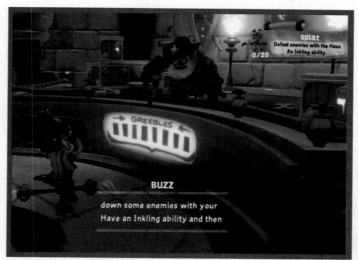

FIGURE 7.3 Buzz and his protégé, Agent 11 3/5ᵗʰ, are keen to put you to the test. Strap in and show them what you're made of!

Shark Shooter Terrafin & Shark Tank

Quest 1 (SuperCharger Only)

Defeat 20 enemies using the "Surface to Air to Surface" ability to win +5 Armor.

Quest 2 (SuperCharger and Vehicle)

Defeat 50 enemies using the "Street Swimming" ability to win +25 Armor.

SuperCharged Challenge "Bug It Out"

Shark Shooter Terrafin is caught in a swarm of bugs! The Chompy Gardens track is the setting for this high-speed knockout race. You're on a mission to run over (so no ammo required!) all the bugs along the track (see Figure 7.4). The small bugs will wait in place to be squashed, so if you can line them up, go for it! The big bugs aren't quite so considerate—they're on the move across the path, so you'll have to do some tight turning to hit them. There is a points multiplier on the big bugs, so if you hit a few in a row and then sweep up a trail of the little guys, each bug hit is worth more. You can earn the multiplier bonus on up to ten (big bugs) in a row, but it's tricky.

Your multiplier times out after a few seconds if it's not increased and will drop back to standard points. Focus on getting a few multipliers and then work your way up. If there's a trail of bugs in front of you, slow down to nab a few biggies first and then hightail it through.

Rewards:

- ✪ One Star: Earn 75,000 points to win 25 gearbits
- ✪ Two Stars: Earn 250,000 points to win one Wish Stone
- ✪ Three Stars: Earn 400,000 points to win one special item

Tips:

- ✪ Puddles won't slow you down here, so don't worry about avoiding them. Be careful on the lily pads and bridges, you'll lose seconds if you fall off.
- ✪ As fun as the high jumps are, at best you'll only nab a handful of extra bugs. Stick to the ground trails for a clear shot of what's coming up.

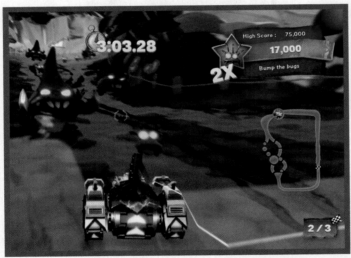

FIGURE 7.4 Insect repellent won't keep these nasties away! Squash the big bugs first for a super-score boost.

Smash Hit & Thump Truck

Quest 1 (SuperCharger Only)

Defeat 20 enemies using the "Connect and Disconnect" ability to win +5% Critical Hit.

Quest 2 (SuperCharger and Vehicle)

Defeat 50 enemies using the "Under Punch" ability to win +5 Handling.

SuperCharged Challenge "Wrack and Ruins"

You're in Chompy Gardens again and, boy, it's a mess! Building equipment, boxes, giant pumpkins, and orange construction cones are all over the track (see Figure 7.5). Luckily for you, there's nothing that Smash Hit loves doing more than plowing down whatever gets in his way. Run over as many items as you can to build up a score multiplier and earn higher points. Again, the multiplier only lasts a few seconds, so you'll have to be strategic. Water puddles on this course will slow you down a tiny bit. Remember to alter your course each time to target different trash. Once you've smashed it, it doesn't come back! There are at least four channels of trash to take out, so you won't run out.

Rewards:

- ✪ One Star: Earn 100,000 points to win 25 gearbits.
- ✪ Two Stars: Earn 375,000 points to win one Wish Stone.
- ✪ Three Stars: Earn 550,000 points to win one special item.

Tips:

- ✪ You'll need to keep up your acceleration to jump the lily pads or you'll fall in the drink (and lose your multiplier as well). There isn't too much to smash on them anyway, so go for speed instead.

- ✪ The tunnels are a great place to take out long straight rows of cones without missing much. Target a different row each time you lap to make sure you don't miss any.

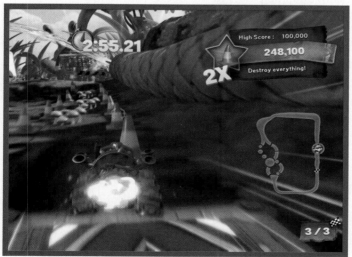

FIGURE 7.5 Build up your multiplier by knocking over construction cones. Everything you smash increases your score.

Fiesta & Crypt Crusher

Quest 1 (SuperCharger Only)

Defeat 20 enemies using the "Solo" ability to win +5 Elemental Power.

Quest 2 (SuperCharger and Vehicle)

Defeat 50 enemies using the "Tune Up" ability to win +5 Speed.

SuperCharged Challenge "Set the Tone"

There's a party on the Dragon's Spine! Blue and yellow musical notes are lined along the track waiting for Fiesta to groove past and pick them up (see Figure 7.6). You don't need to hurry for this one—the race is over whenever you complete three laps. Yellow notes are worth 100 points and blue are worth 50, but there's no shortage of music, as new notes will appear each lap you take. As with the other challenges, you can earn a multiplier by collecting lots of notes in a row; however, use it strategically (aim for a long row of notes to collect straight after). The multiplier will time out after a few seconds. Dragon fire and water will slow you down here, so avoid obstacles in your path. Purple speakers are hovering around the track and some are moving across it. Avoid these; a hit will cost you a massive 5000 points, which will really hurt your final score!

Rewards:

- One Star: Earn 50,000 points to win 25 gearbits.
- Two Stars: Earn 150,000 points to win one Wish Stone.
- Three Stars: Earn 300,000 points to win one special item.

Tips:

- Speakers are hiding at the end of boost pads and mid-air between lap jumps, so watch your aim when landing!
- It's easy to build up a multiplier but hard to keep it. Avoid paths ahead that involve tight turns where you can't see what's waiting—chances are, it will be a speaker.

FIGURE 7.6 Make merry music under the watchful eye of the Dragon—but don't get caught in its fiery flames!

Bone Bash Roller Brawl & Tomb Buggy

Quest 1 (SuperCharger Only)

Defeat 20 enemies using the "Love Bites" ability to win +5 Elemental Power.

Quest 2 (SuperCharger and Vehicle)

Defeat 50 enemies using the "Unfair Play" ability to win +5 Acceleration.

SuperCharged Challenge "The Wild Ghost Chase"

There's a ghostly visitor in Chompy Gardens and everyone is running scared! Who you gonna call? Why, Roller Brawl of course! Chase the ghoul down three times (the undead don't mind a bit of road rage!) to win this challenge (see Figure 7.7). You're on a timer with three laps and a graveyard of creepy tombstones that pop up in your way (often a split second before you are about to hit them), so keep your finger on the Attack button and let Tomb Buggy "Spread the Love" to blow up any tombstones in your path. This attack takes a couple of seconds to charge up before you can use it again, so use it where it counts (that is, right in front of you). Tombstones will appear in random spots during each new lap, so don't waste time blasting anything that doesn't affect you at the time. Puddles will slow you down but tombstones are the time killer. This is a great challenge to practice weaving in and out of obstacles on the road! Tomb Buggy has pretty good handling, but you might like to up your acceleration with the Ghastly Speeders or Boo-ster mod beforehand for that winning edge.

Rewards:

- ⊙ One Star: Beat 3:35 minutes to win 25 gearbits.
- ⊙ Two Stars: Beat 2:55 minutes to win one Wish Stone.
- ⊙ Three Stars: Beat 1:45 minutes to win one special item.

Tips:

- ⊙ Ride as many boost pads as you can to shoot forward; this cheeky poltergeist is super-fast! If you can catch him right at the beginning of lap one, you'll get a much-needed head start.
- ⊙ Memorize the layout of the track to keep one step ahead and try to anticipate its moves. Cut corners and get ahead of the ghost, then slow down (but don't stop) until it appears. Keep your finger ready on that ammo and acceleration—then BAM!

FIGURE 7.7 Don't let the grinning ghoul escape! Boost your acceleration and handling with mods to get off to a super-speedy start.

Lava Lance Eruptor & Burn Cycle

Quest 1 (SuperCharger Only)

Defeat 20 enemies using the "Lava Joust" ability to win +5 Elemental Power.

Quest 2 (SuperCharger and Vehicle)

Defeat 50 enemies using the "Releasing Fire" ability to win +5 Speed.

SuperCharged Challenge "Sheep Shot"

There is a riot of crazy sheep on the loose at Dragon Spine! Lava Lance Eruptor has the noble job of herding them back home, or at least blowing their white wooly jumpers off to scare them back to the paddock (see Figure 7.8). (They look a bit cold without the fuzz!) Sheep jump in and out of the track through swirling blue portals in groups of about ten. Most of the sheep are worth 500 points if you hit them with your attack, but extra-large sheep are worth 2000, and zooming, miniature golden sheep are worth 10,000 (jackpot!). Once you've made it through three laps, your score will be settled and those sheep can head to pasture and grow back their wooly jumpers!

Rewards:

✪ One Star Earn 100,000 points to win 25 gearbits.

✪ Two Stars: Earn 300,000 points to win one Wish Stone.

✪ Three Stars: Earn 600,000 points to win one special item.

Tips:

✪ Keep firing no matter what; this is a numbers game, so you can't lose.

✪ Ice will slow you right down, so try to avoid it.

FIGURE 7.8 Little golden sheep are worth their weight in… gold! They're faster and smaller but worth the chase.

Hammer Slam Bowser & Clown Cruiser

Quest 1 (SuperCharger Only)

Defeat 20 enemies using the "Molten Bowser" ability to win +5% Critical Hit.

Quest 2 (SuperCharger and Vehicle)

Defeat 50 enemies using the "Bullet Bill" ability to win +5 Maneuver.

SuperCharged Challenge "Ham It Up!"

Thieves are flying high with stolen ham-bones through Calamity Canyon (see Figure 7.9). There are plenty of sharp turns, washing lines, and flying food to knock you out of the sky, so hold on tight! It's not too difficult to collect ham-bones from the flying thieves if you use your Koopa Bombers to blow them up. Every ham-bone is worth 1000 points, and you can't really lose points here, just time. Gold boost rings will speed you through in clear patches of sky. You'll begin with six minutes on the clock, and any time left over after three laps will up your score with a time bonus.

Rewards:

● One Star: Earn 15,000 points to win 25 gearbits.

● Two Stars: Earn 50,000 points to win one Wish Stone.

● Three Stars: Earn 100,000 points to win one special item.

Tips:

● Ham thieves respawn after each lap, so you'll never run out. Keep your finger on the ammo to hit every target.

● The thieves split in the canyon tunnels and take different paths—follow the majority for the highest hit count.

FIGURE 7.9 Duck and dodge your way through Calamity Canyon to catch the ham-bone thieves. This challenge is no picnic!

Spitfire & Hot Streak

Quest 1 (SuperCharger Only)

Defeat 20 enemies using the "Flamenado" ability to win +5 Elemental Power.

Quest 2 (SuperCharger and Vehicle)

Defeat 50 enemies using the "Nitro Blaze" ability to win +5 Acceleration.

SuperCharged Challenge "Where's the Fire?"

Are you a speed demon? If so, this challenge is for you! Your goal is to get through three laps as fast as possible, which is a pretty easy ride on the Dragon Spine track. Flaming boost rings are set along the course (see Figure 7.10), and you'll need to hit as many of them as you can. Each boost ring is worth 5000 points, so they're definitely worth your attention. Boost pads can help push you through and give a bonus 1000 points, so hit as many of these as you can as well. Just when you thought Hot Streak couldn't get any faster....

Rewards:

- ✪ One Star: Earn 100,000 points to win 25 gearbits.
- ✪ Two Stars: Earn 350,000 points to win one Wish Stone.
- ✪ Three Stars: Earn 600,000 points to win one special item.

Tips:

- ✪ Avoid ice on the track; it's the only obstacle here to slow you down.
- ✪ The locations of boosters are pretty consistent between laps, so memorize them to plan your turns.

FIGURE 7.10 Speed full throttle through the flaming boost rings for gold and glory!

High Volt & Shield Striker

Quest 1 (SuperCharger Only)

Defeat 20 enemies using the "Traveling Light" ability to win +5 Elemental Power.

Quest 2 (SuperCharger and Vehicle)

Defeat 50 enemies using the "Crowd Control" ability to win +5 Speed.

SuperCharged Challenge "Shooting Bolt!"

High Volt will need all his military precision for this task. Diamond thieves are racing through Dragon Spine with their precious cargo floating above them. You need to shoot down as many as you can in three laps of the course to beat a high score and win some treasure for yourself (see Figure 7.11). This is a tricky one, because although the course is familiar, Shield Striker isn't too easy to handle, especially on slippery ice. Get a group of bad guys in close range and keep your finger on the Crowd Control attack to create a stream of electricity; just stay as straight behind them as you can. This will help you take them out a lot quicker than picking them off one by one. Alternatively, you can try your Doomproof Forcefield attack up close and personal, but you'll need to be right on your target for it to work, with the risk of spinning out.

Rewards:

- ✪ One Star: Earn 10,000 points to win 25 gearbits.
- ✪ Two Stars: Earn 40,000 points to win one Wish Stone.
- ✪ Three Stars: Earn 90,000 points to win one special item.

Tips:

- ✪ Follow the majority; don't try to chase down thieves that stray from the pack.
- ✪ Keep on the boost pads as often as you can; High Volt needs a helping hand to keep the speedy bad guys in close range.

FIGURE 7.11 High Volt makes short work of bad behavior. Catch as many diamond thieves as you can to pull them into line.

Double Dare Trigger Happy & Gold Rusher

Quest 1 (SuperCharger Only)

Defeat 20 enemies using the "Breaking Cannon" ability to win +5% Critical Hit.

Quest 2 (SuperCharger and Vehicle)

Defeat 50 enemies using the "Triggered Happy Mines" ability to win +5 Handling.

SuperCharged Challenge "Crazy on Fireworks"

This is quite a tricky challenge, so you'll need to multitask. Speed through the boost rings, earning multipliers, and then gain extra points as you fire at boxes of fireworks lying around the track at The After Party track (see Figure 7.12). The more fireworks you hit, the higher your score will be. There are multicolored orbs to knock out as you speed past, so do your best to hit them. Fireworks are your biggest point scorer, though, so make them your priority. You don't have to go super-fast because you have as much time as you need to get through three laps, but if you are hitting those boost rings on target, this challenge will be over before you know it.

Rewards:

☼ One Star: Earn 100,000 points to win 25 gearbits.

☼ Two Stars: Earn 225,000 points to win one Wish Stone.

☼ Three Stars: Earn 425,000 points to win one special item.

Tips:

- ❂ Hit those boost rings to build up your multiplier, then make it count by blasting fireworks.

- ❂ Hitting your targets is more important than speed, so slow down for better aim if you're missing boxes.

FIGURE 7.12 Double Dare Trigger Happy is always keen to crack some fireworks and get the party started!

Stormblade & Sky Slicer

Quest 1 (SuperCharger Only)

Defeat 20 enemies using the "Cyclone Surge" ability to win +5 Elemental Power.

Quest 2 (SuperCharger and Vehicle)

Defeat 50 enemies using the "Pigeon Flock Missiles" ability to win +5 Speed.

SuperCharged Challenge "The Lightning Run!"

Get ready for some seriously topsy-turvy air action in this challenge! Stormblade is up against an obstacle course at the Cloud Factory (see Figure 7.13). There are golden boost rings everywhere. Your aim is to make it through three laps as fast as you can; the quicker you are, the greater your reward. Boost rings will help you speed through, but you'll need to choose a specific path because you can't hit every one. But beware, there's a storm brewing! Dark clouds shoot purple lightning at the boost gates, turning them into hazards as well. If you fly through a dark purple boost gate, you'll lose points, which loses you time. A tornado will loop you through the laps to begin each time, but watch out for the purple hurricanes as you arrive—they'll spin points off you, too.

Rewards:

- ✪ One Star: Beat 5:30 minutes to win 25 gearbits.
- ✪ Two Stars: Beat 4:40 minutes to win one Wish Stone.
- ✪ Three Stars: Beat 3:45 minutes to win one special item.

Tips:

- ✪ Stay alert if lightning is heading toward the boost gate you're aiming for— duck and cover!
- ✪ Boost gates stay in the same position each lap, but some will have new target boards covering them. Shoot ahead to clear your path.

FIGURE 7.13 Fire ahead to break down targets over boost rings to speed through, but beware of a last-moment lightning strike.

Hurricane Jet-Vac & Jet Stream

Quest 1 (SuperCharger Only)

Defeat 20 enemies using the "Somer Assault" ability to win +5% Critical Hit.

Quest 2 (SuperCharger and Vehicle)

Defeat 50 enemies using the "Avian Razors" ability to win +5 Handling.

SuperCharged Challenge "Balloon Popper!"

It's party time at the Cloud Factory with red, blue, and green balloons floating all over your flight path (see Figure 7.14). Your goal is to pop as many as you can as you speed through, but there are a few things to keep in mind as you do. First, aim for the green balloons, which are smaller and floating slightly off course (so a bit harder to hit), because they are worth higher points than red or blue (worth the least). Hitting green balloons in a row (up to five) will earn you a point multiplier. Purple hurricanes will spin you out and cause you to lose points, so watch out for them as you come out from the eye of the tornado that loops between laps.

Rewards:

- ❂ One Star: Earn 100,000 points to win 25 gearbits.
- ❂ Two Stars: Earn 275,000 points to win one Wish Stone.
- ❂ Three Stars: Earn 415,000 points to win one special item.

Tips:

- ❂ Beware of random purple boost rings and purple hurricanes (which move)—they'll set back your score.
- ❂ Although you can pop the balloons by flying into them, the jolt will knock you off course, making for a bumpy ride. Keep your finger on the ammo to deflate your targets ahead and you'll create more collateral damage.

FIGURE 7.14   Green balloons will score you multipliers and higher points, so they are worth slowing down for.

Super Shot Stealth Elf & Stealth Stinger

Quest 1 (SuperCharger Only)

Defeat 20 enemies using the "Circle Slash" ability to catch four enemies at once, 20 times to win +5% Critical Hit.

Quest 2 (SuperCharger and Vehicle)

Lose 50 enemies using the "Forest Fog" ability to win +5 Handling.

SuperCharged Challenge "Buzz Off!"

Calamity Canyon is in complete chaos. Swarms of bees are overtaking the course, appearing and then disappearing from magic portals in the air (see Figure 7.15). You'll have to be quick to shoot as many down as you can within three laps. Giant bees are floating around, particularly near the entrance to the canyon. The little bees are worth 50 points (big bees are worth 500). Aim for the big guys and consider the little ones collateral damage if they happen to get in your way. Tagging five big bees can get you a five times multiplier, so any biggies you hit after that (before the multiplier expires) will earn you mega points.

Rewards:

- ✪ One Star: Earn 10,000 points to win 25 gearbits.
- ✪ Two Stars: Earn 40,000 points to win one Wish Stone.
- ✪ Three Stars: Earn 70,000 points to win one special item.

Tips:

- ✪ Keep your finger on the ammo. You'll need a couple of seconds of on-target firepower to bring the big guys down—but they're worth it.
- ✪ Focus on targets, not speed. Racking up points on a big bee is worth more than hitting a boost ring in the long run.

FIGURE 7.15 Little bees are on the move, but big buzzers stay put, which makes them easier to swat.

Turbo Charge Donkey Kong & Barrel Blaster

Quest 1 (SuperCharger Only)

Defeat 20 enemies using the "Bongo Barrel" ability to win +5% Critical Hit.

Quest 2 (SuperCharger and Vehicle)

Defeat 50 enemies using the "Barrel Blaster" ability to win +5 Maneuver.

SuperCharged Challenge "Going Bananas!"

Everybody at Chompy Garden has gone bananas! Zoom through the course on the Barrel Blaster, collecting as many bananas as you can to beat the high score (see Figure 7.16). Bunches are worth more than single bananas, but every fruit will add to your score. Collect bunches to build up a score multiplier to boost your points. Your multiplier will expire after a few seconds, so hit as many bananas as you can before it does. You'll earn bonus points if you complete three laps before your time runs out (there are five minutes on the clock). Lines of TNT barrels are randomly placed and also laid out in the underground tunnel area, so slow down—hitting one could cost you 5000 points (that's fifty bananas!), and you'll lose your multiplier as well. Stick to the outside edges of the tunnel to steer clear of them. Don't slip on a banana skin!

Rewards:

- ✪ One Star: Earn 100,000 points to win 25 gearbits.
- ✪ Two Stars: Earn 325,000 points to win one Wish Stone.
- ✪ Three Stars: Earn 550,000 points to win one special item.

Tips:

- ✪ Keep ammo streaming ahead to take out any TNT barrels in your path; they won't respawn for the next lap.
- ✪ Take care with your aim while hopping lily pads—spinning off the side or driving too slow will cost you precious seconds if you land in the drink.

FIGURE 7.16 TNT barrels litter the track at Chompy Gardens to slow you down and steal your hard-earned banana points. Dodge them to stay safe!

Thrillipede & Buzz Wing

Quest 1 (SuperCharger Only)

Block damage 200 times using the "Cocoon" ability to win +5% Critical Hit.

Quest 2 (SuperCharger and Vehicle)

Defeat 50 enemies using the "Insect Swarmer" ability to win +5 Handling.

SuperCharged Challenge "Bug Rescue!"

You're back in Calamity Canyon (see Figure 7.17) in another swarm of bugs, but this time, they're the good guys! Thrillipede has to save his insect family from terrible clouds of poisonous green gas. Collect as many blue butterflies as you can while you dodge rocky outcrops and gas clouds within three laps of the course. The timer is set at five minutes, so you can focus on aim rather than speed.

Rewards:

- ✪ One Star: Earn 100,000 points to win 25 gearbits.
- ✪ Two Stars: Earn 200,000 points to win one Wish Stone.
- ✪ Three Stars: Earn 400,000 points to win one special item.

Tips:

- ❂ This is a tricky course with lots of obstacles to steal your health, so take it slow.
- ❂ Butterflies gather in rings, so if you're careful with your aim, you can score multiple hits in one.

FIGURE 7.17 Thrillipede's blue butterfly brethren are counting on you! Net as many rings as you can to keep them safe from poisonous gas.

Dive-Clops & Dive Bomber

Quest 1 (SuperCharger Only)

Defeat 20 enemies using the "Ping" ability to win +5 Armor.

Quest 2 (SuperCharger and Vehicle)

Defeat 50 enemies using the "Torpedo Tubes" ability to win +25 Armor.

SuperCharged Challenge "Go Like a Bomb"

This is a seriously tricky challenge! The Frozen Fossil Festival course is overflowing with mines, both above and below the water (see Figure 7.18). Every time you hit a mine, you'll lose a bar of health. There are 24 health bars—once they're all gone, unfortunately so are you. Your ammo has a homing device, so you'll hit the target if you shoot ahead to clear the path; however, Dive Bomber's Waterpedo missiles take a few seconds to charge up. This means you can't shoot as many bombs as you need on-the-go to clear them all out. Hitting them will be unavoidable. The best you can do is keep it to a minimum by going slower than you'd like on the first round to keep your health up while you figure out where they are and then taking the path of least resistance. Practice makes perfect with this challenge.

Rewards:

- ✪ One Star: Beat 4:00 minutes to win 25 gearbits.
- ✪ Two Stars: Beat 3:00 minutes to win one Wish Stone.
- ✪ Three Stars: Beat 2:45 minutes to win one special item.

Tips:

- ✪ The underwater path is slightly clearer than the surface, so you're more likely to make it through unscathed, but you'll need to take it slower to avoid bombs because you can't fire missiles underwater.
- ✪ There's no avoiding bombs on the rapids as you're forced to the surface, so use your firepower here to clear them out.

FIGURE 7.18 The Frozen Fossil Festival is exploding with danger. Missile as many bombs as you can to clear a safe path through.

Deep Dive Gill Grunt & Reef Ripper

Quest 1 (SuperCharger Only)

Defeat 20 enemies using the "Typhoon Turbine Jetpack" ability to win +5% Critical Hit.

Quest 2 (SuperCharger and Vehicle)

Defeat 50 enemies using the "Ocean Upheaval" ability to win +5 Handling.

SuperCharged Challenge "Something Fishy"

There are plenty of fish in the sea—or at least there are plenty of fish at the Golden Temple. Gill Grunt must speed through and hit (catch) as many fish as possible, using boost pads to keep up speed (see Figure 7.19). Sounds easy, right? Not so much! The timer is ticking down, and when it runs out, your challenge is brought to an abrupt end. Aim to dive through the blue time rings you find on your path; each one adds five seconds to your clock. You'll begin with 30 seconds but won't get far unless you hit every blue ring you cross. Focus on these blue rings, and if a fish swims in your path, by all means duck underwater if necessary to grab it. You'll hit plenty of blue fish because they are most common. Prioritize red fish, then green over blue, as they are worth highest points. Don't change direction unless you have to; find a path and stick to it because indecision may lead you off the ramparts into the channels below, where time gates are few and far between.

Rewards:

- One Star: Earn 10,000 points to win 25 gearbits.
- Two Stars: Earn 50,000 points to win one Wish Stone.
- Three Stars: Earn 95,000 points to win one special item.

Tips:

- The longer you stay in game, the more fish you'll be able to take out, so make those blue time gates your priority.
- Hitting the sides of the tunnels will slow you right down, so take care with your aim.

FIGURE 7.19 The elusive red fish are the ones to catch, but don't let your timer run dry!

Splat & Splatter Splasher

Quest 1 (SuperCharger Only)

Defeat 20 enemies using the "Have an Inkling" ability to win +5 Elemental Power.

Quest 2 (SuperCharger and Vehicle)

Defeat 50 enemies using the "Oiled Ink" ability to win +5 Acceleration.

SuperCharged Challenge "Show Your Colors!"

You're back at the Frozen Fossil Festival and it's a riot of color! There are golden boost gates set along the track, and each is dripping with either yellow, green, or pink paint (see Figure 7.20). You need to make it through the course three times, as quickly as possible, to beat the high score (within a five-minute time limit). Each time you pass through a colored gate, you'll earn a multiplier (up to a massive 25 times). However, there's a catch (of course!). If you use the same color gate more than once in a row, you'll lose health, spin out, and slow down. What a stroke of evil genius! The gain in points is just not worth the loss of time in getting back on the waves, so alternate between colors with every ring you pass through. Each time you use a gate, the color of the Splatter Splasher vehicle will change to match. Use this to help remember what color gate you last used. You need to think quick for this challenge!

Rewards:

- ✪ One Star: Earn 75,000 points to win 25 gearbits.
- ✪ Two Stars: Earn 225,000 points to win one Wish Stone.
- ✪ Three Stars: Earn 450,000 points to win one special item.

Tips:

- ✪ Get to know your track—choose the same turns each lap to anticipate where gates will be. Colors may change, but your boost rings don't.
- ✪ There are a few underwater gates, but most of the course is above water, so for the sake of getting through faster, keep afloat.

FIGURE 7.20 Splash a little color around, but make sure you switch it up to gain bonus points!

Big Bubble Pop Fizz & Soda Skimmer

Quest 1 (SuperCharger Only)

Defeat 20 enemies using the "Genetic Engineering" ability to win +5% Critical Hit.

Quest 2 (SuperCharger and Vehicle)

Defeat 50 enemies using the "Alchemic Admixture" ability to win +5 Handling.

SuperCharged Challenge "Alchemixology!"

There's magic afoot at the Mystical Vault! Glowing red and blue potions are floating on and under the water (see Figure 7.21). Collect as many as you can before the timer runs out (you have seven minutes on the clock). This challenge will really test your reflexes—only red *or* blue potions are active (and collectible) at any one time, and the color changes every ten seconds. You'll have to look ahead to choose the path where you'll be able to collect the most. Prioritize big potion bottles over small ones because they are worth five times more. You'll have to hit a pretty high score to pass this challenge!

Rewards:

- ✪ One Star: Earn 50,000 points to win 25 gearbits.

- ✪ Two Stars: Earn 120,000 points to win one Wish Stone.

- ✪ Three Stars: Earn 250,000 points to win one special item.

Tips:

- ❂ If you're heading for a potion and the color changes, there's often one of the alternate color just under the surface—dive down to check before you change course.

- ❂ As a general rule, red potions tend to be on the left side of the path and blue on the right, although they occasionally switch. Zigzag your way through each lap.

FIGURE 7.21 Big potion bottles will score you a multiplier and are worth five times more—chase as many down as you can.

Nightfall & Sea Shadow

Quest 1 (SuperCharger Only)

Defeat 20 enemies using the "Whip Lash" ability to win +5 Armor.

Quest 2 (SuperCharger and Vehicle)

Defeat 50 enemies using the "Abyss Cannon" ability to win +25 Armor.

SuperCharged Challenge "A Shot for the Dark"

Buckle your seatbelt because you're in for a super-fast ride in this challenge! Nightfall is gearing up to speed through the water channels of the Mystical Vault, firing at light crystals that are scattered throughout the course (see Figure 7.22). On the right of the screen, a "Dark Gauge" will fill up gradually as you hit crystals on target and turn them purple. Blue and red speed rings will boost you along your way (remember, in the Mystical Vault the active color changes every ten seconds), but you'll make good time without them if necessary. You have five and a half minutes on the clock to pass this challenge, but you'll be able to complete it in far less. Keep your ammo firing to take advantage of the homing feature of your Abyss Cannon attack. You'll have enough Dark Matter to win in no time.

Rewards:

- ✪ One Star: Beat 5:30 minutes to win 25 gearbits.
- ✪ Two Stars: Beat 3:40 minutes to win one Wish Stone.
- ✪ Three Stars: Beat 2:20 minutes to win one special item.

Tips:

- ✪ You can dive underwater, but there are fewer crystals to hit and your orb attack won't work, so you'll have to drive through crystals to take them out.
- ✪ The boost gates aren't as helpful in this challenge because they may make you miss crystals on the way—focus on firepower and fill that gauge first.

FIGURE 7.22   Hit light crystals to fill up the Dark Gauge on the right side of your screen, but watch the clock—once it ticks down, you lose!

Astroblast & Sun Runner

Quest 1 (SuperCharger Only)

Defeat 20 enemies using the "Starsault" ability to win +5% Critical Hit.

Quest 2 (SuperCharger and Vehicle)

Defeat 50 enemies using the "Satellite Support" ability to win +5 Handling.

SuperCharged Challenge "A Guiding Light!"

Wow, this is the trickiest challenge yet! Sun Runner must gather (fly through or shoot) as many light bulbs as possible during a three lap voyage of Clock Rock (see Figure 7.23). There's a Light Meter on the right side of the screen that decreases as your health and time do (the screen also dims as you lose health and time, so be careful or you'll soon be flying in the dark!). As soon as the Light Meter is empty, the challenge is over. Your aim is to make it through the asteroid belt three times without running out of health. It doesn't take much to lose all your light, though, so every light bulb you can pick up helps. Big yellow bulbs will boost your Light Meter up by half, so don't miss any. Smaller bulbs will help incrementally, but you can easily fail by missing a few. This challenge is a hair-raiser! Keep at it and you'll get through—there's light at the end of the tunnel!

Rewards:

● One Star: Beat 6:00 minutes to win 25 gearbits.

● Two Stars: Beat 5:00 minutes to win one Wish Stone.

● Three Stars: Beat 4:45 minutes to win one special item.

Tips:

● Giant asteroids, laser gates, and other obstacles move into your path and make it difficult to catch bulbs, so go *slow* around these.

● Yellow bulbs are few and far between, so make a big effort to grab them whenever they appear.

FIGURE 7.23   Giant yellow bulbs are your lifeline in this challenge—you need every one!

Great Grizzo's Elemental Challenges

When you'd like to have a bit of fun without moving forward in the adventure chapters, why not visit the Great Grizzo at Skylander Academy? He is waiting just to the right of Persephone at a swirling element gate (shown in Figure 8.1). Chat with him to switch the gate to match the element of your current vehicle (the Skylanders' element doesn't affect the gate). There are ten challenges to choose from, one for each element. Have a blast shooting enemy fighters from the sky, dodging lava explosions, chasing down nasty sheep thieves, and rescuing squeaky twitterpillars from spider webs! Every challenge is a race against the clock—how fast can you go!? Beat the timer to win shields that reward you with stardust. These mini-challenges are a fantastic way to boost your Portal Master rank and gain serious skills in flying, driving, and diving. What are you waiting for?

FIGURE 8.1 Find the Great Grizzo near Persephone to prove your mettle in an elemental challenge (look for the little guy in the crazy wooden mask!).

Earth Zone

Earth vehicles will bring you a land challenge. You're dropped into a dust bowl that has pyramids made of giant boulders placed around it. These boulders need to be knocked over and maneuvered toward circular air vacuums that suck them up (see Figure 8.2). You only need to vacuum away 12 boulders to get through this challenge. Sound easy? Not quite!

There are hazards of course! The first obstacle is blocks of rock that are in your way. You can smash through these easily to reach your goals (and score the gearbits underneath), but don't waste time hitting them unless you really need to. Remember, the clock is ticking! Some of the blocks are covering the entrance to the fans and will smash as they are hit by your well-aimed boulders. Clearing them out of the way first can be a big help, though, especially if your vehicle's turning circle isn't as tight as you'd like and your aim suffers for it. In a hurry, you can leave the boulders close to the mouth of the vacuum, and they'll be sucked in while you're busy rounding up more.

The second hazard you'll come across are giant robots intent on throwing boulders at you. You'll see a target appear on the ground right before the boulder hits, so watch your step. These boulders crash and burn up, so they won't get in your way once they land. If you get hit directly, though, it'll set back your health a little. Avoid the robots, but don't try to destroy them because you'll waste precious time (and they recover immediately anyway).

TIPS TO WIN!

- Ignore the hazards and focus on boulders. Knock down one pyramid at a time and score multiple hits by guiding each boulder in before moving on—you'll clock up your tally faster.

- This challenge is all about angles and tight-turning skill, so choose a land vehicle with good handling (such as Thump Truck). It's better to drive slower and aim correctly than to speed around and miss your target.

- Let gravity be your friend. Try knocking a heap of boulders into the bottom pit; then dash down and aim for the lower vacuums. Boulders won't roll back uphill (unless you push them), so they're easier to manage in a confined space.

REWARDS!

- To achieve the first shield, you just need to finish the challenge.
- To achieve the second shield, finish in under 90 seconds.
- To achieve the third shield, finish in under 60 seconds.

FIGURE 8.2   Round up boulders and herd them toward the air vacuums for a quick win—but watch your step because the robots have good aim!

Fire Zone

Another land challenge awaits you, but this one's all about speed! This challenge is a two-tiered racing track with plenty of gearbits to pick up on the way. You're racing against the clock, but you can take time off your final score by driving through stopwatches (see Figure 8.3). There are plenty of them to pass, so don't worry if you miss a few. The golden speed gates and arrows will zoom you along to cut time if you pass through or over them. The coast is clear for the first section of track—no hazards here. In the second section, you'll need to dodge puddles of lava that will slow you down. You can learn where they are to avoid them on each play-through, but you can't predict the lava meteors falling from the sky in the third part of the track. Slow down to weave your way through safely. It's worth collecting the stopwatches because they'll make a big difference to your time overall, but look ahead because a couple of them will land you in a lava puddle if you hit on the wrong angle. Wherever possible, take the high road (literally) for more reward and less mess. If you're distracted by the lava meteors, focus on where you want to go (in the distance) and let your peripheral vision (the edges around where you are focused) take care of where and when to dodge the fireballs. You'll do a lot less twisting and turning and get to your goal faster!

TIPS TO WIN!

- ❂ The first top track you hit (on your left) will have lava puddles on it, but not as many as below, so you can gain some speed by taking it.

- ❂ Hold off on heavy steering on this track; there are no super-tight turns to maneuver.

- ❂ Take the treasure-laden top track on your way to the finale to score a few last-minute stopwatches (no lava here!).

REWARDS!

- ❂ To achieve the first shield, you just need to finish the challenge.

- ❂ To achieve the second shield, finish in under 65 seconds.

- ❂ To achieve the third shield, finish in under 55 seconds.

FIGURE 8.3 Collect as many stopwatches as you can while you dodge lava meteors—your final time score will be adjusted at the finish line.

Undead Zone

Exterminate! Exterminate! Nasty bugs are on the loose! (Or are they just misunderstood arthropods looking for a friend?) In any case, your mission is to destroy 55 of the little critters as fast as you can. You'll begin in a graveyard full of tombstones (yikes!). Smash as many tombstones as you can, releasing the critters from underneath so they can swarm the surface. Keep your finger on the attack button because these creepy crawlies will be every which way you turn. There are different types of bugs to kill: the enormous Rhino Rampage Beetle (slow but deadly), quick Beetle Bouncers (easy to destroy), nosey Snot Catchers (dodge those sticky tongues!), and nasty fire-hose buzzing beasties. You can go crazy in this arena, swerving and smashing with your finger on the trigger, causing as much damage as you possibly can. Watch the counter at the top to determine how close you are to your goal. Your tally is for bugs, not gearbits, so don't slow to try to pick them all up or you'll lose precious time.

TIPS TO WIN!

- Spin off to the edges to zoom through purple glowing stones held by skeletons (shown in Figure 8.4) to gain extra gearbits and power-ups.
- Rhino Rampage Beetles are hard to take down—you have to hit them at the correct angle or your ammunition goes to waste.

✪ Focus on the little guys. They're easier to take down *en masse*, driving your score higher, faster.

REWARDS!

✪ To achieve the first shield, you just need to finish the challenge.

✪ To achieve the second shield, finish in under 180 seconds.

✪ To achieve the third shield, finish in under 90 seconds.

FIGURE 8.4   Zoom through skeletons to grab power-ups and shields as you zap nasty bugs—you'll need strong repellant for these creepy crawlies!

Dark Zone

Oh dear! Five very waterlogged sheep are floating in the sea and are in dire need of rescuing! Better pull on your scuba gear, Skylander! This challenge is a little trickier than it looks. Follow the paths of coins under the water until you track down the sheep, one by one, moving from left to right. Some take a little exploring to find. But take care—a giant eel (shown in Figure 8.5) is on the lookout for lunch! It will let off sonar blasts as it follows you around, waiting for the perfect moment to strike—CHOMP! The jaws will gobble you up! (Don't worry, you'll reappear in the same spot as it retracts, minus a few health points.) To avoid becoming dinner, keep your eye on the eel in the background and hide (in a small alcove, behind metal bars or rocks, and so on) as soon as you see it turning red. If it turns red, the eel will strike out at you. Argh!

TIPS TO WIN!

- ⊗ Don't stress if the eel nabs you a few times—the damage to your health is minimal. Focus on finding the sheep as fast as you can; your real enemy here is the timer.

- ⊗ Remember to accelerate—even though it's harder to handle your vehicle, floating toward your goal won't find you those sheep fast enough.

- ⊗ The position of the five sheep changes each time you play, but the hiding spaces don't. Memorize those nooks and crannies for a quick win.

REWARDS!

- ⊗ To achieve the first shield, you just need to finish the challenge.
- ⊗ To achieve the second shield, finish in under 240 seconds.
- ⊗ To achieve the third shield, finish in under 135 seconds.

FIGURE 8.5 Don't get scared—but there's an enormous EEL trying to eat you! Duck and cover to complete your mission—five innocent scuba sheep are counting on your courage!

Air Zone

Are you ready to fly? A long air battle awaits you in this challenge as you must defeat 40 enemies in the clouds. You'll begin with a handful of fighter jets, but tracking them down one by one will waste your time. There are three turrets on the top of towers that have extra enemies waiting inside for the chance to escape. Destroy these turrets straight away (see Figure 8.6) to fill the sky with enemy flyers (that are easy to spot) and then have a field day shooting them all down. As your enemies begin to thin out, use direction arrows to find them. If you have a few baddies on your tail, fly in close to a tower and do a barrel roll away or quick dive to leave them crashing while you make an escape. As long as your own (white) target is close to your enemy's (green) target, your ammunition will home in and do damage. This challenge is a tough gig because of the sheer numbers required to reach your goal—but remember, practice makes perfect!

TIPS TO WIN!

- Fly through the top of towers to find hidden power-ups to give you a boost.

- Go hard with firing ammunition; every shot counts, including destroying carrier ships and turrets!

- Barrel roll your way out of a tight spot to get enemies off your tail, then spin back to retaliate.

REWARDS!

- To achieve the first shield, you just need to finish the challenge.

- To achieve the second shield, finish in under 180 seconds.

- To achieve the third shield, finish in under 120 seconds.

FIGURE 8.6 A sky full of feisty fighters are on your tail—you'll need serious stamina and super skills to shoot them all down.

Water Zone

This challenge is a super-fun obstacle course! Your new best friend the scuba sheep needs to get through a series of challenges in a shipwreck to reach the finish line, and you're just the Skylander to lead it through! First, shoot the gate directly in front of you to reach a gold button (see Figure 8.7). Float up and hold it to the roof, which releases a hatch so the sheep can pass through, dropping another gate in front of you. Continue on until you reach another gate with two flapping hatch doors above it. You need to attack this gate to remove it, which gives the flaps room to hang down properly. Float upward into the top space and blow up the right-side gate that is keeping your sheep trapped. Return underneath and hold up the left flap, then the right, to create a bridge for your sheep to cross. As it crosses, your own gate ahead will be triggered to drop as well. Pass through. A second gold button needs to be pushed upward to release a new gate trapping the sheep. More hatches to lift; left, then right so the sheep can pass overhead, then you destroy the gate below to gain access to a water wheel. Push the wheel around in a clockwise direction to guide your scuba sheep over to safety. A third gold button is up high above you; push it to release another two gates, one up top for you, and another down below for your wooly friend. Float through to the end and your scuba sheep pal will use a red bounce pad to join you at the finish line. Well done, Skylander! Your sheep-herding skill is world-class!

TIPS TO WIN!

- ✪ Keep those golden buttons and hatch flaps pressed right up until the sheep is safely through, or you'll knock your sheep out baaadly!
- ✪ To beat the clock, ignore the glittering gearbits that are floating in corners to distract you.
- ✪ Take your sheep over the top of the water wheel, rather than below, so it doesn't get stuck.

REWARDS!

- ✪ To achieve the first shield, you just need to finish the challenge.
- ✪ To achieve the second shield, finish in under 90 seconds.
- ✪ To achieve the third shield, finish in under 60 seconds.

FIGURE 8.7 It's time for some teamwork! Break down barriers, hold buttons, spin gates, and build bridges to help your wooly scuba-pal to the finish line. Hooray!

Life Zone

Twelve tiny twitterpillars have found themselves in terrible trouble! They're all tangled up in spider webs strung between the thorny branches of a forest with no chance of escape—so of course it's up to you, super-Skylander, to save them! This is a sky vehicle challenge, and your main concern will be on maneuverability and handling. You need to fly to each twitterpillar in turn and collect it (see

Figure 8.8), then drop it down onto the flowery nest in the center. Take it slow to start. If you hit a red thorny branch with a twitterpillar onboard, the little guy will fall squealing to the ground and be lost. (Oops, sorry buddy!). Don't worry, they'll reappear in a nearby spider web. Hitting a plain tree branch won't cause you to drop your charges, but there are some very tight turns between webs as you progress, and some are tricky to navigate. Take care!

TIPS TO WIN!

- As you fly in toward the twitterpillar you intend to save, look ahead for the safest route out again. Guesswork on the fly could lead you straight into a bramble patch!

- Try to circle around and pick up the twitterpillar from behind so you are on a straight course to the nest as soon as you have your passenger!

- Pick up more than one twitterpillar at once to save time, but be careful! Your cargo is longer and can hit obstacles more easily.

REWARDS!

- To achieve the first shield, you just need to finish the challenge.
- To achieve the second shield, finish in under 180 seconds.
- To achieve the third shield, finish in under 120 seconds

FIGURE 8.8 Twelve tiny twitterpillars are all caught up! Collect as many as you can and drop them into the flower nest with their cheery little friends before the spiders come home for dinner!

Light Zone

Welcome to an intergalactic smash-a-thon! Sun Runner is all set up beside a rocky lava-filled planet with asteroids orbiting around the outside, as shown in Figure 8.9. Use your laser fire to shoot down as many asteroids as you can to reveal enemy ships hiding inside (purple shuttles), which will then fly around you. This is a fairly straightforward challenge. Shoot down 25 enemy shuttles as quickly as you can to pass this challenge. Focus on locating the enemy ships to beat the timer—there are lots of shiny distractions floating around to tempt you off your target.

TIPS TO WIN!

✪ Use your **Attack 3** button to scan the asteroids ahead to decide if they are worth shooting. Any golden asteroid that has a yellow bar appear over the front of it is hiding enemy ships inside.

✪ Any asteroid that turns green under the scanner has gearbits hiding inside (collect them if you like, but remember that this adds time to your score).

✪ Your white target pointer is quite hard to see against the white backdrop of space light, so use your ship's base for direction assistance.

REWARDS!

✪ To achieve the first shield, you just need to finish the challenge.

✪ To achieve the second shield, finish in under 120 seconds.

✪ To achieve the third shield, finish in under 90 seconds.

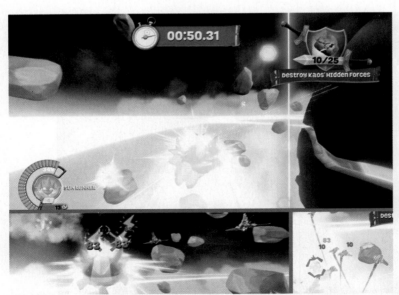

FIGURE 8.9 Search out concealed enemy ships—a golden bar means you're right on target. Shoot them up, but be prepared—up to five fighters will come straight for you.

Tech Zone

There are sheep thieves on the loose! No one knows what dastardly plans they have for the five hostages tumbling above their vehicles as they speed through the sky, but this is definitely not a good time for counting sheep. Well, perhaps just these five. You'll need to intercept the vehicles to rescue sheep, then drop your wooly cargo off at a safe haven (the yellow and red gear platform with a pink laser beam) to deliver them to greener pastures, as shown in Figure 8.10. You can carry two sheep at a time (they won't fall off once collected), so save time by chasing down multiple vehicles before delivery. Two is the limit, though; no more sheep thieves will appear if you already have a full load. Flying vehicles will attack you with missiles to knock you off your game, but they're fairly easy to dodge. Your main opponent here is having a slow and difficult-to-handle vehicle as you battle the clock.

TIPS TO WIN!

○ Unless you're getting heavily hit by enemy fire, ignore the vehicles firing at you and focus on collecting sheep.

○ You don't have to destroy the vehicle carrying a sheep to collect it, just driving into it will do. However, if you have a vehicle such as Shield Striker with difficult handling, a long-range attack will help you gather sheep faster.

○ The disappearing floor is a bit disconcerting, but don't let it hold you back—you can't fall off. Just follow the arrows to chase down sheep.

REWARDS!

○ To achieve the first shield, you just need to finish the challenge.

○ To achieve the second shield, finish in under 150 seconds.

○ To achieve the third shield, finish in under 85 seconds.

FIGURE 8.10 Once again, innocent sheep are in mortal peril! Chase down the sheep thieves and deliver your wooly friends safely to the platform.

Magic Zone

It's time to get your feet wet! Twelve unfortunate Mabu are trapped in bubbles on (or under) this high-speed water course, as shown in Figure 8.11. Lots of hazards are in your way to prevent you from achieving your goal, so put your navigation hat on for this one! Meteors fall from the sky and then obscure your path underwater when you dive, and bombs are floating on the surface to damage your health.

You'll repeat the same short course multiple times by slipping through a swirling portal at the end, so you'll get a feel of where different obstacles lie as you make your way through. Enemy ships start attacking from your third course onward. Keep your attacks going while on the surface to blast them (and those pesky bombs) out of your way. There are plenty of gearbits lying around as a bonus.

TIPS TO WIN!

- ❂ Take alternate routes of the course, traveling under then over the water, or down the left side then the right, to collect Mabu systematically; it's easier than zigzagging across the course with so many obstacles.

- ❂ Look for a blue glow above water—it means there's a Mabu bubble below the surface. Give yourself plenty of time to dive so you don't miss it.

- ❂ There will be two to four bubbled Mabu in each run through. Memorize their typical floating spots so you can anticipate pickups.

REWARDS!

✪ To achieve the first shield, you just need to finish the challenge.

✪ To achieve the second shield, finish in under 120 seconds.

✪ To achieve the third shield, finish in under 90 seconds.

FIGURE 8.11 The Mabu are in a bubble of trouble, but so are you, Skylander! Underwater boulders, floating bombs, and enemy ships will steal your health if you hit them.

SuperCharged Racing

In an entirely new area of Skylanders Academy, Pandergast offers racing tracks where you can spin, dive, and barrel-roll through the competition to win bonus coins, Wish Stones, and special items. He'll always be ready with a new challenge for you as you test your courage on the tracks. When you first arrive at the academy, visit him to try out two new tracks for each type of vehicle. Buy the vehicle adventure packs (sky, sea, and land) for access to the remaining two tracks of each type and the Mirrored Races. You can race as Kaos, in his signature vehicle, the Doom Jet, by placing the Kaos Trophy on your portal (sold separately or included in the Dark Edition Starter Packs).

Blue ammo pods are scattered throughout each racecourse and reappear a couple of seconds after they've been picked up. Gather as many as you can to keep your ammo bar full. It doesn't take long to deplete it.

Magic boxes shine and spin in your path along each track and offer a surprise twist to your race. Inside each box is a power boost to help you, like those pictured in Figure 9.1. There's no way to predict which magic item is inside; the contents change each lap and are completely random. Some magic items will give you a speed boost, shield, or heal your health, or make you temporarily invincible. They can also inflict damage on the other racers to give you a head start. Of course, that works both ways—other racers can pick boxes up, too, and cause harm to you.

FIGURE 9.1 Drive through a magic box on the track for a surprise boost in your performance by scoring one of the magic items inside.

To begin racing, visit Pandergast at Skylanders Academy and choose the type of race you'd prefer. Table 9.1 shows the options available to you, although some, such as the Boss Pursuit, require another challenge to be completed first or require the use of an Adventure Pack trophy on your portal to unlock it.

TABLE 9.1 Racing Challenges with Pandergast

Icon	Race	How It Works
	Online Race	Challenge an online friend to race in a location and vehicle of your choice.
	Single Race	Test your skills against seven other racers.
	Time Trial	Just you at your fastest. Set a new record against the timer. This option opens after you complete a Single Race.
	Boss Pursuit	Chase down a villain, one-on-one. This race becomes available after you earn one star (by winning) in a Single Race for a specific location. After you win, each villain becomes available to race in their own vehicle.

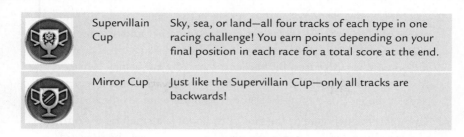

	Supervillain Cup	Sky, sea, or land—all four tracks of each type in one racing challenge! You earn points depending on your final position in each race for a total score at the end.
	Mirror Cup	Just like the Supervillain Cup—only all tracks are backwards!

Choose your track and place the SuperCharger and vehicle on the portal to race. Once you have defeated a villain in a Boss Pursuit, save them into your Trophy (sea, land, or sky). You can then choose to race as that villain by placing the trophy on your portal and selecting the appropriate button on your controller to view defeated villains. You can also view the villain's vehicle stats.

Sea Racing Tracks

Dive under the water by holding down the **Jump** button on your controller to discover hidden rewards, use speed boost gates, and complete obstacle challenges. Often, an underwater path is quicker than an icy surface above. Vehicle attacks don't work underwater during races, so your only defense is speed and agility. Underwater diving often leads to a shortcut on the track. Tapping the **Jump** button will give your sea vehicle a small bounce on the surface, which can help you reach floating rewards above. In the following section, we'll look at each of the sea racing locations in detail, including some tips on how to beat the competition.

Frozen Fossil Festival

This is a super-long racecourse with so many twists and turns you'll get dizzy (see Figure 9.2)! Never fear, though, because we're going to break it down and give you the inside scoop on the fastest ways to stay the coolest contestant on the track! Sliding on ice makes your vehicle harder to manage, but keep your eye underneath the bergs—there could be a hidden shortcut to take instead.

1. Spin off the starting block onto a straight track with a jump into the icy waters below. A fast current takes you on the windy right-side bend. If you dive underwater as soon as you land instead, you'll find a speed boosted shortcut straight underneath the arrows on the ice. Both paths have golden boost rings below the surface to speed you on your way. Chase the white water downstream, jumping up onto the ice to dive through the hoop of another speed boost or two.

2 Your first major decision involves a split in the track. To the right are plenty of blue ammo pods on the surface to gather and a faster ride through; to the left are boost rings underwater and ice up top. You can slide on the ice, it's just a bit harder to control your vehicle while doing so. The paths converge on some surface rapids with a boost jump to hit rings in the air (it's a long shot!) or rings underwater at the base pool.

3 Through the open gate at the end of the pool is a small ramp to the left offering a boosted jump into the pool beyond to meet the right-side path. It's a bit quicker, but will shoot you straight into the brick divider if you don't correct your direction in the air. More rapids lead you to an icy split. Ammo pods tempt you on the right with boost rings underneath to get you to the finish line faster. Take an almighty leap from the end into the open jaws of an enormous skull!

4 More giant teeth! The left skull and center (underneath the ship) paths are similar in terms of reward, but of course the center is more direct so will save you precious time. The right path is very windy with boost rings, so it's more challenging to make it through unscathed. Prepare for a slippery-slide ahead!

5 As you drop into the final stretch, steer to your right to pick up magic boxes on the surface (there's a boost pad on the left). One final leap will see you win or lose. Good luck!

Beware! If you're chasing down a super-villain on this track, you'll run out of ammo very quickly. Grab those blue ammo pods and the magic box to keep your firepower up (before your competition steals them all!).

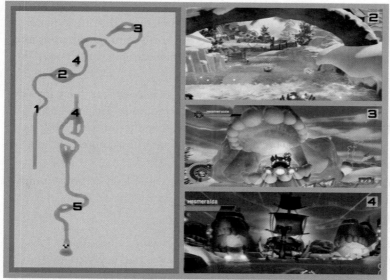

FIGURE 9.2 There's a spine-tingling chill in the air at the Frozen Fossil Festival! Fly into cavernous jaws to win the ultimate sea challenge!

Mystical Vault

Welcome to the Mystical Vault (see Figure 9.3), where nothing is as it seems. The magical caretaker sneezes every ten seconds or so and—*SNAP!*—the active colors of the boost gates change from red to blue! Keep alternating colored gates with each sneeze to zoom ahead as fast as you can. If the active color changes just before you hit a gate, try ducking underwater because there is often a gate of the opposite color waiting for you. The Mystical Vault has a lot of underwater territory to cover. There are plenty of detours to be taken; explore them all to find the best route!

1 You'll begin in a colorful canal where boost rings frequently appear on both sides (remember the active colors change!). A boost pad takes you into a circular pool with boost rings and ammo pods on both sides of the center statue. Continue through to a giant loop, zipping through colored rings as you go.

2 Spin off a boost pad and leap into a deep channel with two lanes. Both sides and underwater are full of boost rings, speed pad jumps, and ammo pods, so just follow the active color and dive from one side to the other.

3 Spin to your right and you'll hit a section where looping channels reconnect in the middle. Watch out for the moving floors (up and down) that shift underwater (depending on the active color) as you come

through here. If you hit a newly raised wall, it'll spin you out, costing time. Next up is a high vanishing platform on either side, one for each active color. If you curve your glide you can score some ammo pods and a boost ring before you land back down. This section has tidal waves in the center, so duck underwater to avoid them.

4 You'll emerge outdoors and the channel splits in two. Take the right-side (top) path to follow red boost rings and ammo pods. The left-side path has both colors and splits again into a higher and lower path. Both have the same features, and the high path drops back down quickly from a boost jump.

5 All paths converge back into a final straight, with plenty of boost jumps and underwater rings to navigate. Leap across a platform to begin the lap again.

Beware! If you don't gather enough speed before your jumps, they'll fall short and stun you, wasting precious time while the bad guy slips away.

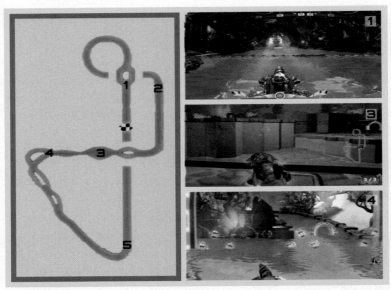

FIGURE 9.3 Expect the unexpected in the Mystical Vault by memorizing your path ahead.

The Golden Temple

There's no shortage of treasure in the Golden Temple—in fact there's so much of it, you may very well forget to race! Even the water here glitters as it rolls along the golden channels. But beware—there are dangers everywhere! Giant boulders tumble down ramps to crush you, and boost rings spin out of reach. As you progress through laps, the water is ever rising, bringing danger closer and closer. Prepare for a rapid-fire race of daring, quick decisions, and soaring risks, as pictured in Figure 9.4.

1 Begin outside in a channel with boost rings leading into a room with two paths. They both jump across a series of steps to a channel below. (If you fall into the water underneath, you'll be pushed toward the same channel.)

2 Speed along through ammo pods and boost gates until you get to the room with falling boulders. You're safe here until the water rises in laps two and three, when you'll need to duck underwater to reach the end safely.

3 The tunnel continues back into the main room where shifting blocks create jumps on the surface. Use these for a bit of leverage to speed ahead into more boost gates, but don't run into them, as you'll be knocked off course and need time to recover. Take a flying leap into a series of boost rings that slide back and forth. They're fast, so you won't need much change of direction to hit them.

4 The channel loops back on itself with a chain of boost rings that slide from the roof down and across the surface of the water. This is a fantastic spot to pick up your speed for a leap across the channel.

5 Huge boulders are heading your way! Duck underwater as they roll toward you down the three lanes of the channel. As long as you dive right down to the bottom, you're safe from being crushed, or you can blow the boulders up as they roll toward you. If you get hit, you'll suffer major damage. There's a magic box (Powered Pods) at the top left of this climb (you'll have to bounce up to reach it). Emerge into the final tunnel for a race to the end!

Beware! This is a complex course with many opportunities to fall off the track, so take care!

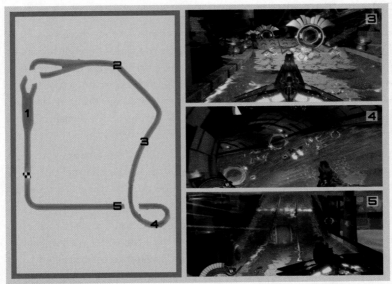

FIGURE 9.4 Battle for the crown in the glittering underworld of the Golden Queen.

Tropic Plunder

Salty Tusk Volcano is about to erupt! Broken shipwrecks are on fire! Giant boulders are falling from the sky! This is a very dangerous island... but oddly enough, the local Mabu are sun-bathing and sipping on coconuts! Brave or crazy?! Tropic Plunder is a fast race with many obstacles to keep you from winning, like those shown in Figure 9.5. There are pitfalls, literally; each new water pit you fall into will have a large hazard, or a few, in the middle of your path. Decide ahead of time whether to stick to the left or right so you don't run straight into a volcano, rock, or tree.

1 Get off to a flying start with the right-side speed jump. A series of rapids with boost pads is fraught with danger—rocks are jutting up everywhere. Stick to the right for an easier ride into the mouth of Salty Tusk Mountain where magic boxes await you.

2 Drop down into the volcano center where you can choose a path on either side to get around it. Both sides have underwater boost rings and ammo pods on the surface. On your first lap through, take the right path around the volcano and steer right immediately after the underwater boost rings to find a little cave with a magic box (Powered Pods) inside. It's worth losing a few seconds to have constant firepower.

3 Continue through a second set of underwater boost rings to find yourself in a shallow channel with sandbars along the sides. You can move across

the sand without slowing here, which is easier than hitting the next two boost rings underneath the water, which each have an obstacle (tree branch) around it. Hitting the branches will knock you off course.

4 A series of boost pads line the next stretch, but they are dangerously close to the edge. These are fantastic for catching up with other racers—if you can hit them all in a row—but it's a tricky feat. Falling off the side of the channel here is not a bad thing, though—there's a boost pad at the end that will speed you to the next section. Just aim straight as you come out of the end jump, then veer left in the air so you don't get caught in the greenery!

5 If you managed to stay on the main path following the boost pads on the edge, you're soon given another split. The right-side path up a ramp is slightly longer but has central boost pads to speed you up without much effort. Stay left for a straighter ride, but boost pads are hidden under waterfalls to your left, which are harder to navigate without hitting the wall. The two paths converge in a pool filled with rock islands and magic boxes. Stick to the left to find a hidden shortcut through the sand (look for a single magic box under a rocky arch) to reach the starting gate again for another lap.

Beware! Giant boulders begin falling in the second lap and increase in numbers in the third. They create big waves that throw you off track.

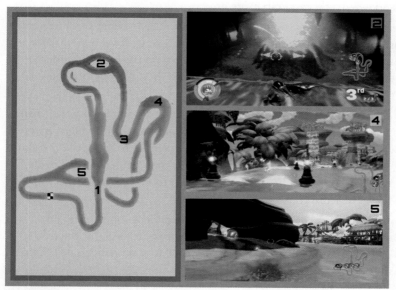

FIGURE 9.5 Beware the flaming boulders falling from the sky and rocky hazards in your path. Tropic Plunder is not for the faint-hearted!

Sky Racing Tracks

You'll find plenty of adventure waiting for you among the clouds. If you have trouble on your tail with a target lock, try spinning away with a quick barrel-roll (the **Jump** button on your controller). Learning to race in the air takes a bit of work. If you find you're having trouble getting the hang of your controls, try inversing the up/down control under Controls in the Main Menu. In this section, we'll discover the tricks and traps of all sky racing locations.

Calamity Canyon

Dodge and weave through a frightful food-fight, rocky outcrops, washing lines, and enemy fire to win your rightful place as champion of the canyon (see Figure 9.6)!

1 Take off on a clear course through some rocky archways, dodging flying food toward magic boxes. A tiny shortcut to your right boasts a boost ring and then a high-set magic box (follow the ammo pods).

2 The paths join back together and lead you under a covered track with an immediate, sharp right turn. This tunnel is full of blue ammo pods, so hit as many as you can to boost your firepower. Again, the tunnel splits, one above (ammo pods) and one below (magic boxes). You'll need solid handling for these caves; there are many tight turns and a sharp right at the end where you can grab more ammo.

3 Emerge through a fog to find yourself in clear sky. A series of three golden boost rings line up to your right with magic boxes between them. One boost ring is on your left as well. As you progress through laps, these may appear with targets on them that need to be shot away before you use them.

4 Turn left back into the canyon to pick up some more ammo pods; then take a sharp right to decide between two main paths with magic boxes between them. Follow the majority of your enemies to score the highest hits. The left path has three boost rings and the right has ammo pods, but both have washing lines that you'll need to dodge (they slow you down and obscure your view).

5 They'll come back together at a tunnel with another boost ring. Just ahead is the waving arm of a giant Chef Pepper Jack sign. Sneak over or under the hand to keep from hitting it (you'll lose time if you do). Cross the start line and begin again!

Beware! An exploding airship will collapse from above in lap three. Dodge the flying pieces, or you'll get knocked off course!

FIGURE 9.6 The crazy crowd at Calamity Canyon has started a food-fight! Watch out for flying vegetables as you navigate the caves.

Clock Rock

Are you ready to rock? The hands of time are turning forward and zapping you into the future at Time Town, where Wolfgang the Werewolf is shredding his guitar to the tune of evil! Each lap is broken into two parts: old Time Town with Mabu cheering from the sidelines, and a future space-rift of flying meteors and laser music bars, as shown in Figure 9.7.

1 Begin in Time Town, where giant clock gears fold down to open a portal into the future. As you spin toward a shining light, move slightly left or right to grab the ammo pods floating in the tunnel—you'll need them!

2 You'll emerge into a zany space-tunnel through future Time Town, where psychedelic holograms of Wolfgang adorn the skies. Within the confines of the tunnel, you'll hit ammo pods and giant rocks. The outer wall slows but doesn't damage your health; the inner, molten core brings epic damage if you hit it. Stick to the right side where three golden boost rings can speed you through a clearer path.

3 Emerge into outer space where huge asteroids are floating. From lap 2 onward, they'll fly toward you and there will be more of them. Blast them out of your way. Just in front of the right side tunnel, floating behind an asteroid, is a magic box with Powered Pods in it (in Boss Pursuits you'll find it where the tunnels converge on the right edge). Pick it up for

unlimited ammo. The right-side path has ammo pods and three red laser beams (vertical/horizontal/vertical) obstructing your path that cause damage. The left-side path (easier) has three gates cutting the tunnel into alternate semicircles (fly over/under/over) with boost rings in between.

4 Both paths converge, and the rest of the tunnel is obstacle free (except for other racers, of course!) Emerge into outer space to be bombarded by meteors again on the final stretch into the time portal to be zapped back home.

5 Back in old Time Town, a boost ring tempts you from the right side, but it's tricky to navigate and better left alone. Head straight for the turning gear gate instead through the perfectly aligned boost ring, grabbing a magic box on the way. Another gear gate is beyond it—both of these will turn faster as you complete each lap. On the right side of the second gear gate (behind a hanging chime) is an open window with ammo pods inside. Fly through for a shortcut and then turn hard right. Some giant rollers have magic boxes above and below (above is easier) if you missed the shortcut window. Before you reach the time portal for a new lap, pass under or over the giant Wolfgang sign with a moving guitar arm.

Beware! Hitting an asteroid without blasting it first will knock you out and cost precious time.

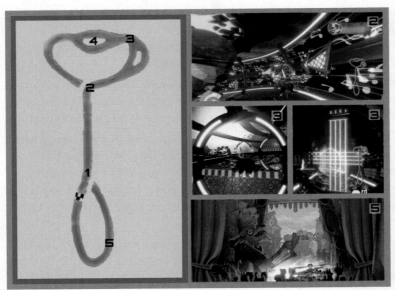

FIGURE 9.7 Do you dare to enter Wolfgang's time warp? Fly through the future to beat your best time!

Cloud Factory

There's a storm brewing at the Cloud Factory (see Figure 9.8), and you *really* don't want to get caught in the rain!

1 Open air and high arches lead you through the first section of this course, which splits quickly into two paths. Both paths have magic item boxes at their beginning.

2 The paths converge seconds later at a gold boost ring. Smash through it to begin your ascent onto the high road with some more magic boxes on the way. Straighten up quickly at the top for a nice stretch of clear sky through arches and more boxes.

3 Immediately left of the first gold boost ring is a shortcut path to the left. Blink and you'll miss it! There are blue ammo pods to pick up on both paths here, but the right-side (main) path also has another boost ring and some magic boxes.

4 The paths converge right in front of a descent tunnel. Hold onto your magic hats! Fly straight down through the eye of the tornado (try not to hit any sheep!). Pull up quickly at the bottom to take off straight.

5 Magic boxes will lure you into a room of purple spinning hurricanes. Keep away from them! Getting caught will lose you seconds of precious time. On the far side are boost rings that open into a big room with magic boxes. Fly through the final boost ring gate to begin another lap!

Beware! As you progress, some boost rings will turn dark purple. These will damage your health, so steer clear of them.

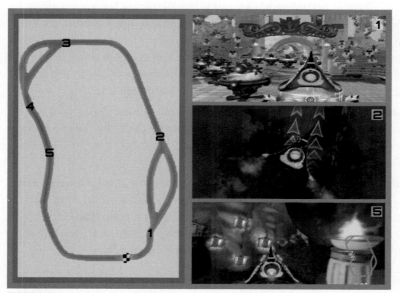

FIGURE 9.8   The open air arches are a fun ride, but beware of your descent into hazardous hurricanes!

Cluck's Cuckoo Nest

Uh oh—the chickens of Cluck's Cuckoo Nest are extra egg-cited! Zoom through the sky in a flurry of feathers as you dodge enormous rolling eggs, conveyer belts of eggy boost rings, and flapping hatch doors in a flying bird bonanza (see Figure 9.9).

1 Take off on a clear path through the wooden halls of Cuckoo Nest with big eggs on nests nearby. You'll quickly arrive at a fork in the road. The left path splits again into three (the right reconnects soon after). Of these, the left is just a small henhouse detour with ammo pods hidden underneath. The middle and right-side paths both boast ammo pods and egg obstructions. Shoot the eggs if they get in your way, but they won't cause too much trouble for you yet. This is a straight run, so take advantage and focus on targets and firepower here to bring down your competition. All paths meet back together soon after under covered walkways.

2 High to the top-right side of the walkway roof is a golden boost ring. It's a small space so tricky to maneuver but worth the effort to get ahead. In the open air, just past it, is a steep ascent marked by moving white arrows. Hold onto your tail feathers! This is a vertical climb with your finger on the **Attack** button as you're bombarded with falling eggs from above. Shoot them apart to clear your way! At the top of the tree, level down quickly to avoid hitting the platform above.

3 Eggs are held in grappling hooks and (after lap three) are moved along by means of a conveyor belt. You can choose either a right or left path. The right has a boost ring and plenty of ammo pods. The left has eggs and ammo pods. This is a super-fun area for a bit of target practice. Every few hooks, you'll see one with a golden ring inside and possibly an egg too. Smash the egg to reach the boost ring and fly through.

4 These paths converge soon after at the Chicken House. Fly up to the top-right side of the building quickly and navigate through the rafters. About two-thirds down the length of the henhouse is a magic box with Powered Pods inside.

5 Through the open barn doors and into the sunshine! More Powered Pods are waiting for you on the path along with alternating rolling eggs and boost rings on a track. A steep descent through the coop leads into a tunnel with many square platforms of eggs that flip down as you shoot them. Clear your path and grab some boost rings in between.

Beware! As you progress, more eggs will roll by on the conveyer belt obstructing your path, and boost gate positions will change.

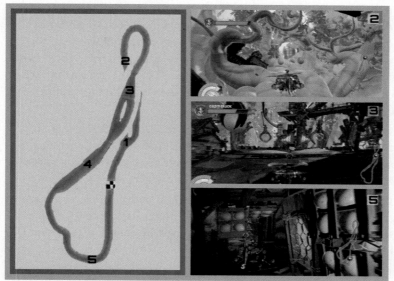

FIGURE 9.9   Prepare for egg on your face as you smash your way through the coop at Cluck's Cuckoo Nest!

Land Racing Tracks

There's nothing more thrilling than ripping through a race track at the speed of sound. Land vehicles are the best way of testing your skill because they're the easiest to become accustomed to. For wide corners with minimal obstacles, try drifting (by using the appropriate button on your controller). You can't steer your vehicle while drifting, so be in a position where it can move forward without hitting anything. As soon as you release the button, you'll surge ahead with extra speed. The longer you drift, the greater the boost once the button is released. This takes a bit of practice because you'll need to compromise control for speed. Each of the land racing locations have special features and shortcuts, and we'll look at them individually next.

Chompy Garden

Everything at Chompy Garden is larger than life, as you can see in Figure 9.10! Churn your way through oversized carrots, radishes, and mushrooms with twitterpillars cheering from the sidelines! Look out for Pandergast's floating blimp passing above while you dodge huge hoses and puddles, explosive barrels of TNT, and lines of sun-fire created by a mischievous Chompy with a magnifying glass!

1 *Zoom!* Straight out of the starting gate, there are puddles to slow you down. Dodge the first one and then pick up ammo pods and a boost gate on the left. Swing to the right for a boost ramp that will send you flying beyond your competitors! This track is laden with magic boxes and ammo pods, so grab as many as you can. Stick to the right side up ahead for a second boost jump, but beware TNT barrels in the short tunnel ahead from lap two onward.

2 A row of magic boxes signifies a fork in the road. The left side has easier ramp jumps and a larger landing space. The right side has boost pads on lily pads, which require good speed and aim to maneuver (if you're too slow or miss the boost pads, you'll fall in the water).

3 Both paths land on a central lily pad. The right path from here is quicker with plenty of ammo pods on the way and more space. The left-side path is a smaller lily pad jump, which holds a magic box and a second ramp, but this time it's a safe land on mudflats and a straight path ahead.

4 The paths converge into a dirt tunnel full of magic boxes and TNT barrels after lap two, which increase in lap three. This is an easy run for knocking out competitors (blow up those barrels before you hit them!).

5 A series of five boost pads (right/center/left/center/right) through the home stretch is marred by moving lines of fire from giant chompies playing with magnifying glasses. Keep away, or you'll get burned! Stick to the left to take a flying leap onto two boost jumps and then bounce off a mushroom to finish the lap.

Beware! On the third lap, two magnifying glass fires will move faster, more water will spill onto the track, and extra TNT barrels will be in your way. Dodge them all or spin out!

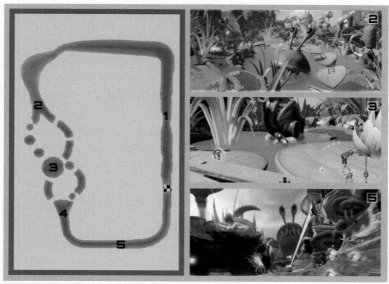

FIGURE 9.10 Gigantic chompies are making pests of themselves among the veggie patch. Avoid their antics as you race to the finish line.

Dragon Spine

Mighty slumbering serpents are curled around the towers of Dragon Spine (see Figure 9.11). Don't wake them up or you're in for fiery fury! Uh oh! Kaos's forces invade the area and bang the noisy gong, tempting the dragons to unleash their terrible morning breath on you!

1 Head to the left side as you come through the starting gate to pick up a row of ammo pods on a ledge; then cross over to the far right to take advantage of a boost pad jump to speed things along. The red dragon breathes fire onto the track, increasing in intensity with each lap (none in the first, two fires to avoid in lap two, three fires in lap three). There are two scale speed jumps approaching. The center scale offers ammo pods.

2 Approach the second scale jump (which is on the left of the track), cutting across the right-side row of ammo pods to get a straight run, and then launch off the very tip of the jump, veering slightly right to land on a shortcut track with two boost pads (you'll need to get some speed up to make this jump). Rejoin the pack to launch off the Red Dragon's tail into the village below.

3 On the village track, two platforms on the left offer a boost pad at the end, or a row of ammo pods underneath (if you have good aim). The second ramp has a magic box (Powered Pods) at the end for a super ammo boost. A row of four magic boxes marks the entrance into the Blue Dragon's domain. On the first lap through, the dragon just yawns. It breathes ice onto the track after lap two (on the right side of the track first, then the left side).

4 Boost jump across to race the Blue Dragon's spine, but beware of ice on the track. Hitting ice will slow you right down and give your competitors the advantage. This long stretch of track with ice in the center is a great place to fire at other racers without risk of crashing.

5 Landing back in the Red Dragon's zone means watching out for fire as you begin a new lap.

Beware! Hitting the shortcut spine jump on the wrong angle spells doom if you're winning. Practice makes perfect in this case.

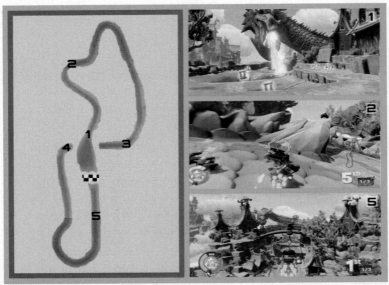

FIGURE 9.11 Speed and agility are the keys to winning a Dragon Spine race. Beware of fire and ice!

Temple of Arkus

A host of woodland folk and a troop of enormous robot monkeys are waiting at the Temple of Arkus track to cheer you on—and smack you down! There are plenty of ammo pods on this track, but you'll have to be quick to score them before your competitors do! Take the opportunity to target and fire at racers ahead of you while you're in the air crossing boosted jumps.

1 A row of magic boxes is hard to miss on a tight turn to the right. Hug the side of the track to take advantage of a boost pad when you pull straight again. Fly under the arm of a giant fallen robot to score some ammo pods, and stay to the left so you don't spin out on the curve.

2 The track splits into two here. A Powered Pod is hidden in a magic box on the right-side path.

3 The first boosted jump flings you through a row of floating magic boxes for an easy score. When you land, alternating left and right side boost pads will speed you up, but beware! Stone monkey statues next to each one will slam down fists to damage you from the second lap onward. A series of three boost pads are coming up on a straight run to speed you across another jump.

4 This is a massive jump with lots of floating obstacles to avoid (and ammo pods to scoop up) The first major obstacle is an island with a tower on the right side, so veer slightly to the left. The second is another island with a stone tower on the left side (so veer slightly to the right). With a bit of practice, you can pass straight between them. Score some more ammo pods as you land.

5 Another row of magic boxes cross on your final turn. Hug the right-side corner, then drift across to the left of the track to take a boost ring back to the finish line.

Beware! Hitting the boost pads after the split means risking a stone fist smashing you up. Time your run through to avoid those statues!

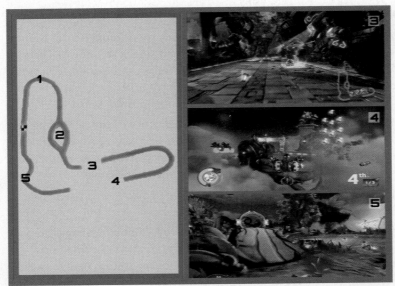

FIGURE 9.12 There are plenty of stone monkeys throwing tantrums on this track, but keep your eye on ammo pods and magic boxes for a quick win.

The After Party

You've been invited to the craziest undead after party in town! This place is a maze of green slime that covers the track in greater amounts as you complete each lap, slowing you down. It's easy to lose track of what's up next, so keep your eye on the map as you out-race your competitors for a confetti-shower victory!

1 It's a downhill ride through a row of magic boxes off the starting block. You'll zoom across a giant spinning record with a playing needle that will entirely spin you out. In the second lap, two needles will play, and in the third, three. Be careful to avoid these (hug the right side, close to the center platform) as they'll cost you a lot of time if you hit them.

2 The track splits into two paths; brown (left) and blue (right). Both paths feature a boost pad and ammo pods. Start on the blue and drop left onto the brown path to score both boost pads before the paths rejoin.

3 A circular area has a platform in the middle with ammo pods on top, but there's a catch—a revolving wall will knock you out if you hit the boost ramp at the wrong time. Save yourself the trouble and take the left-side path around to pick up a magic box with Powered Pods inside. Take advantage of more boost pads and magic boxes on the way out.

4 The track splits again into blue (left side) and brown (right side) paths. The blue side is a pretty straight run with ammo pods and a row of magic boxes. Take the high road along the brown path for a four-disc row of jumps, with boost pads on them. Veer toward the left edge for disc one, then the right edge for disc two, left edge for disc three, and right edge for disc four. It's easy to overshoot the turns and drop off the side early— aim to hop across in as straight a line as possible.

5 The fourth disc is above an epic slime pile in a circular area. If you took the blue path, you'll end up here (dodge the slime!). Zoom through to the starting gate to begin again!

Beware! It's easy to spin out on this track due to so many curves—keep a tight rein on your controller and cut corners for a straighter path.

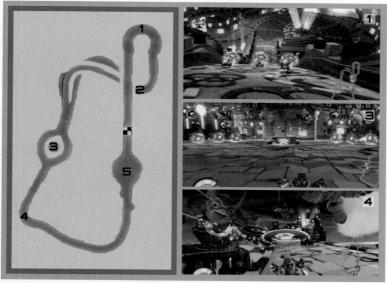

FIGURE 9.13   Take the high road or the low road—either way, you'd better be fast!

Gear Up for Adventure

Are you ready to begin your biggest Skylands adventure yet?

The gloriously evil power of The Darkness has been released, and Kaos is at the helm of a devastating Sky Eater that is consuming all of Skylands! The Mabu are being evacuated from their villages, and nasty minions are running around stirring up trouble. To make matters worse, Master Eon, the greatest Portal Master who ever lived and wise leader of the Skylanders, has been kidnapped! Unless you step up and take control, Skylands is doomed!

In this chapter, you'll find hints and tips on how to make it through each level of the adventure unscathed, as well as clues on where you can find all the hidden collectibles. These collectibles include Epic Treasure Chests, Reward Objects (Soul Gems, piñatas, gems, legendary treasure, and hats), Wish Stones, and Skystones Overdrive stones. In the vehicle sections, you'll find Red Toolboxes, orange gearbits, and puzzle pieces. Keep an eye out for them in hidden alcoves and corners, and search behind you at the beginning of each chapter in case one is hidden in plain sight. It's worth backtracking or playing through again to pick up any collectibles you may have missed.

Are you ready to begin, Skylander? Let's go!

TIP

Line Your Pockets with Gold!

Don't dash through the adventure chapters and miss all the hidden loot! Smash up boxes, vegetables, furniture, and barricades as you pass through each level to find treasure. Then visit Skylanders Academy to spend it on upgrades with Persephone or buy something special at the Academy Shop.

The Rift to Skylands

Oh no! Kaos has taken control of all the portals in and out of Skylands, cutting the poor Skylanders off from the only heroes who can save them. But don't despair... Hugo has cracked the security of the portal and opened a temporary rift into Skylands. Get moving, Skylander, it won't hold for long!

Chapter 1: Skylands in Chains

Jump straight into the adventure to rescue your friends! Escape the Sky Eater and then explore an underground lair guarded by King Chompy the Eighth to rescue Cali, Flynn, and Hugo.

Distress Call: Reach Skylands

The last remaining portal in Skylands is only open as long as Hugo can hack into the security system. Speed through the swirling tunnel in your land vehicle, get a feel for your new controls, and collect as many shining gearbits as you can along the way.

The Great Escape: Rescue Your Friends

A hero always rescues his or her friends! Follow the gold coins to find Hugo, Cali, and Flynn.

There's a green button, on the right-side ramp of the first step, leading to an **Epic Treasure Chest**.

A **Wish Stone** is on top of the furthest left cage after you jump up the second green button.

King Chompy and his snoring friends guard an **Epic Treasure Chest** on the right-side cage (glowing yellow door), as shown in Figure 10.1.

A **Reward Object** is on the top of Cali, Flynn, and Hugo's cage.

Use your controller to move the Gremlin through the **Live Wire Lock** near Cali and collect three lightning bolts. Avoid hitting the light bulbs.

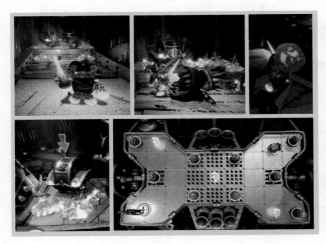

FIGURE 10.1

Gather treasure, including King Chompy's gold, but don't wake him!

TIP

Live Wire Locks

Live Wire Locks are found throughout the adventure, usually on rewards and doorways to secret areas. To open these locks, you'll have to complete a little puzzle by moving a green gremlin around a playing board to pick up three lightning sparks and then turning the ignition key to exit. Be very gentle on your directional controller because it's easy to overshoot and fall off the edge of the board, or get knocked off course by a light bulb shock. These puzzles get harder as you progress through the game, but completing them earns you the reward inside as well as additional stardust.

Chapter 2: Motley Meadows

It's racing time! Head to Motley Meadows where Kaos' flagship is keeping innocent Mabu as prisoners inside—can you save them?

A **Reward Object** is on the immediate right-side path where you begin.

On the end of the ramp opposite Cali is a **Wish Stone**.

Land Star: Save the Pit Crew

Collect four puzzle pieces to earn extra gearbits. One piece is hidden behind boxes on the right side under a ledge.

Blow up the rock wall under the right-side ledge to find a boost pad leading to the "Break the Barrels" challenge. Zoom around to collect six barrels.

Save the Pit Crew sharks by launching off high ramps (see Figure 10.2).

An iron equalizer, chompies, and other enemies attack here.

Grab the **Red Toolbox** on the ledge above before you leave.

Land Star: Get Back to the Fleet

The right-side ramp has a small jump (stay right) with another **Red Toolbox** reward.

A final **Red Toolbox** is in a mid-air jump after the Kaos Cruisers attack.

Defeat all the Kaos Cruisers to move on to your next challenge.

FIGURE 10.2
Launch off high ramps to pick up Fender, Socket, and Clyde before the Sky Eater devours them!

Chapter 3: A Fuel's Errand

Track down Cali and the crew from among a sea of floating crates. Beware of red target rings on the ground—mines fall here and explode, causing damage!

Jump down to the lowest crate to collect a **Reward Object** and treasure.

A **Wish Stone** is above the moving crate to your left side.

James Prong has a Sea Challenge for you after you destroy the Electroclops guards. You can skip this challenge by entering a golden hatch to his right.

Sea Star: Destroy the Catalytic Cyclotron

Destroy all enemy ships and three Cyclotron valve covers.

Attack the overhanging pipes to find a hidden **Red Toolbox**.

Escape Through the Outtake Valve

Dive into the outtake valve. Stay left (underwater) for a **Red Toolbox**.

There's a **Reward Object** on the small island in the main room.

A **Red Toolbox** is at the back of a large pipe to the left of the island.

Return to James Prong to continue on foot.

Jump into the glowing cylinder where you dock for a **Reward Object**, piles of treasure, and a game of **Skystones Overdrive** with Aimee. Bounce up to her cage roof for more treasure and your way out.

On the left-side ramp, trailing coins along a cylinder lead to a **Wish Stone**.

Jump in the orange liquid falling from the ceiling to maximize your damage in a tussle against Chompies, Shifty Sticklers, and Electroclops.

Continue past the Live Wire Lock on the right path to enter a glowing pipe. Jump across fast-moving rafts to find an **Epic Treasure Chest**.

Back at the **Live Wire Lock**, press the red button to spin the right-side circular platform to access the lightning bolts (see Figure 10.3).

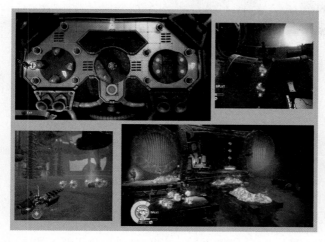

FIGURE 10.3

You can pass a Live Wire Lock by collecting just one spark, but you'll miss out on earning extra stardust.

Chapter 4: The Great Breakout

Kaos' troops are sending you a message—get off their ship!

Follow the fighters' flight path at the start for an **Epic Treasure Chest**.

Avoid the Kaos Cruisers by zigzagging to reach treasure platforms.

A **Reward Object** is on the furthest center platform.

To skip the Sky Challenge, talk to Hugo for a Land Star challenge instead.

Sky Star: Save the Escape Pods

Shoot down enemies trapping the three escape pods to set them free.

Two large ships have a **Red Toolbox** on board to pick up.

One large ship has a mini-game flag; break nine barrels to win gearbits.

Sky Star: Protect Sharpfin's Ship

Attack five enemy fighters to save Sharpfin's ship (see Figure 10.4).

Sky Star: Destroy the Cannon Ship & Capture the Flag Ship

Destroy the three ship turrets on the Cannon Ship of Doom.

Land on the flag ship to end your first adventure in Skylands. Brilliant work, Skylander!

FIGURE 10.4
Destroy enemy fighters to allow prisoners to escape from the Sky Eater.

Chapter 5: A Safe Place

Kaos is gleefully celebrating that his own nasty Darkness plan is progressing quite well, while Count Moneybone rattles in fear! Glumshanks, as always, is worried though... The Darkness is more powerful than they expected and the Troll minions aren't happy.

Meanwhile back at Skylanders Academy, Pandergast arrives with his fast fleet of racing legends to go for a spin. You can now access 6 of the 12 racing tracks available. For access to the other six tracks, you'll need to purchase the adventure racing packs. There's a new quest waiting for you called Beacon of Hope, from Mags, and you'll need to chat with Persephone and Sharpfin before you move on. Hugo is on a mission to discover a way to rescue poor Master Eon, who is still languishing in his prison cell. It's time to explore Skylanders Academy before your next adventure begins.

The Cloudbreather's Crag

Legend has told of a magical dragon living in the Cloudscraper Mountains that can sniff out a missing person (or spirit, in Eon's case) with the help of something that belonged to them. Luckily Hugo has secretly kept one of Eon's old socks (which is a little weird) that he can take on this mission.

Chapter 6: Conquered by Kaos

Whoa! That was a rough landing! Kaos' forces have taken over the villages of Cloudbreather's Crag. Nayu (who is most definitely not staging a revolution) offers advice. Get to the top of the mountain and ring the gong to wake him!

Eon's Sock: Talk to the Cloudbreather

There's a **Reward Object** floating on the lower ledge in front of Nayu.

At the top (left side) of the stairs above the sleeping Drow soldiers, enter a glowing door to find a secret garden with an **Epic Treasure Chest**.

Witch Pitcher is waiting to set off the alarm and call in minions to battle. Destroy the spinning alarm as quickly as possible to turn it off.

Assemble the lower gate gong and ring it, but explore before you continue.

There's a **Wish Stone** on a ledge to the left near a triangle gate gong.

A square gate gong is on the balcony with some food hidden behind.

Hit each of the three gate gongs in the order on the sign above the villager to open a secret door leading to an **Epic Treasure Chest**.

Continue on to battle small enemies and destroy the second siren.

Land Star: Ring the Dragon Gong

Dodge the red mines and collect as many gearbits as possible. Destroy the red alarms along the way, like the one shown in Figure 10.5.

The orange gearbit above where you land briefly spawns gearbits.

There's a **Red Toolbox** hidden under tents at the very top of the hill.

A **Red Toolbox** is up above a boost jump on the high area near the gate.

Gather power-ups and then destroy all enemy vehicles to open the gate.

FIGURE 10.5
Knock out any alarms as quickly as possible—they summon enemies!

Chapter 7: City Under Sea

You've woken the dragon, but now Flynn's ship is under enemy fire! A SuperChargers work is never done....

Drop down from the left side of the path for an **Epic Treasure Chest**.

When Twilight Twisters appear, wait until they stop spinning to attack.

If you don't have a sea vehicle, skip the Sea Star by following the right path past the waterwheel and fishing boat.

Sea Star: Destroy the Blockages

Clear three blockages that are flooding the village. Pink pufferfish will damage your health—avoid them!

After you're done, Matzi is in a small house nearby with a game of **Skystones Overdrive**.

In the second Sea Challenge, a **Red Toolbox** is floating on the left side of the lake.

Ride the whale's spout into the air to gather four puzzle pieces.

Exit on the back right-side docking bay and jump across the waterwheels to find a **Reward Object** on the left, along with plenty of treasure.

The left-side house is your exit back to the waterwheel. Ride the wheel to a high ledge for food and gold. There is also treasure to the right side of the stairs.

Persephone is floating in the left-side alcove after the stairs to offer upgrades. Beware of enemies here.

Break the barrier to jump into the airship. Once enemies are defeated, you can take off! Be prepared for a crash landing! **Sharpfin** and his crew are ready to upgrade your vehicle.

Kitemaster Azko

A mini-game is at the top right of the stairs where you disembark the ship. Shift the kite under falling gold to collect 30 coins.

Rescue the Miners

Three miners are trapped in the Firestone Mine to the right of Sharpfin. Break down the barricades to free them and score a **Reward Object**.

Reassemble the circle gong to open a gate ahead. Before you go through, hit the gong pattern on the sign above a closed door to score an **Epic Treasure Chest** (see Figure 10.6). The triangle gong is at the front end of the sleeping tents. Treasure and a square gong are on a high ledge above.

FIGURE 10.6

If you see a sign with symbols on it, hit the gongs to reveal hidden treasure.

Chapter 8: Scaling the Road

Jump in your land vehicle ready to race! You're getting close Skylander; enemies are on your tail!

Immediately off the starting block is a **Red Toolbox** on a very high ledge above you, as shown in Figure 10.7.

An underpass in the middle of the first field rewards you with a power-up.

After you boost-jump across to the Cloudbreather's back, you'll find another **Red Toolbox** atop the middle shelter structure in the center. Score as many gearbits as you can to the end of the track.

FIGURE 10.7

Take a fast run-up in your vehicle to reach high ledges for toolboxes, orange gearbits, and power-ups. You can drive almost vertically if you need to.

Chapter 9: Temple of the Cloudbreather

There are plenty of rewards on the Temple of the Cloudbreather ship, so keep a sharp eye out for them!

To your immediate left is a path down some stairs. Break the barricades to reveal a **Live Wire Lock** on an **Epic Treasure Chest**. You need some speed behind you to ride the electric arrows across the gap on either end of the lock to collect the sparks.

On the right side of the deck is treasure—dodge the drifting red mines!

On the center path, jump onto floating rafts. Break the barrier on the left of the first raft to continue across to a **Reward Object**.

Sky Star: Destroy Kaos' Fleet

Talk to Chicha on the right side of the platform to get the low-down on your challenge. Destroy four giant fighter ships to win this challenge.

Pick up the **Red Toolbox** under the building on the Cloudbreather's back.

Extra enemy fighters join in but don't count toward your goal.

Sky Star: Save the Temple

Destroy two large carriers to save the temple (see Figure 10.8).

Back on the ship, ride the floating raft opposite Chicha across to the left. Destroy enemies and dodge mines to reach the front of the ship.

Ride the raft all the way to the left side to find a **SuperCharger Gate**. Inside, dodge mines and jump from one giant wheel to the next to reach the left platform. You're in for a big fight to score a **Reward Object**.

Back on the main ship, take the right-side ramp near the SuperCharger gate to find treasure.

Gather gold on the center platform and hit the gong to summon your final fight with Rush Crusher. After he lunges, he becomes vulnerable.

Once Rush Crusher is defeated, use his key to open the first lock. Take down waves of smaller enemies and then a Twilight Twister to recover the final key. Set the dragon free!

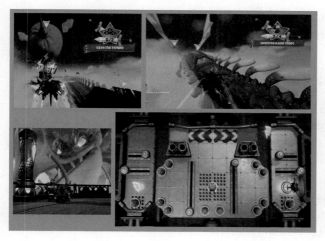

FIGURE 10.8
Take down sky fighters and fight enemies using hand-to-hand combat to free the dragon from its chains—he'll thank you by sharing important information.

Chapter 10: Call Down the Thunder

The Cloudbreather Dragon declares that Master Eon is trapped in the Land of the Undead! It's going to take some serious fighting to free him. Mags suggests you spend some time on the Vehicle Test Zones so she can recalibrate your engines while you're back at Skylanders Academy. Visit Flynn when you're ready to continue to the Cloud Kingdom!

The Cloud Kingdom

Queen Cumulus has promised to lend Mags the Thunderous Bolt to upgrade the SuperChargers' rift engines, but Lord Stratosfear has stolen it! Navigate the Cloud Kingdom to find a large foghorn to clear the skies before you teach Lord Stratosfear a lesson in manners.

Chapter 11: The Brewing Storm

Blow the Stormhorn

Fog covers all paths here, so beware of hidden enemies! Explore all areas to find treasure. Use small foghorns to get a glimpse of the paths ahead.

A **Reward Object** is on the right side of the water paths where you start.

Bitning Bugs explode when they hit you. Destroy them first!

Inflatrators are hiding along the main path to the right. Destroy them before they breathe in and expand to twice their size. Watch out for flying gas clouds from the fountain.

To the right side of Ukko ahead is a set of stairs heading downward. Defeat a pack of Inflatrators here to score an **Epic Treasure Chest**.

Sky Star: Destroy the Transport Ships

Destroy nine transport ships on the Cloud Kingdom race track.

Fly low at the very start on the right side of the track to pick up a **Red Toolbox** in the middle of the four blue columns (see Figure 10.9).

A **Red Toolbox** is atop a large blue column on the right side of the path.

Back on land, jump across a series of floating platforms near Ukko to reach a **SuperCharger Gate**. Use the foghorn to look ahead at the spinning gears. Jump across to the large left gear first, then continue downward.

Always land in the center of each gear to avoid the damaging rolling orbs.

A **Wish Stone** is hidden on the lowest platform on the right.

The final (lowest) gear has a central platform with three Meteo-Trollogists shooting from it. Take them out first, then collect the **Epic Treasure Chest** and treasure from surrounding platforms.

Return to the central garden path between Ukko and the SuperCharger Gate. Walk around the laser platform until the two lasers connect with the lion heads. Spin the second platform until the two lasers connect with the smaller statues, while the smaller ones are both pointed to the gate.

FIGURE 10.9

It's tricky to spot Red Toolboxes on the Cloud Kingdom track. Do a few laps before you take on the bad guys so you have a chance to pick them up.

Chapter 12: All Roads Lead to Ruin

Plenty of treasure lays on the road ahead, but there are many obstacles to stop you reaching it. Take on some brain-benders to prove you're worthy!

An **Elemental Gate** is the first stop in this chapter. This is the same Elemental Zone challenge you'll find at Skylanders Academy.

To the left of the Land Star Challenge is a series of platforms in the clouds leading to an **Epic Treasure Chest**.

Land Challenge

Take the left fork at the first track junction to pick up a **Red Toolbox**.

On the green track, take the right fork for another **Red Toolbox**.

Take out three flying fighters on the way.

Ring the Doorbells

Your final leap takes you to a closed arena. Destroy two Iron Equalizers and some minions to take a breather (see Figure 10.10).

You'll need to gather good speed to hit four hanging bells (two low and one from each high jump). This triggers the exit gate. Awesome work!

FIGURE 10.10
Zoom up the curved walls of this arena to grab floating power-ups for extra defense as you take on Iron Equalizers.

Chapter 13: Mayhem at the Market

Uh oh! Lord Stratosfear is very cranky! You're ruining his selfish plans. It's time to make him relinquish the Thunderous Bolt for Mags to use.

First up, **Sharpfin** and his crew are waiting to offer you vehicle upgrades.

Time your dash through the path ahead to avoid lightning bolts.

At the first junction, a **Wish Stone** is on the right ledge, and gold is on the left.

Meteo-Trollogists are waiting to ambush you at the second junction.

A **Live Wire Lock** on the left leads you to a secret room. Move your gremlin from the left to the right, fitting into the grooves of gears to reach the edges.

Guss is inside, hoping to play **Skystones Overdrive**. Pick up a **Reward Object** here and chat with **Persephone** about upgrades.

A room filled with enemies and treasure marks the end of this section.

Sea Star: Destroy the Storm Sequencer

A **Red Toolbox** is underneath the center tower (underwater) where you find two marked arrow paths on this track.

A second **Red Toolbox** is just inside a secret path off the main track.

In the main pool, attack the Storm Sequencer with maximum firepower. Defensive ships with red targets (this means they're about to strike!) will attack you as well. The shields will drop on the Storm Sequencer right before it generates a tidal wave, so use that moment to attack.

Once the force field comes up, the Storm Sequencer is impenetrable. As soon as the smaller fighters are destroyed, it will become active again.

Back on dry land, a Storm Spawner and Bitning Bugs are ready to attack down the path to the right of the Sea Star. Defeat them to reach an **Epic Treasure Chest**.

A foghorn will show you the way across a new series of platforms. There is an **Epic Treasure Chest** on the far-left platform and another foghorn on the far right with a Troll guarding each.

In the garden below, all enemies have to be defeated before the gate will unlock. Walk on the circular platforms to connect gargoyles to the gate gargoyles with green laser beams (shown in Figure 10.11). A **Reward Object** on the left side of the exit gate also unlocks.

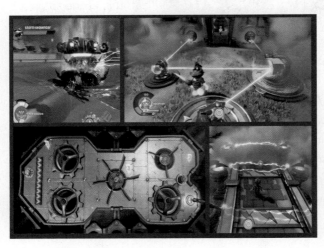

FIGURE 10.11

Laser beam locks can be tricky. First, figure out what the final point of connection needs to be; then work your way backward by spinning platforms.

Chapter 14: Clear Skies Ahead

There's a big storm brewing ahead in the shape of Lord Stratosfear!

An **Elemental Gate** is just through the doors, if you want a practice run!

Land Star: Catch Lord Stratosfear

Chase his windy Highness down the track until you reach the first jump, after which minion fighters join in, as shown in Figure 10.12.

Stratosfear alternately drops lightning orbs and damaging clouds. Swerve to avoid the rolling red mines on the track as you gather gearbits. This is an easy course with few jumps or turns.

Keep Stratosfear in your crosshairs with constant firepower as you drive, and you'll defeat him very quickly.

FIGURE 10.12
Enemy fighters join in quickly. Destroying them won't affect Stratosfear's health, but it will clear the skies so you can focus on him.

Chapter 15: The Land of the Undead

Back at Skylanders Academy, visit Buzz to learn all about the Greeble Dispenser on his Battle Arena for some Super Ninja Commando training. Agent 11 3/5th wants to take you on a run through of the SuperCharged Challenges, which are always open for business now. Mags amps up the Rift Engine at Sharpfin's Pit Station while you have a look around. When you're feeling brave enough to visit the Land of the Undead to rescue Master Eon, go back to talk with Flynn.

Land of the Undead

As soon as Buzz gives you the go-ahead, gather your wits and jump on board—you're off to the Land of the Undead! It seems that Count Moneybone has a rather strange *perspective* on how to keep his prisoners.

Chapter 16: Not as Advertised

Grab some explosives and start your next adventure with a *bang!* You'll have to get used to viewing battle floors upside down and sideways from here on in—it's very confusing. Take your time to figure out new directional controls.

Rescue Master Eon

Blow up the gate as well as the small pipe entrance to the left side of the path to find an **Epic Treasure Chest** inside a cave.

You'll find a **Wish Stone** on the left side of the main path.

Enter the swirling portal at the back of the path for a **Reward Object**.

Blaster Casters guard a second portal to the right side. Chat with Agent Softpaw and then jump inside the portal.

An **Epic Treasure Chest** is just inside, but you'll need dynamite to crack it. Continue through to the next portal, which is laden with dynamite and treasure. Return with dynamite to claim your prize; then continue on to the second portal area. At the back is a land vehicle challenge.

In the first section of the track, a **Red Toolbox** can be found on the left-side hanging ramp after you break through the second chained gate.

The second section of the track is a battle arena. Stay clear of the green spotlights; they draw out minions such as Chop-Hoppers that hold tight onto your vehicle. Blast them off as you drive.

Zoom into the blue portal at the back left to retrieve a barrel of dynamite. Return to the arena and place it near the wall embedded with gearbits to score a **Red Toolbox** hidden underneath (see Figure 10.13).

Return to the portal to grab another barrel of dynamite and blow up the exit gate in the arena. Time to move on!

FIGURE 10.13
You'll need to carry dynamite from one perspective gate to another quite often. Watch the yellow timer bar on the barrel and move quickly!

Chapter 17: Upside Downstairs Overtheres

This is a complicated area with many perspective gates. Try not to get lost! Crossing orange firecracker trails while carrying dynamite creates a colorful, big *bang!* and a shower of coins.

Sharpfin's Pit Crew is waiting at the start to offer you upgrades. Now's the time to improve your sky vehicle, ready for the challenges ahead.

Follow the main path to the left for your first perspective twist. Defeating the guards inside the portal opens two cells. Go to the furthest (top) cell first. Defeat a couple of Blaster Casters and Spin-Offs (which only attack when they stop spinning) to score a **Wish Stone** and some dynamite. Carry the dynamite to the second (lower) cell and blow up the chained **Epic Treasure Chest**. Play a game of **Skystones Overdrive** for fun.

Before you exit the portal, grab one more barrel of dynamite from the top cell and run fast. Drop it at the chained **Epic Treasure Chest** further down the main path on the left side (seriously, run fast!).

On the right side of the same path is a **SuperCharger Gate**. This one is tricky. The switch beside the portal spins the cross-ramp upside down, or right side up. Start right side up and run across the ramp into the top platform. Grab the dynamite (ignore the red targets and alarms; they'll put you off). Dash back across the ramp to the switch outside, spin the ramp upside down, and then cross it to enter the platform underneath. Deposit the dynamite by the **Epic Treasure Chest** on the far side. Once it blows, all alarms stop. Gather top-side treasure before exiting.

Back on the main path, the right-side portal leads to dynamite guarded by Trolls. Grab it and return to blow up the left-side gate.

Sky Star: Help Prisoners Escape

Mabu transport ships are trying to escape, but Moneybone is holding them with grappling hooks! Destroy the fighters (two per ship) to let the Mabu prisoners escape, as shown in Figure 10.14.

Look for red gems to determine which ships need help.

A **Red Toolbox** is floating in the middle of the air arena near a power-up.

Sky Star: Blow Up the Statue

Grab dynamite from the docking station and through the portal to drop it at the statue blocking the ships' escape route.

Return a second time for more dynamite to blow up the **Reward Object** near the portal door. Jump back in your vehicle.

Three more transport ships are caught in tractor beams. Destroy the fighter jets to finish the challenge.

Continue along the main path (avoiding green spotlights) and battle a few Chompies to enter another portal.

Run along the underside of the path to retrieve a **Reward Object**; then return to the perspective gate to follow the top path. Before you follow your tracks above, come back in the direction of the entrance to follow gold coins to an **Epic Treasure Chest**.

Continue along the top path toward the back of the room. Defeat Spot Bite by lunging in for an attack before he gets the chance. Wait for the Spin-Offs to stop spinning before you attack them.

Complete the level with a quick land vehicle challenge. If you get caught in a green spotlight, spikes will pop up on the road.

There's a **Red Toolbox** on a jump, halfway along the track on the right side.

FIGURE 10.14
Destroy the enemy fighters connected to each transport ship and then dock to blow up the gold statue with dynamite.

Chapter 18: Eon's Escape

There are pointy spikes (ouch!) and green spotlights (that summon enemies) all along the road to Eon's tower, so tread very carefully!

An **Elemental Gate** is on the immediate right from where you start.

Sea Star: Destroy Blockage

Destroy the blockages in your sea vehicle for Cora.

A **Red Toolbox** is on the very bottom of the left-side tunnel.

The blockage is to the far right end of the top area.

Take some time to explore this challenge as there are plenty of gearbits to collect. Going through the perspective portal halfway down will change your dive button from up to down.

Beware of exploding mines and water fans that knock you off course.

Back on the land, **Persephone** is on a ledge near the sea challenge. Battle a few little Bonehead Chompies to reach her.

Inside the perspective gate near Persephone are a couple of Spot Bites. They won't attack unless you get caught in their beam. Follow the path across spikes (time your jump!) into a second perspective gate.

Follow the left path for a **Reward Object**.

Follow that same path backward and to the right to defeat a Spot Bite and **Live Wire Lock** (Figure 10.15) for an **Epic Treasure Chest** reward. To defeat the lock, roll the gremlin over the lower red button to release the side barrier to access the top lightning spark. This then releases the lower barrier to access the third lightning spark.

The final path (near the Live Wire Lock) leads to another portal. Take a deep breath—you'll be bombarded with baddies inside. Use the dynamite on the right path through the portal to blow up the gate ahead to score a **Wish Stone**. This gate takes you to the final land challenge.

FIGURE 10.15

Live Wire Locks take a bit of practice. Move the green gremlin around the board with tiny, gentle touches on your controller—a mistake will send you back to the beginning.

Chapter 19: Moneyback Guarantee

It's time to catch Warden Moneybone and put him in his place (jail!). Gear up for a difficult land vehicle challenge ahead!

Land Star: Defeat Moneybone

Warden Moneybone's first attack is to shoot purple energy rings across the floor, which damage your health. It's difficult to avoid these as they reach all the way to the edge, but you can drive through portals into other perspective platforms to avoid them. It's worth taking a bit of damage to keep a constant stream of firepower on Moneybone.

Avoid driving through the flames behind Moneybone as he moves. His laser beams (see Figure 10.16) are deadly, so move fast to keep out of range.

Vehicle fighters will join in midway. If the portals turn red, it means you are trapped inside a perspective gate. All you can do is keep safe and destroy any minions trapped in there with you to earn a green light again.

You can out-run minions through the portals quite easily, but still, focus on Moneybone instead. It will only take a few minutes to defeat him.

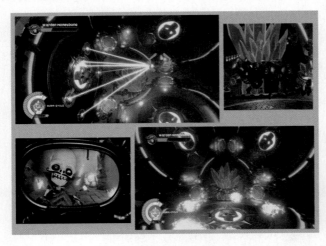

FIGURE 10.16
Moneybone's laser beam attack can be used across platforms, so keep on the move at all times.

Chapter 20: Reunions

Uh oh! The Darkness is alive! All shall fear and obey it, even Kaos! This means gas cloud is planning to conquer every world *in the world!* Back at Skylanders Academy, Master Eon is finally free. He reveals that The Darkness is growing ever more powerful. The Core of Light is the only thing keeping it at bay... for now. Pandergast has new races and challenges available, so check them out and then return to Eon for the next stage of your journey.

Battlebrawl Island

It's time for a rumble in the ring! Your next mission is to enlist the help of a Spell Punk, who has secret knowledge about a magic book.

Chapter 21: Cast a Deadly Spellslamzer

Bubbles offers you some advice on how to get into the arena to find the Spell Punk. Before you go, grab the **Wish Stone** hidden behind some crates in the back right-side corner. There's another **Wish Stone** in the cage beside Frothy on the back-left side of the room.

Pay Frothy 25 gold coins to change the arena element to match your SuperCharger (this will boost your damage in the upcoming fight).

The glowing door to your left leads to a potion master called Shank. Buy a flask of Wake the Dead and take it back into the main room to Crabby, the sleeping crab in front of the elevator. You can also buy some additional potions that increase your stats.

The glowing door to the right takes you to the audience area of the arena (you won't have to fight here, yet). To the right, once you're inside this door, is an **Epic Treasure Chest** with a **Live Wire Lock** on it.

To unlock it, ride the top fan across to the right side, then the middle vent over the center platform, to turn the green button red. Cross again to the right side and let the moving button push you across the lower air vent into the spark.

Up the stairs, the academy crew is waiting with **Persephone**. Pick up a **Reward Object** here and then play a game of **Skystones Overdrive**.

Get into the Arena

Go back through the glowing door to Crabby (you woke him up a bit earlier) and take the elevator to the Colosseum.

Defeat Brimstone and Boulders

Stage 1: Percussion Pounder sends rings of damage across the floor; jump over them while you attack him. Fired-Up Frontman flings Bitning Bugs into the arena; take them out as collateral damage while you attack Pounder.

Stage 2: Frontman uses a flamethrower; attack him from behind as soon as the flames are done. Pounder throws rocks from above; watch for red targets on the ground.

Stage 3: Both hop off the arena floor to throw rocks and Bitning Bugs at you instead. Just keep out of the line of fire.

Stage 4: All in! Both competitors jump back in the ring for a final chaotic showdown. Pick one at a time and keep your attacks constant to win.

Intermission: Attack some bouncing sheep to score coins and food. After your health is full, leave extra food on the arena floor to pick up later.

Defeat the Pirates

Stage 1: Captain Bristlestache and his Pirate Henchmen are up next. The Henchmen can be taken out close range easily enough.

Stage 2: Grinnades are thrown directly at you by Bomb Brawls, so step out of the line of fire each time. The Grinnades explode after a few seconds, so you can either just keep clear of them or step in to take them out yourself first. They won't stop coming though until you destroy the Bomb Brawl itself.

Stage 3: When Captain Bristlestache joins in, give him your full attention. With some solid attacks on your part (attack from behind to avoid his sword), he'll be down in 30 seconds flat.

Intermission: Attack the Food Thief like a piñata and, once full, leave remaining food on the arena floor. You'll need it later during the final fight to restore your health.

Defeat Spellslamzer

Stage 1: Spellslamzer shoots blades directly in front of himself that cause damage, so keep to the side or jump! He has a second attack that shoots a purple gas from his hood to damage enemies. You'll need to move fast to avoid it.

Spell Punks attack you. The last one destroyed in each wave spawns three new Punks. There are different Spell Punks for each element, and their attacks reflect this. Air Punks speed up other Punks, Undead Punks summon Ghastly Greebles, Water Punks throw snowballs, Fire Punks throw fire, Magic Punks turn other Punks invisible, and Life Punks heal their friends.

Stage 2: Spellslamzer transports you to a snowy field where many Spell Punks attack at once. Destroy them before they attack and prioritize Life Punks and Undead Punks to minimize their numbers.

Stage 3: Back at the arena, Spellslamzer has a new explosive attack that causes damage over a bigger area. You'll see target marks on the floor so you know which spots to avoid (see Figure 10.17). Never get directly in front of him or you'll score big damage from the hood attack. More Spell Punks appear, and the final one destroyed in each wave spawns another four.

FIGURE 10.17

A series of arena battles brings you ever closer to defeating Spellslamzer—and winning the information you need to search the Spell Punk Library.

Chapter 22: Book Report

No one is particularly impressed with Spellslamzer, but he gives the Mabu crew the information they need to get into the Spell Punk Library. Ari opens the Academy Store, which has an ever-changing range of hats, Skystones Overdrive cards, and trinkets to buy. Go visit him and then head back to Eon.

The Spell Punk Library

Eon is sure that finding a special book is the key to ending Kaos' reign and the devastating power of The Darkness. Everyone is joining in this mission!

Chapter 23: The Spell Punk Library

This is no ordinary library—the books come alive! Explore the area for treasure before you explore Cali's book. Inside the books, you will be trapped in a two-dimensional battleground, as illustrated in Figure 10.18. Battles here are a bit easier to manage, but rewards are harder to recognize.

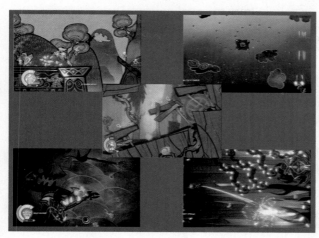

FIGURE 10.18

Each book tells a unique story with familiar enemies and rewards. Pay attention to the stories, though; there are clues on new challenges ahead.

Big Book of Secrets: Investigate the Spell Punk Library

Shift the bookcase near **Persephone** to reveal treasure and a Mabu called Poppy, who wants to play **Skystones Overdrive** with you.

Push the bookcase near Mags to reveal a hidden **Reward Object**.

Jump on chairs to reach hidden food and treasure on top of furniture.

A **Wish Stone** is floating on the bookshelf above Hugo (he's on a ladder).

A **Reward Object** is on a circular platform above Flynn (use the chair).

Push the bookcase behind Flynn to find an **Epic Treasure Chest** with a **Live Wire Lock**. To unlock it, hit the top right-side green button to turn off the lower-right fan and collect two sparks. Hit the center right-side green button to turn off the lower-left fan. Then hit the lower-left green button to turn off the top-left fan and collect the final spark.

Push the bookcase behind Sharpfin to find a hidden **Wish Stone**.

Above the **SuperCharger Gate** you'll find treasure and another book. Play the story mini-game to score a **Wish Stone** and an **Epic Treasure Chest** before they are destroyed by a spiked rolling machine.

An open book near Persephone has a short challenge. Destroy the Life Spell Punk that is healing bigger enemies and defeat some fire and water Spell Punks. Your reward is an **Epic Treasure Chest**.

Talk to Cali

The ancients used Rift Engines to explore worlds—but The Darkness was unleashed!

Book 1: The Darkness—Get to the Temple

First up, grab the pile of treasure behind you up a small hill. Destroy any crates you find on your journey to reveal more treasure.

Cross the first platforms and then drop down following a line of gold coins to find a **Reward Object**.

Baddies appear with a sword and shield but are easy to defeat with a few well-placed attacks. Unless you see coins trailing down, try not to fall.

Time your jump onto flipping platforms to land as soon as they flip so that you have the longest time left to cross them and jump again.

Three flipping platforms lead you back the way you came but a level higher, where you'll find a **Reward Object**.

Spell Punks aid the baddies. If you see a (green) Life Spell Punk, take it out first to stop it healing them. Then deal with the big guys.

An **Epic Treasure Chest** is under the boxes to the left side of a trail of coins trailing downward from more flipping platforms.

Sky Star: Book 2: Charge of the First Light Squadron—Destroy the Mothership

Destroy the large blue crosses to reveal a **Red Toolbox** and the smaller blue crosses to reveal power-ups; then grab them before they disappear off the screen.

Small planes and larger fighters that fire red missiles are easy to destroy if you keep a steady stream of firepower on them (Stealth Stinger is good for this) and move into their vulnerable spots to attack. Some attack horizontally and some vertically, so adjust your angle to keep out of the line of fire.

The Mothership is more difficult to destroy. It has many missiles and shoots lightning from its base. Dodge the missiles by zipping from one side to the other in gaps, and attack the Mothership as soon as the lightning clears.

Book 3: The Ancients Plan—Reach Ancient's Peak

Jump off the end of the wooden ramp and head back toward the start (underneath) to find a **Reward Object**.

Avoid the purple spiky weapons; you can't destroy them.

Jump onto a higher platform ahead to reach a **Wish Stone**.

Continue hopping on lower platforms until you reach the right-side purple spiky weapon at the end; then jump up the platforms and head left again for another **Reward Object** hidden under an alcove.

An **Epic Treasure Chest** is hidden below a trail of gold coins on the bottom-left side of the main path. A bounce pad will take you back up to the top platform.

Sea Star: Book 4: The Hydra—Get to the Bottom

Avoid mines in the first part of the story; then swim away from the multiheaded hydra monster at the end of the story as fast as possible.

There are multiple power-ups on this course.

Find a **Red Toolbox** at the far-right side near the end of the challenge. It's on the bottom of the sea floor.

Land Star: Book 5: The Core of Light—Defeat the Darkness

Hugo has the final story book. Zoom along the track behind The Darkness, zipping from side to side to avoid being hit with the laser beams and black clouds that shoot out from behind it. This feels like a sign of things to come!

Grab power-ups and gearbits on your way through, but don't go out of your way for them. As soon as The Darkness reaches the Core of Light, this story ends.

Chapter 24: Feathered Friends

What an amazing library! Back at Skylanders Academy, Hugo is off to do some research on how to track down Pomfrey LeFuzzBottom to learn more about how to defeat The Darkness. Have a chat with Master Eon about how Portal Master ranks work. Tessa and her giant phoenix, Whiskers, arrive to let you know that Woodburrow has been overrun by Kaos and The Darkness. Everyone has evacuated, so she has come to Skylanders Academy to join the fight. Find Flynn when you're ready to fly to Gadfly Glades.

Gadfly Glades

Professor LeFuzzBottom has some important information about how to defeat The Darkness. No one has seen him in years, but Hugo has tracked him down to Gadfly Glades, where the professor was planning to retire. Prepare for a new adventure of miniscule proportions as you track him down.

Chapter 25: A Teensy Problem

Of course, there's a very *small* problem. Honey, she shrunk... the Skylander?

Shrunk Down to Size

A trap on the top left of where you start has a couple of enemies—Flea Jumper and Cootie Trap. They're super easy to beat.

Ignore that crazy Mabu with the magnifying glass and jump off the path to your immediate right to claim a **Wish Stone** and a **Reward Object**.

Sea Vehicle Challenge:

A **Red Toolbox** is in the hollow tree trunk (looks like a cylinder) on the right side of where you begin. Head to the bottom right of the underwater channel to pick it up (see Figure 10.19), but beware of spiky pufferfish.

At the back on the left land port is some treasure. At the back on the right land port is a **Reward Object** atop some bouncy mushrooms.

Jump in your land vehicle to take out all the bugs in an arena to open the gate. A **Red Toolbox** is on a ledge opposite the gate.

A Bunch of Barrels

Speed through the garden. A **Red Toolbox** is on a ledge to the left side of the giant rabbit.

Take the boost jump into an arena to battle many bug enemies. Keep away from the shadow on the ground—that's a giant foot ready to stomp you!

As soon as the back boost gate opens, you're free!

FIGURE 10.19

It's easy to miss the tree trunk leading to the underwater pond challenge; look for a yellow glowing cylinder to score another Red Toolbox.

Chapter 26: Fungi Funhouse

That lunatic collector won't hand over the Professor unless you pass some challenges first. Get ready to bounce into trouble!

Before you bounce up the giant mushrooms, veer right to a golden door with **Persephone** inside. Try a **Live Wire Lock** to score an **Epic Treasure Chest**. To access the sparks, hit the green button via the spinning platforms; work your way around the board counterclockwise to pick up the first and second sparks, then clockwise to reach the third. Counterclockwise again around the platforms gets you back to the ignition.

An **Elemental Gate** is at the top of the mushrooms on the main path.

On the left side of the second watermelon is a **Reward Object**.

On the right side of the Sea Star is a high cave with a **Reward Object** and a game of **Skystones Overdrive** with The Pillar.

Above this cave (bounce on mushrooms) is an **Epic Treasure Chest**.

Defeat a few bugs for a **Random Reward** that appears near the cave.

An **Epic Treasure Chest** is on high land near a giant gardening trowel.

A **Wish Stone** and **Epic Treasure Chest** are inside a **SuperCharger Gate**, but you'll have to battle bugs to claim them.

Sea Star: Save the Twitterpillars

Five twitterpillars are stranded, floating on clover in the water. Four are in plain sight (in three pond sections) and one is hidden in a small cave.

A **Red Toolbox** is behind the cave in the first (biggest) pond.

Beat the Bee

Rev up the engine, it's time to take your land vehicle for a spin! Zoom through a short run full of gearbits (including an orange gearbit on a sheep's head!) to land in the beehive (see Figure 10.20).

Lots of bees attack, but it's the Queen Bee you must defeat to win a **Red Toolbox**. Once all insects are destroyed, the exit gate will open.

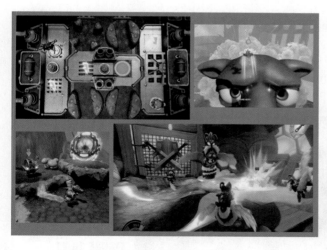

FIGURE 10.20

That crazy Mabu collector is sending you on a wild-goose chase (or sheep chase?!) to win Professor LeFuzzBottom's freedom back.

Chapter 27: Waterdrop Way

You're on the home stretch to rescue Professor Pomfrey LeFuzzBottom from spending the rest of his life in a jar. It's time to pick up some speed!

Sharpfin and **Persephone** are here to greet you. Right at the start on your right side is a **Reward Object** on a low ledge.

A **Wish Stone** is on a tall flower on the left side of the path. Jump off the right side of the path onto a high bouncing mushroom; then land on the flower next to the one with the Wish Stone. Jump across to claim it.

Sky Star: Shut Off the Water

Flooded Franny needs some help. Destroy four faucets in the garden to stop the twitterpillar village from washing away, as shown in Figure 10.21.

Two **Red Toolboxes** are close to the ground in the corners of the veggie patch.

Land at the two flowerpots with Sky Star docks to pick up two **Reward Objects**.

When you are done, pick up a **Wish Stone** next to Franny on a white flower. Jump up the flowers (head right) to the top of the pot near Franny to collect treasure and battle some bugs. Drop down the other side of the pot for an **Epic Treasure Chest**.

Chat with Wheeler and Heeler about the Land Star Challenge.

Land Star: Rescue Pomfrey

The great foot shadow is back!

This is a long fight in a small arena, so keep moving! Big bugs and other enemies are after you in full force, so keep your finger on the ammo at all times. Remember—you're tiny now, so don't get underfoot!

A vehicle with speed and a tight turning circle (such as Burn Cycle) is good here. Fling up the side of walls near the gate to pick up defensive shields and power-ups as you progress—they'll make a big difference.

As soon as all enemies are defeated, the gate opens. Head through it to teach that bad-tempered, giant-footed collector a lesson!

FIGURE 10.21

Before you destroy the leaky faucets, take a quick spin through carrot-tops and turnips to pluck out some treasure.

Cap'n Cluck's Chicken HQ

The undeniably regal Lord Kaos has decided to take over not just Skylands, but the whole universe! Sheesh! Master Eon has some advice that might help. You'll need to gather a Kolossal Kernel from Cap'n Cluck to battle the Titans in the Monstrous Isles. You're up for a BIG challenge ahead!

Chapter 28: Cap'n Cluck's Chicken HQ

At Skylanders Academy, Professor LeFuzzBottom reveals that you'll need to reclaim the missing piece of the Core of Light, called the Eye of the Ancients, to create a weapon to banish The Darkness. And it seems poor Glumshanks needs some career advice.

Chapter 29: Fowl Play

There's a revolution taking over Chicken HQ! Scooter reveals that the chicken feed is growing and shrinking chickens. Anything that glows purple can be grown or shrunk as you move through this area. Use this ability to help you get through obstacles.

Expand the bag of chicken feed next to Scooter to lower a bridge.

An **Epic Treasure Chest** is hidden behind a rock next to the mechanical chickens. (Expand the acorns that the mechanical chickens are holding to crush them.)

At the coop, expand chicken feed bags to roll a chicken through (it will drop into the outside bucket), which opens the gate, like in Figure 10.22.

You'll end up in a cage fight with Hammerhead and some mechanical chickens. Shrink your enemies and grow the weapons so they blow up the bad guys. You'll soon fall through a chute to a new area underneath. Wiggle around to catch coins as you fall.

FIGURE 10.22

Chicken coop puzzles are all about timing. Practice a few times so you can expand the purple bag at just the right moment to send a chicken flying.

Chapter 30: Running Afowl

Begin to the right side of your landing place to open an **Epic Treasure Chest** behind a **Live Wire Lock**. To open the lock, collect the top-left spark first because it's a clear run. For both other sparks, ride the spinning platform by standing on the button and hopping off as it hits the right position (the platform will stop turning when you get off the button).

Sea Star: Drop Feed in Water Supply

Buckley needs you to pour the chicken feed into the water supply to shrink and grow hens.

Growing the purple water pump creates a spout of water you can ride between sections of the water supply.

Enter the giant tube in the second water pool to score a **Red Toolbox**.

Play a mini-game, Break the Barrels, by hitting the flag in the third pool.

Shrink the purple water pump at the back of the third pool to turn off the jets. Then dive up the center water channel (follow the gearbits).

Jump onto land in the fourth pool, cross crates to collect treasure, and grow the purple pump. Jump up the crates again and then shrink the pump on the top deck. Expand the final pump and watch that chicken feed fly! Cross the water using the chicken feed bucket as a step.

Grab a **Red Toolbox** off the high jump on the right side of the ride home.

Shrink the giant chicken beside Buckley to find a **Reward Object**.

Shrink all giant chickens for coin rewards along the path. Follow the ramps above the torpedo chickens for an **Epic Treasure Chest**.

Defeat a few mechanical chickens (grow their acorns) to score an **Epic Treasure Chest** on the circular egg platform. A **Reward Object** is on the platform behind it.

At the chicken coop behind the egg platform, hit the purple feedbag with your shrink attack three times to fling a chicken over the arrow into a feed bucket. The gate will open. Dodge the chicken torpedoes to reach Rusty.

Land Star: Chicken Shoot

Take it slow as you roll giant chickens into vacuum shoots to open gates, as shown in Figure 10.23. There's no trick to this. Let the buzzing bulbs help you move the chickens around, but don't get caught in them yourself.

FIGURE 10.23

If you roll a puffed-up chicken close to the red-and-white-striped vent, the air vacuum will suck it in without your help. Take it easy and don't overshoot your mark, or your chicken will bounce away instead.

Chapter 31: Cuckoo's Nest

It's chicken time! Take to the skies and rustle a few feathers. You're getting closer to finding that Kolossal Kernel.

Reach a **Wish Stone** on the shed by jumping onto giant buckets.

Grow the purple feedbag to raise platforms that bridge to the main path.

Sky Star: Defeat CockadoodleDoom

CockadoodleDoom shoots eggs at you that do a small amount of damage, as shown in Figure 10.24. Follow him to the main arena; keep zigzagging ahead to avoid getting egg on your face!

FIGURE 10.24

Avoiding eggs is pretty easy in such a large arena, but you'll need to get on his grill and destroy those Shield Ships to fry CockadoodleDoom.

A **Red Toolbox** is on the left side of the main arena.

He calls in reinforcements when his health gets low. The big guy can't be damaged while the Shield Ships are protecting him, so you'll have to destroy pairs of these ships to make him vulnerable again. Fighter ships can damage you but leave CockadoodleDoom exposed, so take the opportunity to blast him whenever you knock his force field out.

Grab any balloon power-ups you see to boost your performance.

Back on land, catch a chicken in the box below the see-saw to open the exit gate. **Sharpfin** is waiting behind this puzzle.

To the right of the chicken puzzle, use the purple feedbag to raise a spinning platform bridge. It leads to a **SuperCharger Gate**. Expand, then bounce on enemies to get to higher platforms. When you reach the chicken coop, expand an enemy as it hits the base of the ramp. Then expand a chicken as it rolls down the ramp so it bounces off the enemy and lands in the feed bucket. Your reward is an **Epic Treasure Chest**.

Backtrack to your left on the main path across new, smaller platforms for another **Epic Treasure Chest**.

Continue along the main path to find enemies waiting. Use your shrink/grow weapon on all of them. The mechanical chickens collapse under the weight of giant acorns, Hammerheads hilariously shrink their heads to a miniscule size, and other enemies become bite-sized and easy to defeat.

Grow the purple feedbag hanging at the arena and then jump on new platforms behind you to grab a **Reward Object** and **Wish Stone** and find a **Skystones Overdrive** player.

At the final chicken coop, hit the left feedbag once, then the right once, then back to the left once, to catch a chicken in the bucket and lower the gate. Jump in your land vehicle, ready to fry Cap'n Cluck once and for all.

Chapter 32: Big Boss Cluck

In this land arena, Cap'n Cluck is overseeing a tricky challenge you have to complete. As you succeed, his health decreases. You'll be given one chicken at a time, which you need to push gently into one of three air vacuums (see Figure 10.25). This starts off easy, but you're soon dodging enemy fire from other vehicles on the track, as well as eggs thrown by Cap'n Cluck from his plane above you.

Keep a cool head and focus only on moving the chickens close to the air vacuum so they can be sucked up. It's unlikely that you'll sustain enough damage to lose your SuperCharger from enemy fire if you're moving. There are seven or eight sheep to deal with, then this challenge is deep-dished.

FIGURE 10.25

Puffed-up chickens are light, like balloons, so be gentle knocking them around.

Monstrous Isles

Mags has popped, percolated, and lightly salted the Kolossal Kernel back at Skylanders Academy! That's a big piece of popcorn!

Chapter 33: Monstrous Isles

Visit Hugo and Glumshanks at the Wishing Well to try it out. Head back to Flynn to begin your search for the Eye of the Ancients.

Chapter 34: The Last Resort

Trolls are guarding the Titans and do their bidding at any cost—prepare to defend yourself! These Titans are huge, as you can see in Figure 10.26, so you'll need huge help to defeat them. Eat the Kolossal Kernel—you're in for a BIG surprise, Skylander!

To your right is a small island building with a **Reward Object** inside.

Smash up the village and grab heaps of treasure.

Ride the lava vent in front of the mountain to grab extra treasure.

At the back of the mountain is a path with a **Wish Stone**.

Jump in your land vehicle for a super-sized ride. A **Red Toolbox** is halfway up the right-side wall about five seconds in (before the arch).

FIGURE 10.26

You've suddenly got very big shoes to fill, Skylander! Stomp, smash, and squish your way through the next few chapters!

Chapter 35: Basalt Basin

Have you ever wanted to jump on a giant sandcastle or leap tall buildings in a single bound? Now's your chance, Skylander! The world is at your feet!

Pick up the **Wish Stone** under a small house to your right.

Stomp across another village, wreaking havoc as you go.

Sky Star: Destroy Clam Bunkers

A **Red Toolbox** is directly ahead of your starting place, hiding behind a large stone on a small island.

A **Red Toolbox** is on an outlying island with two medium-sized stones.

A flag mini-game is under an arch on the big, central island. To win, collect five barrels floating around the same island (one is on top of a high arch).

Destroy 12 Clam Bunkers to stop Trolls stealing giant bird eggs to feed to the Pterashark (see Figure 10.27). This isn't too tricky, but you'll get a few enemy fighters on your tail, so keep on the move to be rid of them. Look for power-ups floating near islands to improve your defenses.

Battle the Pterashark

Stage 1: The Pterashark has three attacks. First, it disappears under the ground. A shark fin slides along the surface, damaging anything in its path. Follow its trajectory, so that when it resurfaces (slightly stunned and vulnerable) you can attack it straight away from behind.

Stage 2: Second, it shoots boulders from its mouth. These are slow and easy to avoid (don't stand directly in front of its mouth when you know these are coming).

Stage 3: Finally, it jumps three times, and each time it slams down on the earth causing a shockwave (jump over these shockwaves to avoid damage and then attack again while it's vulnerable).

Stage 4: These three attacks are repeated again and again, until you wear the Pterashark's health down. There's a burger stand in front of the temple. Smash it up for sustenance on the go.

Once the Pterashark is gone, ride the steam vent in the temple to the roof for treasure and the best **Epic Treasure Chest** you've ever seen.

On the path to the left of the temple is a movable block. Push it backward and then jump up to the raised area. Head right to three movable blocks. Shift them against the right-side cliff so you can jump up and claim the **Epic Treasure Chest** up top.

Rearrange the three blocks again to reach the **Reward Object** atop the left-side cliff.

Head for the land challenge gate, stomping all the way! Pick up the **Red Toolbox** in the center of the track after lava bursts in the initial takeoff.

FIGURE 10.27

Giant birds will be jumping for joy after you stop the Trolls stealing their eggs to feed to the slobbering Pterashark. His bounce is far worse than his bite!

Chapter 36: Exclusive Shores

The Squid Titan is a little bit... fancy, and not willing to help you at all. You'll have to chase her into the depths of the pool for the help you need.

First up, locate the **Epic Treasure Chest** to the right side of Beachcomber's lake. It has a **Live Wire Lock** on it. To unlock it, grab the spark on the center spinner; then cautiously move onto the right side spinning platform and down into the lower ramp to pick up the second spark. Cross the two left-side spinners (carefully!) to reach the third spark. Head back to the center spinner to reach the ignition on the right.

Sea Star: Catch Beachcomber

Follow the haughty squid down a vertical tunnel collecting gearbits as you go, as shown in Figure 10.28. Squid arms poke through the walls of the tunnel to cause damage. Try to navigate around them as best you can. Little floating crustaceans will hit you and cause damage, as will the hot water vents that erupt every so often.

A **Red Toolbox** is hidden in a high alcove, above a hot water vent, midway along the first horizontal stretch.

A **Red Toolbox** is on a ledge in front of a hot water vent, not far from the beginning of the second horizontal stretch.

Grab any power-ups you see to boost your chance of making it through!

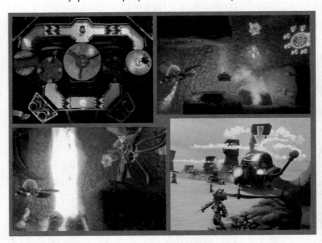

FIGURE 10.28
It's almost impossible not to get damage in this challenge because the tunnel is crowded with crustaceans, hot water vents, and Beachcomber's squid arms. Just do your best!

Chapter 37: Titanopolis

It's time to clean up the beaches, beginning with some cranky crustaceans that are larger than life!

Fight Beachcomber

Beachcomber has a few strong attacks. Follow her pattern of movements to anticipate them and stay a step ahead. Attack her at any opportunity.

Stage 1: Her first attack is to lunge forward twice. She'll turn red first, so you can anticipate this and jump aside.

Stage 2: Her second attack is to disappear underwater and poke tentacles up through the ground at you. Look for the red targets on the ground and keep moving.

Stage 3: Beachcomber will spin with four tentacles outstretched; you'll need to jump these. Stay close to the center where the tentacles are thinner. Keep your firepower constant and you'll wear her down between attacks.

On the left-side village of the first bridge is an upgrade statue. Jump on the lava vent at the end of this area for a **Wish Stone**.

To the right of the next lake are an **Elemental Gate** and a food stand. Jump on the lava vent at the beginning to reach a higher plateau with a SuperCharger Gate.

SuperCharger Gate: Push over blocks to form a bridge ahead. A single block can be moved to the left. Another pile of four blocks on the left-side platform can be pushed back, then right and then front, to form another bridge (look for the floating coins to show where the bridge should fall). On the right-side building, push both the single block and then the pile of four blocks to the left-side building, across the bridge (see Figure 10.29).

FIGURE 10.29

Moving bridges into the right position takes a bit of shuffling. Use a crate on an opposite corner as a blockage so that the bridge stops midway.

Shuffle the blocks around so that they are in opposite corners. You need to use the smaller block as a "stop" to allow the bigger pile to finish in the center of the row. Then it can be used as a bridge off the left of the platform. There's an **Epic Treasure Chest** here for you. Continue up onto the higher area using the single block as a step. Repeat the block puzzle to form a new bridge reaching the back platform to claim a **Reward Object**.

Land Star: Destroy Sandcastles

Pick up a **Red Toolbox** in the second section of sandcastles on the furthest right at the edge of town.

Destroy three large sandcastles that each block the way to the next section of land. Once these are destroyed, use them as boost jumps. You can shoot fighter jets and artillery towers if you like, but it's not necessary to get through.

Defeat Thundertow

Now, this is a big fight (but with a casual, laid-back attitude)! Ultracool Thundertow jumps (he curls over first) and then slams straight into you, causing big damage. When he bends, jump to the side. He will most often come after you with a double punch—but the good news is, both of his attacks are pretty sloppy. If you stay ahead, he'll mostly miss you!

The final attack Thundertow has is a rain of green lightning that surrounds you. If you get stuck in one of these as he holds you in place, your health will quickly deplete. Keep out of range if you see red targets on the ground (lightning will strike in these spots). As soon as the skies are clear again, attack him from behind or the side. Stay nimble, Skylander, and this lobster will be quickly foiled!

Ridepocalypse Demo Derby

The Core of Light has been completely destroyed and poor Glumshanks is missing in action! Help Mags out in the Engine Room by moving blocks to reconnect the engine power; then visit Sharpfin to rev things up at the derby.

Chapter 38: Ridepocalypse Demo Derby

It's show time! Get your battle gear on, Skylander. The Demo Derby is a dirty fight on wheels, not for the faint-hearted!

Chapter 39: Win, Lose or Glumshanks

There's plenty of treasure around the arena, if you're up for a battle of wits! Then put your thinking cap aside and prepare for a battle of fists and fun against some mechanical bruisers in the ring (shown in Figure 10.30). Glumshanks is counting on you, Skylander!

Find a **SuperCharger Gate** to the left of your starting place. Jump down the coins on your right to retrieve a **Wish Stone** on the high rocks.

Defeat Claws, Slick, and Scrag in successive games of **Skystones Overdrive** to score a **Wish Stone**, **Reward Object**, and **Epic Treasure Chest**.

Near **Sharpfin**'s Pit Crew is a shed with an **Epic Treasure Chest** and
Live Wire Lock. Hit the top right-side red button to spin the lower-
right platform. Grab the first and second spark. Use the third platform
button (jump off at the last second) to reach the third spark.

On the rooftops above **Persephone** is a **Reward Object**.

Land Star: Defeat the Enemies

The Chew Crew: Smaller enemies on wheels and wings bombard you.
Grab a **Magic Item** from one of the small jumps on either side of the
arena for extra defense. If you drive over the yellow button in the center,
damaging spikes shoot up from the floor.

Dread Roller: This guy has some serious armor and is surprisingly fast. He
shoots cannon balls and a red laser beam. The laser is narrow and easy
to avoid, but not so for the cannons. Keep on the move and attack from
behind. If Dread Roller is over the spike holes, smash that yellow button.

Turbo Teeth: This little guy is pretty slow but has a contingent of minions to help him out. Use the boost pad under an overhang to change
positions if you're under heavy fire, and jump off the cliff to pick up a
Magic Item. Ignore the minions and focus constant firepower on Turbo
Teeth from different angles to keep him turning to catch up.

Wreck O' Saurus: Be careful of the bombs dropped by this monster
truck—you can't damage them but they'll definitely damage you! He
has a red laser beam to avoid. He can spin and roll deadly fast, so this
is a quick fight. Use the two boost ramps at the back of the arena to
change position and smash into him when he becomes invincible, so he
loses his shield. Then, go crazy on the ammo to keep him quiet.

FIGURE 10.30

Fight tooth and
claw against metal
jaw when you take
to the ring to save
poor Glumshanks
from being sold to
the highest bidder!

Vault of the Ancients

Glumshanks is saved! Not only that, but he has important news. The Dark Rift Engine is hidden away and heavily protected in the Vault of the Ancients. This mysterious machine may just be the clue to sending The Darkness back where it came from. Chat with Flynn to track it down.

Chapter 40: Vault of the Ancients

Uh oh, Flynn is not happy at having to travel to the dangerous Vault of the Ancients. He's staging a silent protest, except, well... without the silence!

Chapter 41: Whispering Wilds

Pluck, the last of the Watch Wraiths, triggers the first gift of the ancients. Use your controller to attract objects, just like a magnet. This gives you a blue glow. You'll use this ability a lot during the next few chapters, so try it out by switching the magnet on and off to draw treasure out of trees, pull the bridge out, and open the gate.

Land Star: Restore Sentry Statues

To progress through this challenge, find missing heads (each head is broken into two parts) for the two statues and return them, as shown in Figure 10.31. Enemy vehicles will attack as you search.

Beware of the blue homing missiles, as they'll damage your health quite badly. Knock the culprits out with a well-placed long-range attack as soon as you enter each area so you don't have to keep dodging them as you search.

Area One: The first statue head is near a small building on the right of the course. There is also an orange gearbit near this building that will spawn more gearbits to collect (for a brief time). The second statue head is at the far back of the area near a stone wall surrounded by stairs.

Area Two: A **Red Toolbox** is on the right side as you enter, under a tree. Two statue heads are near the back gate. A boost pad in the back-left corner will allow you to access a third area.

Area Three: Take down the enemy vehicles and then grab the first statue head on a pillar to the left. A little further along is a **Red Toolbox** (left) and another statue head (right). Take a final boost jump back to Area Two to fix the statue and open the gate.

Open the giant doors near Pluck by using your magnet switch to pull the lever along the floor track and draw the bridge toward you.

FIGURE 10.31
Gather the statue heads to return them to their former glory—and return you to your mission in search of the Rift Engine!

Chapter 42: Riftward Road

The second gift of the ancients is the gift of repelling objects away from you. This gives you a pink glow. You can now switch between pushing and pulling objects using your controller. To attract treasure, use your "pull" ability (blue glow). To push objects away from you (opening doors and such), use the "push" ability (pink glow).

Ascend the staircase behind your starting place to find a **Reward Object**.

Push open doors and drop bridges and walkways using your "push" ability.

Across some platforms to the left of the main path is an **Epic Treasure Chest**.

The next left-side platforms off the main path have another **Epic Treasure Chest**, this time with a **Live Wire Lock**. To unlock it, head downward through the spinning gears and then left into the wedge between spinning light bulbs to pick up your first spark. As soon as a row of light bulbs is out of the way, hit the red button they spin over. This drops the barrier to the top right of your starting point. Take the top right-side red button to get back to the start and then collect sparks 2 and 3.

Persephone is waiting on a small platform opposite the Live Wire Lock.

A **Wish Stone** is on a curved bridge to the left side of the main path. Follow it to the end and then jump onto a platform under enemy fire to collect a **Reward Object**.

Backtrack to the left and cross the magnetic bridges again to find Pluck waiting at a sky challenge.

Sky Star: Ring the Chimes

Area One: Shoot or drive through long, hanging chimes to bring the Watch Wraiths back to life, as shown in Figure 10.32. This is a slow, scenic challenge, flying through cliffs over lakes. Attract gearbits and chimes using your magnet ability. Repel floating bombs.

A **Red Toolbox** is tricky to find; it is at the very top of a huge mountain that splits into three arches underneath. Fly high above the chimes to reach it.

Area Two: Up in the open air, small groups of fighters attack you. There are no chimes here, but plenty of gearbits to collect with your magnet. Finally, you're back in Area One with enemy fighters *and* floating bombs to contend with. Keep searching out those chimes—you're nearly done.

A skirmish is awaiting you when you step out of your air vehicle. Gather treasure as you continue through the vault and have a game of **Skystones Overdrive** with a sleepy Wraith.

On high platforms opposite the Skystones table is an **Epic Treasure Chest**.

Use your magnet switch to spin the end walkway to reach a **Wish Stone**.

Use your magnet to lead each of the three spheres in the end puzzle to their circular groove. Focus on one sphere at a time. Once in place, they don't move.

Land Challenge: Repel the land mines and attract the gearbits. The attract (blue) switch will create bridges over mined areas.

A **Red Toolbox** is in the center of the track, just after the first boost pad.

You finish in an arena. Use your magnet to repel or attract the giant wrecking ball hanging from the center to ring each of the six hanging chimes.

Drive behind the chimes with a blue magnet to hit the four closest to the exit. Drive behind the ball and push it toward the outer two chimes for a bit more momentum.

FIGURE 10.32

Every time you hit a chime, it's music to the Watch Wraiths' ears! Wake the sleeping guardians by clanging as many chimes as you can.

Chapter 43: Slumbering Spires

Does your SuperCharger have a magnetic personality? You'll need every ounce of it for these new challenges!

Head left immediately down some stairs near **Persephone** to pick up an **Epic Treasure Chest**. There is also an **Elemental Gate** here.

Use your magnets to spin the Energy Guardian villains around and attack their backs (their front shield is invulnerable). To move around in this chapter, you'll need to pull blocks in and out to create steps.

At the top-left side of the main platform is a **SuperCharger Gate**.

On either side of the puzzle within this gate is a glowing fan on the floor that allows you to float onto a high tower to collect treasure. Pull the sphere in the track on the floor to the left and loot the high tower by climbing blocks that move in and out. At the top of the left tower are a **Reward Object** and a switch. Repel the switch into place to shift the outer door of the central platform down below; then jump down.

At the top of the right-side platform are more treasure and another switch. This switch shifts the inner gate for the central platform. Jump down to claim your prize of an **Epic Treasure Chest**.

Back in the main area, you'll find **Sharpfin**'s Pit Crew.

Sea Star: Power the Core

In this area, using magnets to repel mines and attract gearbits is, again, your main challenge. The machinery in this chapter is composed of giant screws with mechanical arms at the top (see Figure 10.33). Push or pull the arms (one at a time) to wind them higher or lower so they latch on to their side counterparts.

Area One: Right at the start, dive under (or jump over) some crystals on the right wall to find a **Red Toolbox** in a tiny alcove.

Area Two: This pool has enemy ships and mines. Switch on your repellant and go crazy with the firepower. You can pick up gearbits when they are gone and the gate drops.

Area Three: Ride the cascades with your "pull" to grab gearbits; then hit the "push" at the base to repel mines. There are two more mechanical arm screws here. Once they are in place, another gate drops.

Area Four: This is a closed pool with plenty of mines and enemies. Forget the gearbits and go hard on the ammo. The final gate drops when all enemies are down.

Area Five: The final pool has enemies, three mechanical arms, and a **Red Toolbox** on a crystal island to the right. Each time you fix a set of mechanical arms, new enemies arrive. Take time to clear the pool before you keep working. Nearly done, Skylander!

Back on dry land, there are a couple of additional areas to visit.

Ride the magnetic block to the right of Pluck up to a higher platform. Switch the air vents to ride the breeze upward. Be prepared for a fight at the top of the tower against some Energy Guardians.

Ride the air current across and then lower a ramp to a third tower to continue fighting. After the fight, search for a hidden staircase on the left side behind a Watch Wraith and jump off the end for a **Wish Stone**. Reverse the air current to float back up.

Head right and ride a series of air vents up and down to find another **Wish Stone**, an **Epic Treasure Chest**, and a **Reward Object**. Pluck is waiting for you on the roof with a land vehicle puzzle.

First, destroy all enemies that appear. This unlocks the floor puzzle. Next, push or pull each of the three spheres (focus on one at a time) from the floor track up into its corresponding wall holder. The Rift Engine is revving and ready to go!

FIGURE 10.33
Use your fancy new powers of repelling and attracting to shift objects, open gates and doors, spin mechanical arms, and draw in treasure from afar.

The Bandit Train

The giant, glowing Rift Engine is back at Skylanders Academy, and Buzz isn't too happy about it. Stakes are high, and that Sky Eater is getting more savage by the minute!

Chapter 44: Aerial Ambush

Oh no! The Academy is under attack! Take five Pirate Henchmen down with a quick *Smash! Bang! Pow!* to clear the deck. Great work! But one of the crew has been kidnapped. This can't be good. It's time to track down the dastardly Sky Bandits and save poor Mags!

Chapter 45: Highway Robbery

Grab the **Reward Object** on the platform behind Flynn before you head inside the caboose. Check each carriage thoroughly for treasure before you move on; this is a one-way trip.

Carriage 2: Use the key floating midway to open the exit door.

Carriage 3: Reconnect four blocks to start the engine. The two movable blocks need to be next to each other, connected to the light bulb.

Carriage 4: A battle with Pirate Henchmen awaits you! Be prepared for a dozen scathed critters, with a mean right hook. One of them is carrying a key. When they are all defeated and you have the key, use the door.

Carriage 5: A spinning block with coins is halfway along. Jump off and on to collect them all. Use the bounce block at the end to leap up and backtrack on the outside roof to score an **Epic Treasure Chest**. Drop through the hole in the roof into the next carriage.

Carriage 6: This carriage has more henchmen and a Brawlrus with a key. Be careful smashing (there's a hidden **Wish Stone**); some of the boxes hold Grinnades. Another **Wish Stone** is behind you in the entrance walkway.

Carriage 7: Keep on your toes! As you reach the halfway point on this walkway, a pirate ship begins to shoot cannon balls through the carriage wall (see Figure 10.34). Use the bounce pad on the spinning block to jump up onto the outside roof to backtrack for a **Reward Object**. Drop back down. The moving platform on the other side of the spinning block requires good timing and a bit of good luck.

Carriage 8: Persephone is hiding here with some training dummies. An **Epic Treasure Chest** has a **Live Wire Lock** on it. The top right-side spark is easy to pick up by riding through the top gear. Creep in on a wide angle, almost horizontal, so that you don't bounce straight out again. Do the same for the lower-left spark and then the lower right. The top left will then turn off the fans, so you can reach the final spark. Ignite!

Carriage 9: A block puzzle is here. Shift three blocks to form an upside-down "L" shape to connect the engine to the light bulb. One block needs to be in the top-left corner spot, with the others against its two edges on the floor.

Carriage 10: Dash through as fast as you can. You have more spinning blocks, sliding platforms, and cannon balls to navigate, so your best bet is to keep moving, even if it means backtracking for a few seconds to hit the ground running over a jump. This one takes practice.

Carriage 11: A giant Brawlrus and a few little Grinnades are on guard. Attack them straight up with a good melee and claim their key.

Carriage 12: Loot this area by jumping between platforms. You'll find a golden key, but beware of bombs hidden in boxes.

Carriage 13: This one is another dash through cannon balls and spinning blocks. Right at the end, though, drop down from the large platform to find an **Epic Treasure Chest** underneath. Bounce back up and keep moving!

Carriage 14: Another puzzle lock is waiting for you. Shift the blocks so that there are two between the engine and the left-side platform, and one between the light bulb and that row of blocks. Remember, the aim here is to make sure each block in the path from the engine to the light bulb is touching another block. Grab the **Wish Stone** off the platform when you have them in place.

Carriage 15: It's an ambush! A Brawlrus and his Grinnade and Pirate Henchmen pals have set you up. You can't unlock the **Epic Treasure Chest** or reach the key until they're all down for the count.

Carriage 16: The final block puzzle rests here. The two blocks just need to form a straight line between the engine and the light bulb.

Carriage 17: Run fast—all platforms are on the move! Two Brawlruses are waiting at the exit.

Defeat Blubberbeard

That was an epic effort, but you're not finished yet! The dread pirate Blubberbeard has Carriage 18 packed with Grinnades, Pirate Henchmen, and Brawlruses, all eager for a fight!

First things first, you need to take out all those minions. Choose a heavy-hitting Skylander with a fast and heavy direct attack, such as High Volt or Eruptor, to throw his weight around.

Pre-empt an extra army of Grinnades by smashing the boxes of critters in the middle of the floor any time the fight gets quiet. That way, you can clear them out when it suits you, rather than have the extra burden of running Grinnades to deal with when the boxes are deliberately hit by other enemies.

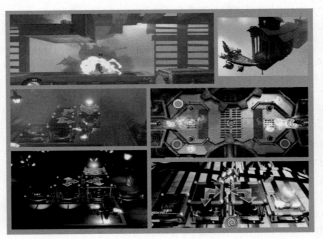

FIGURE 10.34

This is a fast-paced chapter with lots of moving parts (such as cannon balls)! Put on your thinking cap to solve mini-puzzles on the go.

The Sky Eater

Awesome work, Skylander! You've saved Mags from the clutches of evil pirates! That's worth celebrating back at Skylanders Academy. Unfortunately, The Darkness has other ideas!

Chapter 46: Gathering of Friends

Poor Kaos is a little confused and, perhaps, not as evil as he wishes he was. Imaginary Glumshanks offers some words of wisdom to his old Master. The big battle is looming as the Mabu crew prepare to take it inside the belly of The Darkness itself! Hold onto your magic hat, Skylander, the road ahead is about to get rough!

Chapter 47: The Sky Eater

Complete destruction of Skylands commencing in 3... 2... 1... Oh no!

Infiltrate Sky Eater

Stage 1: Fly around the middle of the geode and destroy five giant yellow geode crystals growing from the side of a large crack (see Figure 10.35).

Stage 2: The geode cracks open like a half-eaten apple core, exposing more geode crystals inside. Destroy another seven crystals. Enemy fighters are buzzing around, but if you're fast they won't have time to bother you.

Stage 3: The passage into Kaos' ship splits into two paths. A **Red Toolbox** is in the left path. Both paths have opening and closing gates and mechanical objects to avoid.

Stage 4: Inside the main chamber of the landing bay, destroy four moving crane claws. Enemy fighters will make this hard for you, so clear them out as well. Remember to barrel-roll if you get caught in an enemy laser; they'll wear your health down very quickly.

FIGURE 10.35

Breaking into the Sky Eater is suspiciously easy. That means trouble ahead!

Chapter 48: Grinding Gears

Glumshanks has fallen off the deck! That Troll has some seriously bad luck. The full fist of Kaos is about to come down on you too, so prepare for battle!

Wait for the spinners to stop spinning before you hit them; dodge spells and take the big guys out from a distance if you can. This is a long fight.

Some of the minions drop food when they're hit. Gobble it up to keep your health high. Once they're all taken care of, go exploring.

A pink button to the left of Flynn's ship unrolls a platform bridge to treasure.

A building with a **Live Wire Lock** leads to an **Epic Treasure Chest**. To open the lock, cross the right-side air vent first from top to bottom to pick up the first spark. Then return to the top via the middle air vent. Ride the left-side vent back down to the bottom to grab spark two. The center air vent will take you back up to pick up spark three on the far right. The left-side air vent will take you back to the bottom to reach the ignition. Memorize the safe path of blocks to reach the treasure chest inside the building and ride the elevator back up.

Behind the Live Wire Lock building, blow up some barrels on a platform to drop another bridge. You'll find an **Epic Treasure Chest**.

On the opposite side of the area, some more platforms with barrels drop a bridge that leads to a **Reward Object**. Glumshanks is waiting nearby.

Land Star: Get Past Kaos' Defenses

Area 1: Beware of giant blocks that pop up from the road as you zoom through this challenge. Look at the ground ahead and avoid the square metal cases they are hidden inside. These blocks shoot laser balls at your vehicle, causing damage, so you'll need to anticipate these and dodge them.

Area 2: You'll land inside a metal arena with Kaos' giant pink fist smashing you from above (see Figure 10.36). Wait on the pink buttons until just before Kaos' fist hits it (speed off before you get squashed!). While Kaos is hitting a button, a corresponding tunnel opens on the back wall. Speed through each one. The right tunnel has a **Red Toolbox** off a jump inside.

Area 3: Speed down similar tunnels you faced in Area 1, with blocks popping up. This one quickly splits into two. The right side has an orange gearbit (which briefly spawns other gearbits) and another **Red Toolbox**.

Area 4: Back in the arena, this time you have enemy vehicles, laser shooters, *and* Kaos' giant fist. Geez! Take care of all of the enemies first to clear the floor. There are three pink buttons with corresponding tunnels now. Take the left tunnel for a **Red Toolbox**, then the right tunnel for another **Red Toolbox**. The center tunnel is your way out.

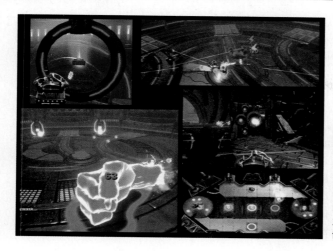

FIGURE 10.36

Beware the iron (pink?!) fist of Kaos! Trick him into pressing the buttons so you can zoom through the tunnels ahead.

Chapter 49: Darkest Goo

You're nearly there, Skylander!

Run left of your starting point to find an **Epic Treasure Chest**, two **Wish Stones,** and an **Elemental Gate**.

Cross the security platform and memorize a safe passage across the bridge.

Persephone and **Sharpfin**'s crew are waiting on the other side.

Sea Star: Hunt and Destroy the Hydra

The Liquification Chamber must be shut down to weaken Kaos and The Darkness. Watch out for the (ginormous!) baby hydra lurking in the depths of the water!

Area 1: Blow up the center hatch and dive down. A few enemy ships show up, but you can leave them behind.

Area 2: There's a **Red Toolbox** caught in a spinner on the right side. Blow up the lodged coins and jump up to reach it.

Area 3: Enemy ships appear again, and this time the hatch shoots lasers from above. Blow up the hatch as quickly as possible and dive inside.

Area 4: A murky pool filled with enemy ships, floating mines, and an enormous baby hydra isn't anyone's idea of a good time! To win this battle, keep the ammo flowing. Every so often, stand still and just wait for a moment to draw the hydra out from under the water (see Figure 10.37). You'll see a ripple and an antenna and then—*whoa!*—out it leaps, directly underneath you! Move away at the last second and spin around to attack it. You'll need up to ten solid firepower opportunities to take down the hydra, which is tricky. It mostly stays underwater and only gives you a second or two when it jumps. Grab power-ups to boost your defenses while you hunt it down.

Back on dry land, you need to make your way out of the chamber. There are two docks. The right side has a **Reward Object**, a **Skystones Overdrive** robot player, and some treasure.

Jump back in your sea vehicle and follow the water channel past the central gate to a back pool. Jump up to claim the **Red Toolbox** attached to a moving crane. Finish up at the central dock to continue on foot.

A series of red memory paths lead you on. Talk to the robot each time to view the safe places to walk.

The left path leads to a **SuperCharger Gate** (and a few minions), an **Epic Treasure Chest**, a **Reward Object**, and a **Wish Stone**. But you'll have to earn it by crossing memory bridges and facing some nasty minions.

Straight ahead of the main path is your way out. Once you've crossed the bridge, you'll have an epic fight on your hands before the coast is clear.

FIGURE 10.37
Aww, isn't that baby hydra sweet?! That is, until it suddenly launches up from the murky depths to devour you whole!! Swim away, Skylander, swim away!

Chapter 50: Crush of Kaos

Get ready for the biggest battle you'll ever face! The evilest, ultimate overlord, Kaos, is ready to release his most unimaginable DOOM on you!

Stage 1: Kaos' first attack is sending groups of four or five spiky balls rolling across the floor to you (see Figure 10.38). Avoid them but stay close. As soon as he lets them go, attack as hard as you can before he's gone.

Stage 2: The spiky balls come in waves, so jump, jump, jump! Attack him again as soon as they pass. Silver lights appear on the ground and split into four versions of Kaos, all fighting you. Attack the real Kaos (the false versions of Kaos don't have a crown) to do the most damage.

Stage 3: This one hits after Kaos has lost about one third of his health. A giant sword strikes the floor, sending out a shockwave of damage from where it hits. Jump the shockwaves, but don't get too close to the sword.

Stage 4: All of the above attacks will keep repeating in turn, with more Kaos clones as well. Keep jumping and attacking the real Kaos at any chance you get. When his health is half gone, he'll change tactics.

Stage 5: Kaos smashes his two giant magic fists down onto the battle floor. At first they just cause shockwaves, then they create spiky balls that roll outward of where they were created. Jump over the shockwaves. Every time the fists rest on the end of the platform, run up and attack them with the strongest move you've got.

Stage 6: Kaos will rise into the air with an invincibility shield around him and then throw off spiky balls. You can't damage him during this, so focus on jumping to avoid damage. As soon as he lands back on the battle floor, he's vulnerable, so attack him. By this stage, he's almost ready to fall! Hang in there, Skylander. You've nearly done it!

FIGURE 10.38

Kaos will try to spike, zap, slam, and confuse you— stay one step ahead by memorizing his attack pattern so you can beat him at his own game!

Chapter 51: Fear and Obey

Aaagh! Just when you thought it was all over—The Darkness isn't gone! Your most important battle is still waiting for you; step up one last time and be the champion that Skylands so desperately needs! Jump in a land vehicle. It's time to banish The Darkness for good.

Stage 1: Follow The Darkness through the rift, zooming through as many Rift Surge Rings as you can, while avoiding the great spikes that form in your way, like those shown in Figure 10.39. Whenever The Darkness falls, blast him with attacks until he moves again to wear down his health.

Stage 2: Out on an open race track through the rift, The Darkness unleashes Shadow Guardian fighters to attack you. Yellow geode crystals sticking up from the track will damage you as well, so take care to swerve around them. Toward the end of each lap, he'll shoot a giant laser at you. As you dive across the bridge between laps, attack him in full force.

Stage 3: When The Darkness reaches half health, you change back to the rift tunnel, similar to Stage One. This time, however, everything is moving! It will take a long time to get through this last battle. Keep the ammo up and drive through any power-ups you see ahead of you.

You can do this, Skylander! Give it all you've got!

FIGURE 10.39

The Darkness will test you in your longest battle yet. You'll loop through the same attacks and challenges, but they'll get harder each time. It's almost over, Skylander. Send that evil beast back where he came from and save Skylands once and for all!

Fully CHARGED!

Congratulations, Portal Master! You did it! By employing all of your cleverness, bravery, and epic fighting skills against the terrible force of The Darkness, Skylands is finally safe! The Darkness, along with its sinister scheme for universe domination, has been banished to another realm, never to return (we hope!?). What an adventure!

You dived head first into ancient story books, shrunk chickens, and blew up titanic-sized crustaceans! Spot Bites, Witch Pitchers, and Bitning Bugs were no match for your heroic SuperChargers who conquered land, seas, and skies.

But what of that gloriously despicable little Portal Master who got Skylands into such a mess in the first place? For now, the tides have turned and Lord Kaos has set himself up at Skylanders Academy as the resident "Ultimate Evil Consultant of Ultimate Evil." You can visit him any time in his tower above the Main Hall to challenge him to a game of Skystones Overdrive and win his crown. Remember, though, Kaos is a very sore loser—you may need to place your Kaos punching bag nearby to remind him who's boss! While you're there, have a chat with long-suffering Glumshanks as he washes Kaos' dirty socks and cuts the crusts off his master's evil, pointy sandwiches.

The best news yet—Skylanders Academy is now fully open for business! Throw all your Wish Stones into the Wishing Well to cash them in for hard-earned rewards. Ari is waiting in the Academy Shop with a new inventory of magical hats, Legendary Treasure, Skystones, and Soul Gems. Get your speed on with Pandergast and challenge your friends to a burn-out at the Dragon Spine, Calamity Canyon, or Frozen Fossil Festival. Don't forget those Red Toolboxes and gearbits to fully upgrade your vehicles with Sharpfin's Pit Crew.

Most importantly, use the instructions in this book to **access your very own online portal** full of bonus extras on how to win Skystones Overdrive, earn trophies and achievements, get quests from Tessa and Hugo, and much more!

In the meantime, visit me at the **SkyPandaAus** YouTube channel for new gameplay walkthroughs, character unboxings, and the latest Skylander news!

Keep exploring Skylander—the sky's the limit!

FIGURE 11.1   There are so many quests and new areas to explore at Skylanders Academy. A whole new adventure is just beginning!

INDEX

M

N

O-P

T

U

V

W

X

Y

Z

S PRODUCT

SAVE 35%*

ON YOUR NEXT PURCHASE!

🖥 How to Register Your Product

- Go to quepublishing.com/register
- Sign in or create an account
- Enter the 10- or 13-digit ISBN that appears on the back cover of your book or on the Copyright page of your eBook.

🔓 Benefits of Registering

- Ability to download product updates
- Access to bonus chapters and workshop files
- A 35% coupon to be used on your next purchase – valid for 30 days
  - To obtain your coupon, click on "Manage Codes" in the right column of your Account page
- Receive special offers on new editions and related Que products

Please note that the benefits for registering may vary by product. Benefits will be listed on your Account page under Registered Products.

We value and respect your privacy. Your email address will not be sold to any third party company.

* 35% discount code presented after product registration is valid on most print books, eBooks, and full-course videos sold on QuePublishing.com. Discount may not be combined with any other offer and is not redeemable for cash. Discount code expires after 30 days from the time of product registration. Offer subject to change.

quepublishing.com